THE MEDICI POPES

LEO X, CARDINAL GIULIO DE' MEDICI (CLEMENT VII) AND CARDINAL
DE' ROSSI

THE MEDICI POPES

(LEO X. AND CLEMENT VII.)

BY

HERBERT M. VAUGHAN, B.A.

WITH TWENTY ILLUSTRATIONS

KENNIKAT PRESS
Port Washington, N. Y./London

THE MEDICI POPES

First published in 1908
Reissued in 1971 by Kennikat Press
Library of Congress Catalog Card No: 74-118554
ISBN 0-8046-1179-3

Manufactured by Taylor Publishing Company   Dallas, Texas

𝔍𝔫 𝔐emoriam

PIAM ET SEMPER VIRENTEM

FRATRIS CARISSIMI

J. P. V.

QUI AD ALTERAM VITAM

NUPER TRANSIVIT

HUNC DEDICAT LIBRUM

AUCTOR MOESTISSIMUS

MCMVIII

PREFACE

ALTHOUGH the names of the two great Popes of the House of Medici loom large in the annals of the Italian Renaissance, yet the private side of their lives and conduct has naturally been dwelt upon with less insistence by the papal historian than the leading part they took in the development of Italian politics or in the course of the Reformation throughout Europe. Even in William Roscoe's elaborate biography of Leo X., the figure of that famous pontiff is largely overshadowed by the momentous episodes of his reign both within and without Italy; "one cannot see the wood for the intervening trees!" In the present volume, therefore, I have made the attempt of presenting to the reader a purely personal study, from which I have excluded, so far as was practicable, all reference to the burning theological questions of the Reformation, and have also avoided any undue amount of dissertation on the tortuous and complicated policy pursued by these Popes of the House of Medici. For I hope that a simple account of the personal career and character of Leo X. (with whom of necessity my work chiefly deals) will prove of some value to the historical student of the Renaissance, who may thereby become better able to comprehend the varying part played by the former of the two Medicean pontiffs in the political and religious struggles during the opening decades of the sixteenth century.

The earliest, and indeed only contemporary life of any importance of Giovanni de' Medici, Pope Leo X., is the *Vita Leonis X.* of Paolo Giovio, Bishop of Nocera, himself a member of Leo's own brilliant court in Rome, and therefore a person well qualified to undertake such a task. The work of Giovio, or Jovius, which was first published at Florence in 1549, is written in Latin, and though it has been rendered into Italian and French, it has never, so far as I am aware, been translated into English. Giovio's *Life*, which is divided into four books, is a most meagre and disappointing narrative, scarcely a biography at all in the modern sense of the term, for it principally consists of a long rambling account of contemporary politics, albeit the Fourth Book contains a large number of intimate details concerning the Pope, which have often been utilised by succeeding writers. Poor and unsatisfactory as was Giovio's *Life*, this work remained for over 250 years the sole biography of the great Medicean pontiff until 1797, when there appeared an enlarged *Leonis X. Vita* from the pen of the learned Monsignore Angelo Fabroni of Pisa. This biography, which was published in Latin and has never been translated, contains a fuller account, together with a

copious Appendix of original Documents discovered
and given to the world by Fabroni himself. His work
was followed eight years later by the justly celebrated
biography from the pen of William Roscoe of Liver-
pool, who based his study on Fabroni's researches.
Roscoe's *The Life and Pontificate of Leo X.* was soon
translated into Italian, and published in 1817 by Count
Luigi Bossi of Milan, whose splendid edition in twelve
volumes constitutes the best and fullest Life of this
Pope in existence. Amongst more recent volumes on
the same subject, the carefully compiled *Leo X.* of
Professor Ludwig Pastor, published in 1906, may be
mentioned. Free use has been made in the ensuing
work of these various biographies, together with their
voluminous Appendices.

I have treated of Giulio de'. Medici, Pope Clement
VII., in a less detailed manner, for two reasons : first,
because his life before obtaining the tiara is closely
bound up with, and consequently covered by, the
career of his more distinguished cousin, Leo X. ; and
second, because his private biography offers far less
of general interest. Special attention has been drawn
throughout the book to the various existing works of
art in Florence and Rome which are connected with
the personal history, or are due to the bountiful patronage of these two Medicean pontiffs. In accordance
with the title chosen for this work, I have also added
a brief account of the later Popes, Pius IV. and Leo
XI., both of whom bore the historic name of Medici,

although their connection with the senior branch of the great Florentine House was exceedingly remote.

In case it may be remarked that an undue proportion of space has been bestowed on the early years of Leo X. (and thereby also on those of his near kinsman and contemporary, Clement VII.), I would reply that far less is generally known of the youthful struggles and adventures of Cardinal Giovanni de' Medici than of the pomp and power of his pontificate ; and that some acquaintance with the story of Leo X.'s early poverty and insignificance is essential to a clearer understanding of his subsequent conduct as Supreme Pontiff. The vast and ever-increasing mass of material reflecting on the life, public and private, of the Medici Popes has rendered my task of selection and rejection peculiarly difficult ; indeed, an adequate and comprehensive account of the reign of Leo X. alone would afford occupation for a lifetime, as every historian is well aware. Yet I think that from the pages of this book the reader will contrive to obtain a tolerably accurate glimpse into the personality of those two great Popes, whose deeds and influence for good or evil did so much to shape the course of the political, religious, intellectual and artistic development of Europe during the early stages of the Reformation.

CONTENTS

Cellini serves the Pope faithfully during the sack of Rome—
Clement's appreciation of Michelangelo—The master is com-
missioned by Clement to erect the New Sacristy and the Laurentian
Library at San Lorenzo in Florence—Progress of this work inter-
rupted by the siege of Florence—Michelangelo is forgiven by
Clement for his behaviour at the time of the siege—The work at
San Lorenzo left incomplete at Clement's death and never re-
sumed.

CHAPTER XIII

Clement VII. pursues a fatal policy of vacillation between the Emperor
and the French King—The battle of Pavia—Clement persists
in his political folly and defies the Emperor—Cardinal Colonna's
raid upon Rome—The united army of German landsknechts under
Frundsberg and of Spanish veterans under the Constable of
Bourbon advances towards Rome—The Spanish fleet under the
viceroy Lannoy reaches Gaeta—Terrible position of Clement—The
battle of Frosinone—Truce between the Pope and Lannoy—The
army of Bourbon continues to move southward—It turns aside
from Florence—It proceeds by way of Viterbo upon Rome—Unprepared state of the city—Abject folly of Clement—Bourbon
attacks the walls of Rome and is killed—The foreign forces enter
the city—Clement and most of the members of the Roman Court
seek refuge in the Castle of Sant' Angelo—Massacre and sack of
the city—Frightful horrors committed—The return of the Cardinal
Colonna—Position of the Pope in Sant' Angelo—Defence of the
castle under Santacroce and Benvenuto Cellini—News of the
revolt in Florence and of the expulsion of the Medicean bastards
brought to the Pope—Miserable plight of the Pope—He surrenders
unconditionally to the representative of Charles V.—Flight of
Clement to Orvieto—The English Embassy at Orvieto—Clement is
reconciled to the Emperor, whom he crowns at Bologna—Siege
and capitulation of Florence.

CHAPTER XIV

The Pope's relatives, Alessandro and Ippolito de' Medici—Preference
of Clement VII. for the former, who is created Duke of Florence—
Ippolito is made a Cardinal against his wish—Memorials of
Clement VII. in Florence—Caterina de' Medici and Clement's
anxiety to arrange an important marriage for her—The Emperor

LIST OF ILLUSTRATIONS

The illustrations are from photographs by Messrs. Alinari, Florence.

BIBLIOGRAPHY

Amongst the printed works that have been consulted during the preparation of this volume, some of the more important and useful are enumerated below:—

Paulus Jovius [Paolo Giovio, Bishop of Nocera]. *Vita Leonis X.* Florentiæ, 1549. (Quoted as Jovius.)

Angelo Fabroni. *Leonis X. Vita.* Pisa, 1807. (Quoted as Fabroni.)

William Roscoe. *The Life and Pontificate of Leo X.* Bohn's edition, London, 1846. (Quoted as Roscoe.)

Count Luigi Bossi. *Vita e Pontificato di Leone X. di Guglielmo Roscoe.* Milano, 1816. (Quoted as Bossi-Roscoe.)

Francesco Nitti. *Leone X. e la sua Politica.* G. Barbèra, Firenze, 1892.

Professor Ludwig Pastor. *Leo X. Geschichte der Päpste seit dem Ausgang des Mittelalters.* Freiburg im Breisgau, 1906. (Quoted as Pastor.)

Dr. M. Creighton, Bishop of London. *A History of the Papacy from the Great Schism to the Sack of Rome* (vols. v. and vi.). Longmans, Green and Co., London, 1904. (Quoted as Creighton.)

Ferdinand Gregorovius. *History of Rome in the Middle Ages.* Translated by Annie Hamilton. George Bell, London, 1902. (Quoted as Gregorovius.)

Jacob Burckhardt. *The Civilization of the Renaissance in Italy.* Translated by S. G. C. Middlemore. Swan Sonnenschein & Co., London, 1892.

M. Sanudo. *I Diarii* (1496-1533). Venezia, 1879-1902.

Francesco Guicciardini. *Storia d' Italia.* Edited by Gio. Rosini. Capolago, 1836.

Lorenzo Pignotti. *Storia della Toscana.* Pisa, 1813.

H. E. Napier. *Florentine History* (vol. iv.). Moxon, London, 1846.

J. Michelet. *La Renaissance.* Lévy, Paris, 1898.

G. Del Badia. *Diario Fiorentino di Luca Landucci.* Sansoni, Firenze, 1883. (Quoted as Landucci.)

E. Bacciotti. *Firenze Illustrata.* Firenze, 1879.

C. Yriarte. *Florence.* Sampson Lowe, London, 1882.

W. Roscoe. *Life of Lorenzo de' Medici.* London, 1796.

Professor E. Armstrong. *Lorenzo de' Medici.* Putnams, New York and London, 1896.

C. Belviglieri. *Tavole Sincrone e Genealogiche di Storia Italiana.* Firenze, 1885.

E. Grifi. *Saunterings in Florence.* Bemporad e Figlio, Firenze, 1899.

Professor Pasquale Villari. *Life and Times of Niccolò Machiavelli.* Translated by Madame Linda Villari. (Third Edition.) Fisher Unwin, London, N.D. (Quoted as Villari.)

J. C. L. Sismondi. *Histoire des Républiques Italiennes.* Bruxelles, 1839.

Professor R. Lanciani. *The Golden Days of the Renaissance in Rome.* Houghton, Mifflin and Co., Boston and New York, 1906. (Quoted as Lanciani.)

B. Platina. *Le Vite de' Pontefici.* In Venetia, 1685.

Raynaldus. *Diario di Paride Grasso.*

Leopold Ranke. *History of the Popes.* Translated by E. Foster. Bohn's edition, London, 1889.

Count Domenico Gnoli. *Le Caccie di Leone X.* La Nuova Antologia, vol. cxxvii.

Signor Alessandro Luzio. *Isabella d' Este ne' primordi del Papato di Leone X.* Cogliati, Milano, 1907.

Adolphus Trollope. *The Girlhood of Catherine de Medici.* Chapman & Hall, London, 1856.

Scipione Ammirato. *Ritratti d' huomini illustri di Casa Medici.* (Opuscoli, vol. iii.) Firenze, 1640.

Cesare Guasti. *Il Sacco di Prato e il Ritorno dei Medici in Firenze nel 1512.* Bologna, 1880.

G. Milanesi. *Il Sacco di Roma del 1527.* G. Barbèra, Firenze, 1867.

J. A. Symonds. *Renaissance in Italy.* Holt & Co., New York, 1887.

J. A. Symonds. *Life of Michelangelo Buonarotti.* Macmillan, London, 1901.

Benvenuto Cellini. *Vita di scritta da lui medesimo.* Firenze, 1842.

Giorgio Vasari. *Lives of the Painters, Sculptors and Architects.* Bohn's edition, London, 1850.

Eugène Muntz. *Raphael, His Life, Works and Times.* Translated by Walter Armstrong. Chapman & Hall, London, 1896. (Quoted as Muntz.)

Baldassare Castiglione. *Il Cortigiano.* Vinegia, 1556.

A. Braschet. *Les Archives de la Serenissime République de Venise.* Venise, 1857.

PEDIGREE OF THE SENIOR BRANCH OF THE HOUSE OF MEDICI

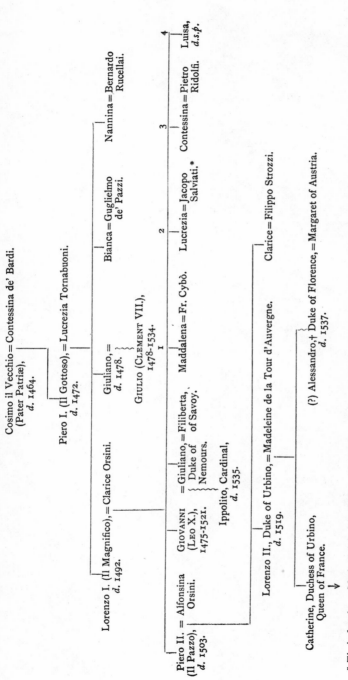

Cosimo il Vecchio = Contessina de' Bardi.
(Pater Patriæ),
d. 1464.

Piero I. (Il Gottoso), = Lucrezia Tornabuoni.
d. 1472.

Giuliano, = *d.* 1478.

Bianca = Guglielmo de' Pazzi.

Nannina = Bernardo Rucellai.

Giulio (Clement VII.), 1478-1534.

1

Lorenzo I. (Il Magnifico), = Clarice Orsini.
d. 1492.

Maddalena = Fr. Cybò.

Lucrezia = Jacopo Salviati. *

Contessina = Pietro Ridolfi.

Luisa, *d.s.p.*

2   3   4

Piero II. = Alfonsina Orsini.
(Il Pazzo),
d. 1503.

Giovanni (Leo X.), 1475-1521.

= Giuliano, = Filiberta, Duke of Savoy.
Nemours,

Ippolito, Cardinal,
d. 1535.

Clarice = Filippo Strozzi.

Lorenzo II., Duke of Urbino, = Madeleine de la Tour d'Auvergne.
d. 1519.

(?) Alessandro,† Duke of Florence, = Margaret of Austria.
d. 1537.

Catherine, Duchess of Urbino,
Queen of France.

* Their daughter, Maria Salviati, was the wife of Giovanni de' Medici, and consequently the mother of Cosimo I., first Grand-Duke of Tuscany.
† Of doubtful parentage, but probably the son of Giulio de' Medici (Clement VII.).

THE MEDICI POPES

CHAPTER I

CHILDHOOD AND YOUTH IN FLORENCE

From the frightful spectacle of poverty, barbarity and ignorance, from the oppression of illiterate masters, and the sufferings of a degraded peasantry, which the annals of England and France present to us, it is delightful to turn to the opulent and enlightened states of Italy, to the vast and magnificent cities, the ports, the arsenals, the villas, the museums, the libraries, the marts filled with every article of comfort or luxury, the factories swarming with artisans. . . . With peculiar pleasure every cultivated mind must repose on the fair, the happy, the glorious Florence, the halls which rang with the mirth of Pulci, the cell where twinkled the midnight lamp of Politian, the statues on which the young eye of Michelangelo glared with the frenzy of a kindred inspiration, the gardens in which Lorenzo meditated some sparkling song for the May-Day dance of the Etrurian virgins (Lord Macaulay, *Essay on Machiavelli*).

IN our efforts to realise the leading events of our own history we experience no small difficulty from the fact that so much of the face of England has completely altered its outward appearance under the stress of modern development, so that we find it particularly hard to picture to ourselves their original setting. Our over-grown yet ever-spreading capital owns scarcely a feature to-day in common with the London of the Tudors or Plantagenets; the relentless pushing of industrial enterprise has turned whole shires from green to black, from verdant countryside to smoke-grimed scenes of commerce. It is therefore well-nigh impossible for us in many cases to con-

jure up the old-world conditions of Merrie England.   But
in writing of Italian annals we are confronted by no such
problem ; altered to a certain extent no doubt is the present aspect of Italy, yet in Florence, Venice, Siena and
most of her cities we still possess the empty stages of the
pageants and deeds of long ago, all ready prepared for us
to people with the famous figures of the historic past.

Standing on the airy heights of San Miniato, where
the golden mosaics of its venerable church have cauhgt
the passing glories of the sunset for nigh upon a thousand
years, or strolling amongst the ilex alleys of " Boboli's
ducal bowers," we can still gaze below upon the Florence of
the Medici, the Florence of Lorenzo the Magnificent and
of Savonarola, the Florence of Popes Leo and Clement,
of Michelangelo and Machiavelli.   For beneath us swift
Arno still shoots under the arches of Taddeo Gaddi's
ancient bridge piled high with its load of tiny shops that
Florentine goldsmiths have inhabited for the past six centuries.   There still dominates the red-roofed city Brunelleschi's huge cupola, and beside it still springs aloft "into
blue aether that no clouds o'ercast" the delicate parti-
coloured campanile of the Shepherd-Painter.   Nearer to
us the graceful yet sturdy belfry of the old civic palace
soars majestically into the clear atmosphere, and hard by
we note the fantastic spire of the Badia, and alongside it
the severe outline of the turret that adjoins the grim castle
of the Podestà.   Westward the slender pinnacle of Santa
Maria Novella greets our eyes, whilst amidst this varied
group of towers there obtrudes on our sight the square
mass of Or San Michele, that sacred citadel of the Florentine guilds.   Oltr' Arno nestling at our feet remains
wholly unchanged, and of a truth the only conspicuous
objects that can interrupt our mental retrospect of the
city of Lorenzo and Leo are the mean tower of Santa

Croce, the long colonnades of the Uffizi, and the clumsy dome that surmounts the gorgeous charnel-house of the Medicean Grand-Dukes. To make the picture perfect, we must blind our eyes to these excrescences of a later age, and by another slight effect of the imagination we must behold the modern raw suburbs and their smoke-belching factories sink into the soil of the Florentine plain to give place to tracts of garden and orchard, to shady groves and smiling vineyards, that lie outside the broad coronal of towered walls, wherewith Arnolfo di Cambio endowed his native city for her protection. We must next conceive the steep hillside of Fiesole less populous than at the present day, less marred by quarries and mean houses, yet freely besprinkled with ample villas. Amidst this radiant scenery the practised eye can easily detect the chief Medicean residences;—that sheltered pleasaunce with its long terraces below the crest of ancient Faesulae; the favourite retreat of the sickly Piero and the Magnificent Lorenzo, with its broad roof peeping forth from bosky thickets of elm and cypress at sunny Careggi; and again by directing our glance across the fertile plain towards Prato, we seem to discover the whereabouts of Sangallo's stately palace at low-lying Cajano, where the luckless Clement VII. spent much of his childhood. No stretch of the imagination is however required on our part to realise the eternal hills which form the northern background to the City of the Lily; for ever unchanged and unchangeable remain the stony stretches of familiar Monte Morello, the green and russet slopes of the heights that rise in endless succession eastward of Fiesole, and the barren violet-tinted mountains bounding the plain above Prato and Pistoja. How exquisite, and also how unaltered even to-day, is the distant aspect of Florence, "la bellissima e famosissima figlia di Roma," as one of her most famous

sons thus addressed his ancient mother !   With so superb
a setting, amid such glorious surroundings, the past history
of Florence becomes a living thing, which it needs no
striving to quicken, for the true Medicean city of the
Italian Renaissance stands before us to-day sharply
defined in the crystal-clear air of Tuscany—

> Dove 'l humano spirito si purga
> E di salir al Ciel' diventa degno.[1]

In the heart of the town itself, almost beneath the shadow
of the vast dome, out of sight of which no true-born son
of Florence is said ever to feel happy, rises that group
of buildings which is so closely associated with the origin
and fortunes of the House of Medici.   Here lies the great
basilica of San Lorenzo with its pitiful naked façade, that
Medicean popes and princes were always intending to
convert into a costly thing of beauty ; at its transepts up-
rear the rival sacristies of Brunelleschi and Michelangelo,
above which looms the red cupola of the Grand-Ducal
mausoleum.   Beside the church extends the long window-
pierced form of the Laurentian Library, overlooking the
quiet cloister in a dark angle of which sits eternally the
robed and mitred figure of the grim-visaged Paolo
Giovio, the venal Plutarch of his age and the earliest biographer of Pope Leo X.   Upon the little piazza before
the church, nowadays the busy scene of a daily market
of cheap or tawdry goods, abuts the massive palace which
was the cradle of the Medicean race.   Much changed
in outward aspect is the mansion that Michelozzi constructed for Cosimo il Vecchio, for the Riccardi, who
bought this historic building in after years, must needs
spoil its original proportions by adding largely to the
structure.   The statue-set garden wherein Cosimo and

[1] *Il Purgatorio*, canto i.

Lorenzo were wont to stroll has wholly disappeared, but
the central courtyard with its antique friezes and its stone
medallions remains intact. A most precious relic of its
former owners it still retains in the exquisite little chapel
covered with Benozzo Gozzoli's renowned frescoes, wherein are portrayed in glowing colours and in gleaming gold
Cosimo the Elder, his son Piero, his grandchildren, and
his Imperial guests from distant Byzantium, all riding
with their trains of richly-clad attendants, with hawk and
hound, and even with trained leopard, amidst a landscape
of marvellous but fantastic beauty. The old Medicean
mansion, lying between Piazza San Lorenzo and the
broad curve of Via Larga, cannot perhaps aspire to the
symmetry and rich decoration of Palazzo Strozzi hard by,
nor can it vie in bulk and majesty with Messer Pitti's vast
palace on the slopes of Oltr' Arno; nevertheless it is
a goodly building, well-proportioned and imposing, and
withal suitably contrived for defence.

It was in a chamber of this historic house that
Giovanni de' Medici, afterwards Pope Leo X., first
saw the light on 11th December, 1475. Of his sire,
the Magnificent Lorenzo—uncrowned king of Florence,
genial tyrant of an adoring populace, statesman, diplomatist, banker, scholar, poet—it will be superfluous to
speak; his mother, Clarice Orsini, a member of the
haughty feudal Roman house, was the first "foreign"
bride to enter the portals of the Medicean palace. She
was a good woman and a faithful wife, but in intellect
the inferior of her brilliant consort, whose versatile nature
and marvellous powers often puzzled or alarmed her.
But she had at least the merit of bestowing on her
second son the pontifical name by which all the world
speaks and thinks of Giovanni di Lorenzo de' Medici.
For on the night before her infant was born the good

Clarice had a dream, wherein she imagined herself seized with pangs of childbirth in the Florentine Duomo, and delivered of a huge but most docile lion instead of the expected infant.[1] Man has always been a superstitious animal, and in the year 1475 dreams such as Clarice's were taken very seriously indeed as intentional warnings or compliments from the Unseen, so that there can be no reasonable doubt that Giovanni de' Medici on being elected to fill the papal throne in after years chose his official title of Leo X. out of deference to his mother's nightmare, over the mystical meaning of which he had probably often pondered.

Of the little Giovanni's brothers and sisters we must speak one word. First, there was Piero, the heir, who was four years old at Giovanni's birth, and last there was Giuliano, born in the year of the Pazzi conspiracy and so named after his ill-fated uncle. Then there were the four sisters—Lucrezia, Maddalena, Contessina and Luisa—of whom the three first-named were married respectively to a Cybò, a Salviati, and a Ridolfi ; whilst Luisa died prematurely on the eve of her nuptials with Giovanni, son of Pier-Francesco de' Medici, head of the younger branch of the Medicean House. To his children, Lorenzo always showed himself an affectionate and indulgent father, even condescending on occasions to take part in their noisy games of the nursery : a circumstance that the merciless Machiavelli records with a sneer in the pages of his Florentine history—" he would forget the dignity of his office in romping with his children, for he would oftentimes indulge in any idle or childish amusement they might put him to ". Nevertheless, most persons will agree with a modern French critic, who de-

[1] Jovius, lib. i.

clares that never could the great Lorenzo have shown himself more human or more lovable than when playing at soldiers with Piero and Giuliano, or rolling on the floor with the future Leo X.

Giovanni must have been far too young to remember the conspiracy of the Pazzi with its terrible scenes, when the mangled corpse of his uncle Giuliano was borne from the cathedral to the palace that was surrounded by angry crowds calling for summary vengeance on the murderers, and professing boundless devotion towards their surviving ruler, who had escaped the assassin's knife as though by a miracle. Later, perhaps, he may have recalled an addition to the Medicean nursery in a little dark-eyed boy with the name of Giulio, the bastard son of the murdered Giuliano, who was sometimes brought to share the lessons and amusements of Lorenzo's own children. In any case he must have been conscious of the change of scene from busy crowded Florence to the quiet and solitude of the family estate of Caffagiolo, whither the Magnificent despatched his household for safety after the Conjuration of the Pazzi. The dark forests of pine and fir, the fleecy flocks, the rough but kindly shepherds of the hills, the keen air of the wind-grieved Apennines, must have had their early influence on any son of Lorenzo the Poet, who loved dearly the life and people of the Tuscan country-side. But in strange contrast with the rural surroundings of airy Caffagiolo on its distant mountain-top must have seemed the conversations overheard by the sharp ears of the children between their tutor, Angelo Poliziano, and the handsome young Pico della Mirandola, or the abstruse arguments indulged in by their father with the learned Marsilio Ficino on the chance occasions when Lorenzo was able to join his family in their country retreat. But more often Politian was left alone with his charges and their mother, whose views by no means coincided with those of their chosen preceptor. Fiercely did the anxious Clarice wrangle with Politian over the methods of education, which she wanted to be conducted on her old-fashioned lines, the tutor complaining meanwhile to Madonna Lucrezia, Lorenzo's mother, a Tornabuoni by birth, to whom in an amusing letter he sends a comically dismal account of the daily life at Caffagiolo, which was by no means a residence to the taste of the fastidious scholar.

"The only news I can send you is that we have here such continual rains that it is impossible to quit the house, and the exercises of the country are exchanged for childish sports within doors. Here I stand by the fire-side in my great coat and slippers, so that you might take me for the very figure of Melancholy. . . . Were we in Florence, we should have some consolation, were it only for that of seeing Lorenzo, when he returned home ; but here we are in continual anxiety, and I for my part am half-dead with solitude and weariness. The plague and the war are incessantly in my mind. I lament past evils, and I have no longer at my side my dear Madonna Lucrezia, to whom I might unbosom my cares."[1]

But besides complaining thus to Madonna Lucrezia, the spoiled Humanist does not scruple to upbraid Clarice to her own husband for wasting the time of his most promising pupil, the precocious little Giovanni, by forcing him to squander his newly-acquired power of reading in spelling through the Psalms of David instead of the masterpieces of antiquity. That the mother and tutor of Lorenzo's children were on the worst possible terms

[1] Roscoe, *Life of Lorenzo de' Medici*, Appendix LIX.

at lonely Caffagiolo is evident from one of Clarice's letters, wherein she relates her side of the case with regard to the thorny question of education, nor does she shrink from abusing Lorenzo's favourite poet and companion to her husband.

". . . I do not like Messer Angelo Poliziano threatening to remain in the house in spite of me. You remember I told you, that if it was your *will* he should stay, I was perfectly contented ; and although I have suffered infinite abuse from him, yet if it be with your consent, I am satisfied. But I cannot believe this to be the case."[1]

At length Lorenzo, growing weary of these appeals and bickerings, advised Politian to withdraw to the villa below Fiesole, where he quickly recovered his equanimity and spent a profitable time in composing his *Rusticus*, a charming Latin poem that his contemporaries did not hesitate to compare with the *Georgics* of Vergil.

With unerring instinct Lorenzo had already perceived his second son's talents, and had decided to turn them to the advantage of his House and his policy, so that the little Giovanni was accordingly marked out for an ecclesiastical career almost from his infancy. Before reaching his seventh birthday the child received the tonsure—the solemn shaving of the scalp which notified his entry into the Church, and he was at the same time declared capable of preferment, whereupon Louis XI. of France, to whom Lorenzo had communicated his intention, at once presented the boy with the abbey of Fonte Dolce, and even promised him the see of Aix, until it was unexpectedly realised that its archbishop was still living. A canonry in each cathedral-church of Tuscany was

---

[1] Roscoe, Appendix LXI.

promptly bestowed on this infantile pluralist, and even Pope Sixtus IV., that implacable foe of the House of Medici, granted him a little later the rich convent of Passignano.   A detailed list of this child's benefices would prove wearisome, but we may mention that he held twenty-seven separate offices, of which the abbeys of Fonte Dolce, Passignano and Monte Cassino were the most lucrative.   No wonder then that the learned Fabroni, Leo's first modern biographer, exclaims in horrified amazement, "Dear Lord, what a mass of benefices concentrated in one single youth!"   Yet it is difficult to dissent from Roscoe's shrewd criticism on such a scandal, that it is of small consequence whether such preferment be bestowed upon an infant who is unable, or upon an adult who is unwilling, to perform the requisite duties.[1]

In the following year, 1483, this young ecclesiastic was confirmed by the bishop of Arezzo in the beautiful Medicean chapel with its Gozzoli frescoes ; a circumstance which Lorenzo naïvely mentions in his *Ricordi:*—

"On the nineteenth day of May, 1483, we received intelligence that the King of France had of his own motion presented to my son Giovanni the abbey of Fonte Dolce. On the thirty-first we heard from Rome that the Pope had confirmed the grant, and had rendered him capable of holding benefices, *he being now seven years of age.* On the first day of June, Giovanni accompanied me from Poggio a Cajano to Florence, where he was confirmed by the bishop of Arezzo, and received the tonsure, and from henceforth was called Messire Giovanni.   This ceremony took place in the chapel of our family."

But it is needless to add that Lorenzo had far more

[1] Roscoe, chap. i., pp. 10, 11.

ambitious ends in view than the mere obtaining of rich
sees and abbeys for his second, who was perhaps his
favourite, son. His many experiences of the Protean
changes in Italian politics, of which he was now becoming the acknowledged moderator—"the beam of the
Italian scales"—had already impressed upon his marvellous mind the paramount importance of a close connection between his own House and the Papacy. The
preponderance of Italian influence in Lorenzo's days was
divided between the duchy of Milan and the republic of
Venice in Northern Italy, and the kingdom of Naples
and the Papacy in the south, whilst in the centre the
wealthy commercial state of Florence under the judicious
sway of Lorenzo himself had for some time past managed
to keep the balance of power between the jarring elements of North and South, and to prevent any dangerous
combinations amongst the four leading states, whose intrigues also shaped the policy of the smaller Italian cities
such as Mantua, Ferrara, Siena, Bologna and the like.
But dangerous and tangled as was the skein of political
threads held in Milan, Naples, Venice and the minor
capitals, it was the uncertain action of the Papacy which
the ruler of Florence had most cause to dread. For it
had been the unconcealed hostility of Sixtus IV. that
had made the Pazzi conspiracy possible, and it was also
the same Pope's aggression that had later forced Lorenzo
to risk his life at the court of the treacherous Ferdinand
of Naples on his famous diplomatic mission of 1480.
From a repetition of past dangers at the hands of the
Pope, Lorenzo had fully determined to guard himself by
obtaining the admission of his younger son into the
College of Cardinals, whenever a favourable opportunity
might present itself. This attempt to obtain the scarlet
hat for Giovanni de' Medici was therefore as much an

act of political foresight as an object of mere family aggrandisement, since a Medicean Cardinal would not
only help to raise the prestige of the burgher House,
already allied with a proud Roman family, but he would
also be able to influence the policy of the Sacred College
and the shifting aims of successive Popes.

So long as Sixtus IV. sat in St. Peter's chair, such
an ambition could remain only a day-dream, but on 13th
August, 1484, the Della Rovere Pope, so dreaded by
Lorenzo, expired unloved and unlamented. The subsequent election of Giambattista Cybò with the title of
Innocent VIII. now placed a personal as well as a political
friend on the pontifical throne, so that a rare chance presented itself to Lorenzo to push his intentions at the
Roman court. Two serious obstacles lay in the way of
his cherished scheme ; the feeble health of the aged
Pontiff, whose tenure of the dignity did not promise to
be of long duration, and the extreme youth of Lorenzo's
own little Cardinal *in petto*. Yet nothing daunted, the
Magnificent at once began eagerly to press his request
upon the new Pope, although the latter was naturally, in
spite of his regard for the father, extremely loth to nominate his infant son a prince of the Church. In fact,
at his election Innocent had in the conclave not only
promised never to admit any candidate to the Sacred
College who was under thirty years of age, but also not
to create any more members of the College itself until
its numbers were in the course of nature reduced to
twenty-four. These restrictions, absurd and illegal as
they undoubtedly were, the new-made Pope could hardly
have been expected to comply with strictly, yet certainly
Giovanni's proposed elevation constituted an extreme
case. To raise a mere child to the highest rank in the
Church, even in that age of universal corruption, would

have caused a grave scandal; nevertheless, Innocent wavered between the fear of offending the Sacred College and a warm desire to serve his true friend, Lorenzo, who kept on demanding this boon from the Pontiff "with no less fervency than he would have asked of God the salvation of his soul".[1] So eager and intimate an appeal the scruples or fears of Innocent were unable to withstand, especially since in the previous year the existing ties between the Houses of Medici and Cybò had been drawn closer by the union of the Pope's son, Francesco Cybo, with Lorenzo's daughter Maddalena. Besides arranging this marriage between the two families, Lorenzo had left no stone unturned to obtain his desired end. By means of his envoy Lanfredini at the Roman court, the two leading cardinals, Roderigo Borgia, whose name was soon to become notorious throughout Christendom, and Ascanio Sforza, brother of the usurper of Milan, were approached on this delicate matter. Both cardinals worked diligently on little Giovanni's behalf, especially the cardinal of Milan, until the Pope, wearied out by this judicious policy of alternate teasing and flattery, finally complied with Lorenzo's wishes, so ardently expressed. On 8th March, 1489, therefore, Giovanni de' Medici was formally nominated a Cardinal Deacon by the title of Santa Maria in Domenica, the small antique church that stands to-day half-hidden amidst the vineyards and acacia groves of the deserted Coelian Hill. The Cardinal de Balue, Louis XI.'s minister, writing after the consistory to Lorenzo in Florence, thus announces the joyful news: "O happy man, what a blessing and what an honour for your most reverend son, for your own Magnificence, and for the city of Florence!"[2] But supreme as

---

[1] Fabroni, Appendix II.　　　　[2] *Ibid.*

was Lorenzo's satisfaction on receipt of this news, his
transports of joy were not a little tempered by certain restrictions which accompanied his son's admission into the
College.   In the first place, Innocent—very reasonably
and properly it will be admitted—refused to allow the
new-made thirteen-year-old Cardinal to wear the vestments or exercise any of the privileges of his rank for the
space of at least three years.   Lorenzo's irritation was extreme at this command, but in spite of shrewd arguments
and persistent entreaties the Pope, to his credit, remained
unshaken in his resolve.   Another stipulation made by
the Pope, who evidently did not consider the education
of a Humanist as altogether sufficient for a cardinal, was
that Giovanni should quit Florence immediately in order
to study canon law at Pisa during his three years of pro-
bation.   Accordingly the boy was sent to Pisa, that
magnificent failure amongst the historic cities of mediæval
Italy, which had lately been endowed with an university
by Lorenzo himself.   For the brooding quiet of the
famous but derelict old city, the cheapness of lodging
within its walls, and its central position near the coast-
line midway between Rome and Genoa, had already
made Pisa a flourishing seat of learning.   Here then
the future Pontiff studied diligently under Decio, Soz-
zini and other learned professors, recently nominated
to the various chairs of Pisa by his father, whilst his
household was managed for him by a young scholar of
great promise, whose career was from this time onward
bound up closely with that of his brilliant pupil, who was
but five years his junior.   This was no less a person
than Bernardo Dovizi of Bibbiena, whose shrewd face
is so familiar to us from Raphael's splendid portrait
in the Pitti Gallery at Florence, and whose attain-
ments will ever shed reflected glory on the humble

village amongst the Tuscan uplands that gave him birth :—

> Fia nota per costui, dicea, Bibbiena,
> Quanto Fiorenza, sua vicina, e Siena.[1]

Meanwhile Lorenzo himself, already ailing in the prime of life, was kept in a perpetual fever of suspense for fear the Pope might die before the close of this probationary period, and there can be little doubt that this continual anxiety contributed not a little to the Magnificent's premature decease.   Nor was he idle in urging Innocent, by means of his ambassadors in Rome, to withdraw the odious conditions, so as to allow his son the full enjoyment of his rank.   But the Pope continued to shut his ears to all appeals and arguments, so that Lorenzo had to rest content with vague assurances of the Pontiff's good-will.   " Leave the fortunes of Messire Giovanni to me," replied Innocent to Piero Alamanni's entreaties on his master's behalf; "for I look upon him as my own son and shall perhaps make his promotion public when you least expect it, for it is my intention to do much more for his interests than I shall now express."[2]

Such promises proved cold comfort to Lorenzo, ever intriguing to shake Innocent's fixed resolve, and ever dreading each post from Rome lest it might bring tidings of the old Pope's death, in the event of which he foresaw only too clearly the certain collapse of all his secret schemes.   For it was highly probable that a new Pontiff, if a virtuous reformer like Pius II., would postpone for many years the desired consummation ; whilst a bad Pope of the type of his old enemy Sixtus would either extort an immense sum for bestowing the hat or else try to repudiate altogether the promises made by

[1] Ariosto, *Orlando Furioso*, canto xxvi., st. 48.
[2] Fabroni, *In vita Laurentii Medicei*, p. 301.

Innocent with regard to a child of thirteen. Nor were Lorenzo's fears of failure unfounded, for, as we shall see, the papal permission arrived only a few weeks before his own decease; in short, but for the frantic efforts of Lorenzo, Giovanni de' Medici would never have received the scarlet hat, and the world's history would have lacked the pontificate of Leo X.

At length the day so anxiously expected by Lorenzo arrived, and on the evening of 8th March, 1492, the young Cardinal, now aged sixteen years and three months, left Florence with a small train to ascend to the ancient abbey that stands on the fertile slopes below Fiesole. This church, commonly known as the Badia Fiesolana, adorns the left ridge of the vine- and willow-clad valley of the Mugnone, and lies within a few hundred yards of the better-known convent of San Domenico with its cherished memories of Fra Angelico. The Badia itself, with its tall tower and its picturesque façade of black and white marble, had long been associated with the name and bounty of the Medici, so that it made a suitable spot for the intended ceremony of investiture, which, probably owing to Lorenzo's ill-health, it had been decided to make as simple and brief as possible. Within the walls, therefore, of this church distinguished by the gifts and emblems of his ancestors, Giovanni spent a long night's vigil in solitary prayer, until with the dawn appeared on the scene Pico della Mirandola and Jacopo Salviati, together with Messer Simone Stanza, the public notary. The young Cardinal now received the Sacrament "with the greatest devotion and humility," after which High Mass was sung. During the performance of the service the Superior of the Abbey pronounced a blessing on the insignia of Giovanni's rank—the *pallium* or mantle, the *biretum* or scarlet cap, and the *galerus*,

the broad-brimmed hat with the long depending tassels
—and these were exposed before the high altar.   In its
proper place the papal brief of 1489 was read aloud, and
attention was openly drawn to the circumstance that the
probationary term of three years had at last expired.
Then the Cardinal was solemnly vested with mantle,
cap and hat of scarlet, and also with the sapphire ring
(emblematic of the Church's celestial foundation) at the
hands of Canon Matteo Bosso, from whose personal
narrative this account is largely drawn.[1]   The choir
having sung the hymn *Veni Creator Spiritus*, the youthful Cardinal stood up to pronounce an indulgence upon
all who had attended the ceremony that day, and also
upon all such as should repair to the altar of the Badia
Fiesolana on succeeding anniversaries of the event.
Returning to the refectory, the assembled company was
now joined by Piero de' Medici, who had ridden up from
the city on a charger of remarkable size and spirit.[2]
Meanwhile an immense crowd of friends and sympathisers
was beginning to ascend the old Fiesole road in order to
witness the ceremony, which was already finished at so
early an hour; but this eager throng's progress was
arrested at the bridge over the Mugnone, where all
persons were compelled to await the return of the two
brothers and their chosen suite.   At the Ponte di Mugnone
therefore the cavalcade coming from Fiesole was duly
welcomed by deputations of the leading citizens, by the
whole body of the Florentine clergy, and by the general
mass of the people, who with cheers and demands for a
blessing from the newly-vested Cardinal, accompanied
Piero and Giovanni to the church of the Anunziata,
where the latter alighted from his mule to perform his

---

[1] *Narrative of Canon Matteo Bosso of Verona*, Fabroni, Appendix V.
[2] *Ibid.*, " Equus mirae ferocitatis et magnitudinis ".

orisons at the Madonna's famous shrine ; thence to the
Duomo, where more prayers were offered up ; and finally
to the Medicean palace, where Lorenzo, sickening with
his mortal illness, was impatiently awaiting his younger
son's return.   Here the Cardinal was presented with a
costly service of plate, said to be valued at 20,000 florins,
by order of the Signory.   Shows and banquets, that
occasioned much grumbling amongst the political opponents of the Medici, were given at the public expense in
honour of the event, which in the words of the republican
chemist, Luca Landucci, "ennobled the city as well as
the House of Medici".[1]

The meeting between Giovanni and his father on
this occasion has been commemorated for us in one of
Giorgio Vasari's frescoes in the *Sala di Lorenzo il
Magnifico* in the civic palace of Florence.   Although
not of contemporary date, this composition is of ex-
ceptional interest, because it affords us one of the very
few extant portraits of Leo X. in his boyhood.   Lorenzo
in a long violet robe appears seated on a throne in a
garden ; languid and suffering, he can yet regard with
proud satisfaction the son who kneels at his feet dressed
in the gorgeous robes of a cardinal, and offering his
scarlet hat to the parent whose indefatigable efforts had
obtained for him so high an honour.   Beside the form
of Lorenzo are introduced Politian, Ficino and other
members of his court, whilst a warrior waves aloft a
white banner emblazoned with the Magnificent's chosen
device of three ostrich plumes, red, white and black,
clasped by a diamond ring.   Above this group towers
the strange head of the giraffe which the Grand Turk
presented to Lorenzo, and the like of which, so Jovius

[1] Landucci, pp. 62, 63.

CARDINAL DE' MEDICI AND HIS FATHER, LORENZO THE MAGNIFICENT

informs us, neither the Portuguese could discover in the Indies nor the Spaniards in the New World.[1] True it is that the spotted ungainly creature, which for some months had been the pet of the Florentine populace, succumbed to the sharp Tuscan climate many years before the event thus commemorated, yet Vasari deemed it not beneath his dignity as a painter to introduce this departed favourite of the people into the scheme of his historical picture. Giovanni himself appears as a tall stripling with light brown hair and a fair complexion, whilst a medallion portrait in the same hall likewise presents him as a youth with a pale heavy face, with flabby cheeks and light hazel eyes. From the peculiar angle at which every portrait of the future Pope has been drawn, it is evident that Giovanni must have possessed a blemish of some sort in the right eye: in any case it is certain that even in these early years he did not share the good looks of his brothers, although his countenance must have been singularly attractive from its marked expression of intelligence and humour. But already at sixteen Giovanni de' Medici gave only too evident promise of that corpulence of body which was destined to become in after-life so great a hindrance to the health and comfort of the Pope.

Three days later Giovanni bade farewell to his father and brothers, and with a well-equipped train of followers took the road towards Rome. Travelling by easy stages, which included halts at his own abbey of Passignano, at Siena and Viterbo, he finally arrived at the Flaminian Gate of the Eternal City on 22nd March. Here he took up his temporary abode in the Augustinian convent of Santa Maria del Popolo—famous in after

---

[1] Jovius, lib. i.

years as the residence of Luther during his visit to Rome
—and made his preparations for his approaching audience of the Pope.

Amongst the Italian cardinals then residing in Rome
during that momentous year 1492, Giovanni de' Medici
was likely to find some friends, notably in the powerful
Roderigo Borgia, papal vice-chancellor, and in Ascanio
Sforza, both of whom had helped considerably in the
matter of his own promotion. He could scarcely expect
much sympathy from the two nephews of the late Pope,
Giuliano Della Rovere and Raffaele Riario, the latter of
whom had been Sixtus' envoy at the time of the Pàzzi
conspiracy, and had actually been present at that
historic service in the Florentine Cathedral, whereat
Giuliano de' Medici had been stabbed to death by innumerable dagger thrusts. According to vulgar report,
Riario had not yet fully recovered from the alarm and
horror of that terrible scene, whilst his nervous pallid
face bore lasting witness to that abominable act of
mingled sacrilege and treachery. Lorenzo Cybò,
Innocent's own son, would of course be well-disposed to
the new-comer, whilst out of the all-too-few members
of the College who were conspicuous for genuine piety
or learning, the Cardinal Piccolomini, nephew of Pius
II., and Oliviero Caraffà of Naples, were naturally inclined to take an interest in the proper development of
Giovanni's still unformed character. And though some
members of the diminished College were disposed to
regard their new brother with disfavour, such persons
with easy Italian duplicity concealed their private
feelings, and openly at least appeared ready to extend
a warm welcome to their young Florentine colleague.
Thus did Giovanni de' Medici, Cardinal Deacon of
Santa Maria in Domenica, make his first appearance

at the age of sixteen in the midst of "that sink of iniquity," as Lorenzo did not scruple in private to describe
the seat of Western Christendom; and his first letter
telling of his arrival and early experiences in Rome to
his anxious father in Florence, although couched in
simple, rather childish terms, is not without human
interest.

"To Lorenzo the Magnificent, Best of Fathers in
Florence

" . . . On Friday morning I was received in
state, being accompanied from Santa Maria del Poplo as
far as the palace, and from the palace back to the Campo
de' Fiori by all the Cardinals, and by nearly the whole
court, although it was raining heavily. I was warmly
welcomed by Our Lord; he spoke scarcely a word, but
the following day our envoys visited him, and they had
a most gracious audience of him. The Pope set aside
the next day for my own reception, that is to-day.
Thither I went, and His Holiness addressed me in as
loving a manner as possible. He has reminded me, and
also exhorted me to return the Cardinals' visits, and
this I have begun to do in the case of all who have
visited me. I shall write another day to tell you who
they all are; they profess themselves to be very well
disposed towards yourself. Of all matters that passed,
I know you are fully informed. I shall write nothing
more concerning myself, except that I shall ever strive
to do you credit. *De me proloqui ulterius, nefas.*
The news of your much improved state of health
has given me great joy. I have no further desire
for myself except to hear such good tidings often,
and for this recent information I beg to thank my

brother, Ser Piero. I recommend myself to you. No
more.

" JOHN, YOUR SON

"AT ROME, 25th March, 1492 "[1]

It was probably on receipt of this simple missive from
his second-born in Rome that Lorenzo indited that
famous letter of advice, which the good Fabroni eloquently
calls the Magnificent's swan-song ("vox cycnea"), seeing
that it was composed within a very few days of his
premature death at the age of forty-two; and indeed,
apart from the intrinsic value of this epistle, such a
circumstance would naturally lend it a pathetic interest.
However early in life Lorenzo's physical powers may
have sunk beneath the fearful strain of his public and
private cares, this letter provides the fullest proof that
his marvellous and versatile intellect continued unim-
paired to the last.   It was indeed a swan-song of peculiar
strength and sweetness, wherein excellent spiritual advice,
not unworthy of a Fénelon, was so blended with worldly
maxims that a Chesterfield might have penned, that it is
well-nigh impossible to separate its component elements
of an exhortation to a Churchman's strict morality and of
a subtle suggestion to turn an ecclesiastical career to the
private interests of the House of Medici.   That a careful
perusal of this remarkable letter is essential to the student
of Leo X.'s career, it is needless to state; whilst it is of
special interest to note the extent to which the young
Cardinal, for whose future guidance this unique piece of
admonition was composed, either followed or deviated
from the path thus carefully pointed out beforehand for
him by his illustrious father.

[1] Fabroni, Appendix VI.

" LORENZO THE MAGNIFICENT IN FLORENCE TO THE CARDINAL DE' MEDICI IN ROME

·" . . . You and all of us who are interested in your welfare ought to esteem ourselves highly favoured by Providence, not only for the many honours and benefits bestowed on our House, but more particularly for having conferred upon us in your person the greatest dignity we have ever enjoyed. This favour, in itself so important, is rendered still more so by the circumstances by which it is accompanied, and especially by the consideration of your youth, and of our situation in the world. The first thing that I would therefore suggest to you is, that you ought to be grateful to God, and continually to recollect that it is not through *your* prudence, or *your* solicitude, that this event has taken place, but through *His* favour which you can only repay by a pious, chaste, and exemplary life, and that your obligations to the performance of these duties are so much the greater, as in your early years you have given some reasonable expectation that your riper age may produce such fruits. It would be indeed highly disgraceful, and as contrary to your duty as to my hopes, if at a time when others display a greater share of reason and adopt a better mode of life, you should forget the precepts of your youth, and forsake the path in which you have hitherto trodden. Endeavour therefore to alleviate the burden of your early dignity by the regularity of your life and by your perseverance in those studies which are suitable to your profession. It gave me great satisfaction to learn that in the course of the past year, you had frequently of your own accord gone to Confession and Communion ; nor do I conceive that there is any better way of obtaining the favour of Heaven than by habituating yourself to a performance of these and similar duties. This appears to me to be the most suitable and most useful advice, which in the first instance I can possibly give you.

" I well know that as you are now to reside in Rome, that sink of all iniquity,—*che è sentina di tutti i mali*,—the difficulty of conducting yourself by these admonitions will be increased. The influence of example is itself prevalent, but you will probably meet with those who will particularly endeavour to corrupt and incite you to vice, because, as you may yourself perceive, your early attainment to so great a dignity is not observed without envy; and those who could not prevent your receiving that honour will secretly endeavour to diminish it, by inducing you to forfeit the good estimation of the public, thereby precipitating you into that gulf wherein they have themselves fallen, in which attempt the consideration of your youth will give them a confidence. To these difficulties you ought to oppose yourself with the greater firmness, as there is at present less virtue amongst your brethren of the College. I acknowledge indeed that several of them are good and learned men, whose lives are exemplary, and whom I would recommend to you as patterns for your conduct. By emulating them you will be so much the more known and esteemed, in proportion as your age and the peculiarity of your situation will distinguish you from your colleagues. Avoid, however, as you would Scylla or Charybdis the imputation of hypocrisy. Guard against all ostentation either in your conduct or your discourse. Affect not austerity, nor even appear too serious. This advice you will in time, I hope, understand and practise better than I can express it.

" You are not unacquainted with the great importance

of the character you have to sustain, for you well know that all the Christian world would prosper, if the Cardinals were what they ought to be, because in such a case there would always be a good Pope, upon which the tranquillity of Christendom so materially depends. Endeavour then to render yourself such, that, if all the rest resembled you, we might expect this universal blessing. . . .

"You are now devoted to God and the Church, on which account you ought to aim at being a good ecclesiastic, and to show that you prefer the honour and state of the Church and of the Apostolic See to every other consideration. Nor, while you keep this in view, will it be difficult for you to favour your family and your native place. On the contrary, you should be the link to bind this city of Florence closer to the Church, and our family with the city, and although it be impossible to foresee what accidents may happen, yet I doubt not but this may be done with equal advantage to all, observing that you always prefer the interests of the Church.

"You are not only the youngest Cardinal in the College, but the youngest person that was ever raised to that rank, and you ought, therefore, to be the more vigilant and unassuming, not giving others occasion to wait for you either in the chapel, the consistory, or upon deputations. You will soon get a sufficient insight into the manners of your brethren. With those of less respectable character converse not with too much intimacy, not merely on account of the circumstance in itself, but for the sake of public opinion. Converse on general topics with all. On public occasions let your equipage and dress be rather below than above mediocrity. A handsome house and a well-ordered household will be preferable to a great retinue and a splendid palace. Endeavour to live with regularity, and gradually to bring your expenses within those bounds which in a new establishment cannot perhaps be expected. Silks and jewels are not suitable for persons in your station.[1] Your taste will be better shown in the acquisition of a few elegant remains of antiquity, or in the collecting of handsome books, and by your attendants being learned and well-bred rather than numerous. Invite others to your house oftener than you yourself receive invitations. Practise neither too frequently. Let your own food be plain, and take sufficient exercise, for those who wear your habit are soon liable, without great caution, to contract infirmities. The situation of a Cardinal is not less secure than elevated, on which account those who arrive at it too frequently become negligent, conceiving that their object is attained and that they can preserve it with little trouble. This idea is often injurious to the life and character of those who entertain it. Be attentive therefore to your conduct and confide in others too little rather than too much. There is one rule which I would recommend to your attention in preference to all others: *Rise early in the morning.* This will not only contribute to your health, but will enable you to arrange and expedite the business of the day, and as there are various duties incident to your station, such as the performance of Divine service, studying, giving audience, etc., you will find the observance of this admonition productive of the greatest utility. Another very necessary precaution, particularly on your entrance into public life, is to deliberate every evening on what you have to perform the following day, that you may not be unprepared for whatever may happen. With respect to your

---

[1] Compare with this Lord Chesterfield's advice to his son, a fashionable layman: "Let your lodging be equal to your means; your living below your means, and your dress above your means".

speaking in the consistory, it will be most becoming for you at present to refer the matters in debate to the judgment of His Holiness, alleging as a reason your own youth and inexperience. You will probably be desired to intercede for the favours of the Pope on particular occasions. Be cautious, however, that you trouble him not too often, for his temper leads him to be most liberal to those who weary him least with their solicitations. This you must observe, lest you should give him offence, remembering also at times to converse with him on more agreeable topics; and if you should be obliged to request some kindness from him, let it be done with the modesty and humility which are so pleasing to his disposition. Farewell." [1]

Scarcely had the young Cardinal received this extraordinary proof of a father's devotion and wisdom, than there was brought to Rome news of the Magnificent's fatal illness and death at the Careggi villa on 8th April. And thus at the very outset of his career in the Church was the youthful Giovanni de' Medici deprived of a loving parent and a judicious guide, who perhaps whilst he was inditing his final letter to his absent son realised only too well the impending disaster of his own death.

[1] Fabroni, Appendix VII. Roscoe, *Life of Lorenzo the Magnificent*, vol. ii., pp. 146-151.

CHAPTER II

MISFORTUNE AND EXILE

O Italy! O Rome! I am going to deliver you into the hands of a people that will wipe you out from amongst the nations. I behold them descending upon you like famished lions. Hand in hand with War stalks Pestilence. And the mortality will be so great that the grave-diggers will pass through your streets calling aloud for the dead bodies. And then will one bear a father to the charnel-house, and another his son. O Rome! again I warn you to repent. Repent, O Venice! Repent, O Milan! . . . Florence, what have you done? Shall I tell you? The cup of your iniquities is full, therefore stand prepared for some great vengeance (*Sermons of Savonarola*).

ROMANCE and mystery have ever brooded over the death-bed of the Magnificent Lorenzo from contemporary times to the present day. Historians still disagree concerning the real facts of Savonarola's undoubted visit to the dying prince at Careggi,[1] whilst his end was accompanied by strange portents or coincidences in Florence itself, which at the moment excited the alarm alike of the learned and the vulgar. Not many hours before he expired, there fell from the cupola of the Cathedral a huge fragment of stone-work with a fearful crash in the dead of night, striking the pavement on the side towards the Medicean palace, whereat it was commonly reported that Lorenzo himself recognised his

[1] The reader is referred to Professor Pasquale Villari, *Life and Times of Savonarola* (book i., chap. ix., Appendix), and to Professor Armstrong, *Lorenzo de' Medici* (chap. viii.) for accounts of this famous incident.

coming dissolution in this mysterious accident. Men told each other also how a fine lion kept at the public expense had sickened and died, and again certain of the more credulous spoke of comets trailing their light over Careggi and of a fire-breathing monster which had been seen in Santa Maria Novella. There was an universal feeling of restlessness and expectancy in the air ; a vague presentiment of coming peril, as men began dimly to realise that the loss of their beloved Lorenzo, "the most glorious man that could be found,"[1] must of necessity cause far-reaching changes not only in Florence, but throughout all Italy. Yet Piero—Piero the Second, as he is sometimes called—was straightway confirmed in the exalted position held by his late father, and in particular the French King's envoy was instructed to recognise the transfer of the dignity from parent to heir, so that outwardly at least, the state of Florence pursued its normal course, as though it had been guided for generations under an hereditary monarchy.

As soon as the fatal news reached Rome, it was at once suggested that the young Cardinal should return to Florence, in reality for the purpose of strengthening his brother's hands, but ostensibly on account of the coming heats, which the Florentine envoy in Rome affected to consider injurious to the health of young persons.[2] During the short space of his residence in the Eternal City it is evident that Giovanni de' Medici had gained golden opinions from the Pope, who had been favourably impressed both by the Cardinal's modesty and by his application to business. How far the papal satisfaction was shared by the Sacred College at large, it is difficult

[1] Landucci.
[2] Fabroni, Appendix V. : " Questa aria a giovani maxime non suol esser buona ".

to determine; yet everyone expressed pleasure when Innocent announced his intention of investing this fortunate youth with legatine authority in Tuscany, so that these additional powers might prove of service to his elder brother, thus suddenly called upon to fill the difficult post of an uncrowned and officially unrecognised monarch. The legatine authority was formally bestowed on Giovanni de' Medici in the Sistine Chapel during the ceremony of the blessing of the palms on Palm Sunday, and the news of this honour, according to the young Cardinal's tutor, Stefano di Castrocaro, made a profound sensation at the Roman court, so that we cannot help reflecting on the gratification which this early mark of favour would have afforded to the ambitious Lorenzo, had he been still living. Yet Castrocaro's report also contains a curious postscript addressed to the Florentine envoy, whom he exhorts to speak seriously to the young Cardinal concerning his present mode of life, which differs much from that pursued by his colleagues, so the writer avers. He will not rise betimes of a morning, and will sit up too late at night, whereat the tutor is much concerned, since such irregular habits are likely to injure his general health.[1] On this vital point, therefore, upon which his father had laid such stress, Giovanni evidently did not intend to follow the excellent advice bequeathed him, and, as we know, his lazy habits in later life are severely commented on by those candid critics, the Venetian ambassadors in Rome.

The Cardinal, who did not return to his native city till 20th May, had early written to his brother, bewailing their irreparable loss and also expressing a subject's deep devotion towards one who was now both an elder brother

[1] Fabroni, Appendix V.

and a sovereign, although Giovanni's profession of un-questioning loyalty is tempered by a delicate hint as to future conduct on Piero's side :—

"JOHANNES FRANCISCUS, CARDINAL DE' MEDICI, TO HIS
MAGNIFICENCE, PIERO DE' MEDICI

"DEAREST BROTHER AND SOLE PILLAR OF OUR
HOUSE!

"What am I to write, brother mine, for there is nought save tears to tell of, and of a truth in dwelling upon the pious memory of our father, mourning seems better than language? And what a father he was to us! That no parent was ever more indulgent to his sons, there needs no witness save his own conduct. No wonder therefore that I lament with tears and find no repose; yet sometimes, dear brother, I obtain consolation in the thought that I have yourself to regard ever in the light of our lost parent. Yours it will now be to com-mand, and mine to obey cheerfully, for it will give me the highest pleasure possible to perform your orders. Despatch me into dangers; command me; for there is nothing wherein I would not assist your ends. Never-theless, I implore you, Piero mine, for my sake to con-trive to show yourself generous, courteous, friendly and open towards all, but especially towards our own followers, for by such qualities there is nothing one cannot achieve or keep. But I do not remind you of this for lack of confidence in your powers, but because I feel it my duty to mention it. Many things go to strengthen and con-sole me—the crowds of mourners at our gates, the grief-stricken aspect of the city, the public lamentations in Florence, and all those other details which help to allevi-ate sorrow like ours—but what solaces me more than aught else is my having yourself, since I trust in you to

a degree I cannot easily express. . . . Fare you well!
As for myself, I am in such health as my grief permits.

" From the City
   " 12*th April*, 1492 " [1]

Of his three sons, Lorenzo had long ago predicted
that Piero would grow up headstrong (*un pazzo*), Giovanni
a scholar (*un savio*), and Giuliano good (*un buono*), and
as usual the Magnificent's shrewd judgment was proved
by time to be correct. The new ruler of Florence,
though not wholly destitute of virtues, for he was
generous, cultured and accounted brave, was far too hot-
headed and fond of pleasure to carry out adequately the
exalted but delicate duties which his father had performed
with such marked ability and success for the last twenty
years. Addicted to street brawling and to nocturnal
amours, Piero was quite unfit to set an example to the
Florentine people. His love of costly tournaments,
wherein his undoubted skill often bore away the palm ;
his excellence at that rough species of Florentine foot-ball,
the *calcio ;* and his acknowledged prowess at *pallone*, the
popular Tuscan game at ball which requires both an unerring eye and brute strength of arm, served to endear
their new ruler to the idle and rich young men ; but such
accomplishments scarcely commended themselves to the
graver citizens, whilst they excited the contemptuous
dislike of the old-fashioned adherents of the Republic.
Piero's mother had been an Orsini, and in her eldest
son's character the feudal pride of the Roman house
dominated the more crafty qualities derived from the
burgher blood ; his wife, Alfonsina Orsini, came of the
same turbulent stock, and her injudicious advice went
far towards increasing her husband's natural arrogance.

[1] Fabroni, Appendix VII.

Tactless and violent, inordinately fond of sports and impatient of the routine of business, Piero could never have held the mastery of Florence for any great length of time, and on the whole it seems rather remarkable that more than two years were allowed to elapse before the offended citizens expelled with ignominy this incapable young ruler from their midst. As to Giovanni and his possible restraining influence over his elder brother, we must bear in mind that he had not yet attained his nineteenth year, when the final catastrophe of 1494 overwhelmed the Medicean family, and even assuming that he tendered good advice, it does not appear probable that the rash and conceited Piero would have consented to listen to a younger brother's solemn warnings. On the other hand, had Giovanni possessed Piero's splendid opportunities and additional years of experience ; had he been educated by Lorenzo as his political heir rather than as a future Churchman, we agree with a modern critic in believing that the forcible expulsion of the Medici in the autumn of 1494 might certainly have been averted.

Of a truth, the times were too fateful to allow of mediocrity, far less of downright incompetence, for the year 1492, that *annus mirabilis*, may be described as definitely marking the boundary line between the world of the middle ages and that of modern thought and civilisation. Europe was passing through a series of changes—moral, social and political—with appalling rapidity. That memorable year saw the expulsion of the Moslem from Granada, and with it the first blow to the overweening power of the Turk and the early rise of the vast but short-lived Spanish empire ; it saw too the voyage of Columbus into the New World, that prelude to the discoveries of Vasco da Gama and of Sebastian Cabot, which were destined to stultify the whole system of

mediæval geography and astronomy, and to prepare the
way for the theories of Copernicus and Galileo. To
Italy itself that year was doomed to be climacteric, for
the death of Lorenzo de' Medici, that typical product of
the earlier Renaissance, broke up for ever the artificial
system of balance of power within the peninsula, of which
the late ruler of Florence had been the main director ;
whilst fresh and unheard-of complications were about to
arise on the decease of the aged Pope. Poor Piero's
abilities were of course quite unequal to cope with this
universal upheaval ; indeed, it is very doubtful if all the
skill of his father could have saved Italy from the terrible
wrath to come.

Scarcely had Piero been three months at the head of
the Florentine state, than news was brought of the fatal
illness of Innocent VIII., "the constant guardian of the
peace of Italy," the firm friend of the Medici and the
patron of Andrea Mantegna. The Cardinal now hastened
to Rome where a conclave of twenty-three members (for
to such meagre proportions had the selfish attitude of the
Cardinals reduced the Sacred College in Italy) met to
select a successor to Innocent. The conclave was of brief
duration, for of the two likely candidates for the tiara—
Roderigo Borgia and Ascanio Sforza—the former by unscrupulous methods soon induced his possible rival to waive
his claims. Five asses laden with bags of gold were seen
to enter the courtyard of Sforza's palace, and even this
was but an earnest of what the Spanish Cardinal promised
to his Milanese opponent in return for his support.
Smaller largesse was sufficient for the other members of
the conclave, all of whom save five are said to have received pay or promises from Borgia in return for their
votes. The opposition of the pious Piccolomini and
Caraffa, of Giovanni Colonna and of the young Medici,

and the fierce diatribes of Cardinal Giuliano Della Rovere
proved of no avail; on 11th August, within three weeks
of Innocent's death, Roderigo Borgia was elected Pope
under the name of the invincible Alexander at his own
request. The elevation of the Borgia was in short almost
an exact historical repetition of that disgraceful incident
during the decadence of the Roman Empire, when the
Pretorian Guard put up the sovereignty of the Roman
world for sale to the highest bidder, the merchant Julius
Didianus. The evil reputation of the new Pope and the
open bribery he had used to accomplish his aims sent a
thrill of horror throughout the courts of Italy. The hard-
hearted Ferdinand of Naples, who had never been known
to weep, even at the death of his own child, burst into
tears of rage and fright at the receipt of this news, whilst
the intrepid Cardinal Della Rovere hurried from the city
to the castle of Ostia, whence he denounced the late election as null and void, loudly appealing to the princes of
Christendom to call a general council to depose this false
Pontiff, this betrayer of the Church. Nevertheless,
Alexander held his own despite the outcry, and at least
in Rome itself his accession was far from being considered
altogether a calamity. For if the new Pontiff had many
acknowledged vices (which Italian historians and gossips
have perhaps unduly blackened in the case of a foreign
Pope) he certainly owned qualities which might have
rendered him an able and even a beneficent administrator.
With justice but without mercy the disgraceful state of
crime and brigandage, which had prevailed in the Roman
States under Innocent's feeble sway, was promptly suppressed, and for this and similar measures on behalf of the
public safety the Roman people felt not a little grateful.
" *Vive diu, Bos!*—O Borgia, live for ever!"—cried the
admiring throngs in allusion to the heraldic bull on the

Borgian shield, whilst during the coronation festivities one
of the many laudatory inscriptions bore the fulsome and
almost blasphemous legend—

In Alexander, Cæsar is surpast,
The former is a God, a man the last ! [1]

But however much the populace of Rome may have applauded on this occasion, such of the cardinals as had
opposed Alexander's election at once perceived the advisability of withdrawing quickly from the city.   Amongst
these was the Cardinal de' Medici, who has been credited,
on the authority of Burchard, the papal master of ceremonies, with a remark addressed to his neighbour in the
conclave, Lorenzo Cybò: "We are in the jaws of a
rapacious wolf!   If we neglect to flee, he will devour us."
Whether or no Giovanni actually expressed himself thus,
it is certain that he deemed it prudent to retire to Florence,
where he resided until the expulsion of his House in 1494,
inhabiting during this period a palace in the quarter of
Sant' Antonio near the Faenza Gate.[2]

The many snares in the existing situation at home
must have been soon perceived by the sharp eye of the
young Cardinal, who did what he could to render the tenure
of the city by his family less insecure.   With the political
world without ready to fall into confusion, Florence itself
was seething with discontent and with a general desire
for reform, a desire which found voice in the impassioned
sermons of the prior of San Marco, Fra Girolamo
Savonarola.   His Advent and Lenten addresses, given
within the spacious nave of the Duomo, were attracting
vast crowds of citizens, bent equally on bewailing their

[1] "Caesare magna fuit, nunc Roma est maxima : Sextus Regnat
Alexander; ille vir, iste deus."—Creighton, vol. iv., p. 189, note 2.

[2] This quarter of the city was dismantled during the siege of Florence in 1529, and its site is now occupied by the Citadel of the Grand-
Dukes of Tuscany.—N. Richa, *Chiese Fiorentine*.

own sins and deploring the wickedness of those in high places. The recent election of Alexander VI. had caused the deepest indignation to the prior, who was already expounding his predictions of impending disaster to his overflowing audiences, ending each discourse with his three famous "Conclusions," on which all his exhortations were based ; namely, that the Church would be chastised for her present state of corruption ; that she would be regenerated ; and that these measures of punishment and reformation were close at hand. From his conclusions the preacher advanced to attack in scathing language the lives and practices of the prelates of the day, who cared only for the outward adornments of Holy Church—for the ceremonies and vestments, the jewelled mitres and golden chalices, the notes of sweet-toned organs and the chaunting of choristers—and who only tickled men's ears with pagan arguments from Plato or Aristotle, instead of attending to the true salvation of the soul. From the princes of the Church Savonarola passed to the condemnation of the secular rulers of Italy, and here his burning indignation knew no bounds ;—"these wicked princes are sent to chastise the sins of their subjects ; they are truly a sad snare for souls ; their courts and palaces are the refuge of all the beasts and monsters of the earth, for they give shelter to ribalds and malefactors". From princes, Savonarola proceeded to "flattering philosophers and poets, who by force of a thousand lies and fables trace the genealogy of these evil princes back to the gods". And in connection with this last piece of fulmination, we can imagine with what degree of disgust the prior of St. Mark's must have heard of the canonry in the Duomo conferred by the Cardinal de' Medici upon his old tutor, the humanist and reputed pagan, Politian.

Names were invariably omitted by the preacher, yet

for this general indictment of secular and ecclesiastical
corruption in Italy, it was no difficult matter for the vast
congregation, much of it already hostile to the Medicean
rule, to apply the prior's statements and warnings directly
to the sins of the prince and prelate in their midst : the
supposed tyranny of Piero and the worldliness of the
Cardinal.   Nevertheless, Piero was unable or unwilling
to take any decided step for the arrest or silencing of
this uncompromising monkish agitator.   For a short
time, it is true, during the summer of 1493, the nominal
ruler of Florence, probably at the suggestion and certainly with the help of his younger brother, had contrived
by means of the superiors of the Dominican Order in
Rome to obtain Savonarola's peaceful transference to
Bologna ; yet by an unaccountable act of folly Piero had
later allowed the all-powerful preacher to return to
Florence, thereby proving beyond the shadow of a doubt
that the great Lorenzo's heir was indeed a positive fool,
wholly unable to read aright the manifest signs of his
times.

The evil effects of Lorenzo's loss and of Alexander's
election soon became apparent, for the three states of
Florence, Milan and Naples were already falling into
political entanglements, which the constant intrigues of
three ambitious women—Alfonsina Orsini in Florence,
Beatrice d'Este in Milan and the Duchess Isabella at
Pavia—made yet more complicated.   Almost immediately after his father's death, Piero had begun to exhibit
a certain degree of coolness towards the usurper of
Milan (whom Lorenzo had always done his best to conciliate) and to coquet politically with Ludovico Sforza's
deadly enemy, King Ferdinand of Naples ; an attitude
which eventually drove the exasperated and nervous
Duke of Milan to take a step fraught with the utmost

importance for the future of Italy.   Dreading a combination of the Florentine state with his arch-enemy, Ferdin-
and of Naples, the Sforza now determined to save
himself from impending ruin by no less a measure than
the total banishment of the dynasty of Aragon from
Naples, by inciting the young Charles VIII. of France
to take forcible possession of that kingdom, which he
claimed as heir of the former monarchs of the House of
Anjou.   The devil, says the proverb, is at all times
easier to raise than to lay ; and in this instance Ludovico
Sforza of Milan has gained an unenviable notoriety as the
original promoter of that detestable policy· of foreign invasion, from the evil effects of which Italy has been
suffering almost until our own days.   But at this period
the aims of every government and ruler throughout
Italy were mean, selfish and provincial to a degree which
we find it hard at this distance of time to realise ;—the
very notion of Italian patriotism, of Italian unity, was
practically non-existent in the year 1492.   Even the
shrewd Lorenzo had always regarded his native land as
a mere conglomerate mass of hostile and disunited states,
which it required a master-hand like his own to manipu-
late, so as to preserve peace throughout the whole
peninsula.   Nevertheless, it was reserved for a Florentine thinker, an obscure and needy citizen, who was
twenty-three years of age at Lorenzo's death, to propound
to an unheeding Italy the tenets of true patriotism and
their surest means of attainment.[1]

After much hesitation and in opposition to public
opinion in France itself, the young French monarch
finally accepted the Sforza's selfish invitation, and at last
the vast army of Charles VIII., 60,000 men strong and
supported by the finest artillery of that age, crossed the

---

[1] Niccolò Machiavelli in *Il Principe*, *Gli Discorsi*, etc.

snowy barrier of the protecting Alps, which, in the words of Michelet, were now levelled henceforth and for evermóre. After a long period spent partly in feasting and dallying at Asti and Turin, and partly in recovering from the ill-effects of his excesses at these entertainments, Charles was again able to proceed, and his splendid army with its fine French cavalry, its sturdy German *Landsknechts*, its Swiss mountaineers and its Scottish archers, once more continued on its course towards Naples, where the aged Ferdinand was making feverish but belated efforts in defence of his coveted kingdom. The king's son, the Duke of Calabria, was meanwhile preparing to oppose the French advance by way of the Adriatic coast-line, but it lay with Piero de' Medici to decide whether or no the invaders were to be allowed to pass unmolested through Tuscan territory on the western side of the Apennines. Intense was the excitement prevailing in Florence at the news of Charles' progress, and the general concern was further increased, when it became known that Piero, anxious to imitate his father's diplomatic methods, had at his own initiative set out for the French camp to treat in person with the king. Both Medicean and popular parties awaited in tense anxiety the result of this mission, and loud were the execrations of the latter party and dire the dismay of the *Palleschi*, the adherents of the Medici, when authentic details of Piero's bungling diplomacy were brought to the city. For the foolish and incompetent prince—" Il Gran Lombardo," as he was styled by the French court for want of a recognised official title—had actually ceded the Tuscan fortresses of Sarzana and Sarzanella, the keys of the road to Rome and Naples, to the King of France. Yet so blind was Piero to the inglorious nature of his late pact with Charles, that he ventured to return to the

city on 8th November, and throwing open the doors of
his palace gave cakes and wine to a number of the populace, whom he assured with a cheerful countenance that
now both he himself and the state of Florence were safe
from danger owing to his judicious treaty with the invincible invader of Italy. But Piero's self-satisfaction, assuming it to have been genuine, was not of long duration,
for on the following day he attempted to force his way
into the palace of the Signory in order to explain his
late unpopular action, with the result that he was ignominiously forced to return to his house amidst the
ringing of alarm bells and shouts of contemptuous hatred.
Terrified at the hostile aspect of the city, Piero after a
short period of wavering finally decided upon flight,
thereby committing the last of the many follies which
had characterised his brief rule of Florence;—indeed,
this final action proved Lorenzo's heir to be not only incapable but also cowardly. Together with his youngest
brother, Giuliano, then sixteen years old, the self-exiled
prince hurried to the Porta San Gallo, where horses
were waiting in readiness to carry them over the passes
of the Apennines to Bologna. Even his voluntary
choice of an objective in his flight proves Piero's hopeless
incompetence, for his natural bourne under the circumstances should have been the camp of the French King,
with whom he had so recently made a treaty in the
name of the state he was supposed to represent. As
it so fell, the unlucky prince richly deserved the taunts,
however ungenerous, of Giovanni Bentivoglio, tyrant of
Bologna, who did not hesitate to twit the head of the
once-powerful Medicean House with his late surrender
of Florence practically without a protest, certainly without a struggle.

During this acute crisis produced by threats of ex-

ternal invasion and by dissensions within the city, what
had been the conduct of the Cardinal? Shortly before
the approach of Charles towards Sarzana, Giovanni de'
Medici had, it seems, been summoned specially to Rome
by the Pope. Not daring to disobey Alexander's explicit message, although the Pontiff's request was generally interpreted as a device to obtain Giovanni's person
as a hostage for Piero's future obedience to the Holy See,
the Cardinal set out for Rome. He had proceeded as
far as his own abbey of Passignano, when he was hastily
informed of Piero's mission to the French King, whereupon he quickly returned to Florence, now filled with
tumult and with the mass of its citizens avowedly hostile
to the House of Medici. On that memorable Sunday
of 9th November, 1494, the Cardinal, in order to assist
his brother's efforts to force an entrance into the palace
of the Signory, issued from his house at Sant' Antonio
clad in his robes and attended by a number of armed
servants. Riding by way of the narrow Corso and
shouting *Palle! Palle!* the young Churchman contrived
to reach the chapel of Or San Michele despite the
threatening attitude of the mob and the repeated cries
of *Popolo e Libertà! Muoiano i tiranni!* with which
the air resounded. Although the Cardinal kept bitterly
reproaching the Florentine crowd for its ingratitude to
his House, the red robe was for a while respected; but
in front of Or San Michele, Giovanni was compelled to
retire at the risk of his life. An attempt to rouse the
poor quarter round San Gallo, hitherto notable as a
stronghold of the *Palleschi*, ended in like failure. The
Cardinal now made his way to the convent of San Marco,
whereupon the monks ungraciously refused to unbar
their doors to a prince of the Church, the son of their
former benefactor, Lorenzo de' Medici. Thus repulsed

at San Marco, Giovanni retired to his own house, where, later, information was sent to him of Piero's unmanly flight. Angry crowds were now gathering round the doors of the palace in Sant' Antonio, where Luca Landucci, no friend to the Medici, declared that he saw the Cardinal's form through the open casement, kneeling in prayer with clasped hands, at which, remarks the good Landucci, " I felt very sorry for him, for I reckoned him to be a worthy young man with excellent intentions ".[1] The beleaguered Cardinal now hastily exchanged his rich vestments for the coarse brown habit of a Franciscan friar, and quitting his palace unnoticed in this garb and mingling with the crowd bent on his own destruction he escaped under cover of the shades of evening to the Porta San Gallo, whence, following in the tracks of his brothers across the Apennines, he arrived a few hours after them at the gates of Bologna.

On hearing of the departure of the three Medici, the Florentine populace grew fiercer and more uproarious, so that the proposal to sack the deserted palaces of their late rulers was greeted with shouts of approval. The Casino of San Marco, with its adjacent gardens and academy provided by the Magnificent for the public study of sculpture, was speedily denuded of its treasures, the ignorant rabble hacking to bits the masterpieces of art, which were too bulky for removal. The Cardinal's residence at Sant' Antonio was next destroyed, and its valuable collections all stolen or scattered ;—so violent was the behaviour of the mob here that the very fabric of the house was threatened with collapse, and the Cardinal's servants were scarcely permitted to escape with their lives. The great palace in Via Larga was

[1] Landucci, p. 75.

however protected by express order of the Signory, not
out of any motive of compassion for its luckless owner,
but because it had been proposed to lodge the King of
France under its roof on his expected arrival. Quantities
of works of art and pieces of plate were, however, pilfered,
and whatsoever the Florentines spared the retinue of
Charles removed a little later, so that it is no exaggeration
to say that all the Medicean palaces were sacked and their
possessors absolutely despoiled of all their private wealth.
Nor was this all, for the Signory, after decreeing the con-
fiscation of their goods, next set a price upon the heads
of the two elder brothers, now declared outlaws, promising by open proclamation 2000 ducats to the slayer
of Piero and half that sum to the lucky assassin of the
Cardinal.[1]

But before pursuing further the fortunes of the exiled
Cardinal, it is impossible to avoid making reference,
although such may naturally be accounted a digression,
to the coming "Restorer and Protector of the liberties
of Florence," as the name of Charles of France was
enrolled officially in the archives of the revived Republic.
Exactly a week from the violent expulsion of the Medici,
late in the evening of 17th November, appeared Charles
VIII. as a conqueror with couched lance at the open
gate of San Frediano. Mounted on a magnificent
charger and clad in black velvet with flowing mantle
of cloth-of-gold, surrounded by the flower of French
chivalry, Charles made an imposing figure at his entry
into Florence. But on his alighting at the portals of the
cathedral and thus giving a nearer view of his person to
the applauding citizens, general surprise and disappoint-

[1] Landucci, p. 75 : "E in questo tempo mandorono un bando
in piazza, che chi amazzava Piero de' Medici guadagniassi 2000
ducati, e chi amazzava el Cardinale n' avesse 1000 ".

ment were expressed at the deformed little monster of a man with the inane face, the staring expressionless eyes, the long nose, the tiny trunk and the spindling legs ending in feet so enormous that vulgar tradition credited their owner with the possession of a sixth toe. " He was indeed a mannikin ! "[1] sighs the aggrieved Landucci, who however adds that all the Florentine women were in love with him, old and young, small and great. But perhaps it might be thought that Nature, who in a malignant sportive mood had bestowed so mean a presence upon a great monarch, had presented him by way of compensation with surpassing gifts of intellect. The King's mind, however, was fully as mis-shapen as his diminutive body, for according to all contemporary chroniclers, Charles of France was weak, vacillating, timid, cunning and appallingly ignorant ; indeed, his sole distinguishing quality, which was not a vice, seems to have been a vague but insatiable craving for military glory. His lust and gluttony were patent to all, whilst his vaunted virtues were imperceptible ; he had the brain of an idiot and the tastes of a satyr. Such was the sovereign whom Ludovico Sforza had called upon to cross the Alps and act as the arbiter of the fortunes of Italy ; such was the creature whom Savonarola now presented to the people of Florence as the scourge of tyrants and the champion of popular rights, as God's own destined instrument to chastise and purge His Church.

It was not long before the three brothers were joined at Bologna by another fugitive member of their House, Giulio, the bastard son of Giuliano the Elder, who had managed to escape from Pisa, where he was then studying. Nearly of an age with his cousin Giuliano the

---

[1] Landucci, p. 80 : " In vero era molto piccolo uomo ! "

Younger, Giulio had originally been brought up as a soldier by his uncle Lorenzo, who had acknowledged him for a nephew and had contrived to get him enrolled one of the Knights of Rhodes ; but later, on the boy's expressing a desire for an ecclesiastical career, he had been nominated prior of Capua and despatched, like his cousin Giovanni before him, to study canon law at Pisa. As a recognised bastard of a great house, Giulio took an unbounded pride in his family, and manifested an intense desire to serve it in every way, so that early in life he began to attach himself to his cousin Giovanni, following and waiting on the latter alike in good and evil fortune till the day of his death. The three brothers quickly dispersed to different parts of Italy ; Piero following the camps, Giuliano chiefly remaining at the courts of Urbino and Mantua, where his accomplishments no less than his buoyant good nature made him a special favourite with the reigning families of Gonzaga and Montefeltre ; whilst the Cardinal, always accompanied by the faithful Giulio, spent much of his time in Rome, although the Eternal City under the rule of the Borgias was scarcely reckoned either a safe or a respectable residence for a young prince of the Church. During the years succeeding the events of November, 1494, no fewer than five attempts were made by the expelled Medici to regain the city of Florence with the assistance of their political friends, but all failed miserably, partly owing to the unforeseen chances of an adverse fate, but largely on account of Piero's unrivalled incapacity. It is wholly beyond the scope of this work to follow in detail the course of these fruitless efforts or their accompanying intrigues, except to state that ere long both Giovanni and Giuliano relinquished all chance of success for the time being. At length, wearied out with the hopeless task of attempting to recover that which seemed for the nonce irretrievably lost, and living in constant dread of Alexander's suspected enmity, the young Cardinal applied to the Pope for permission to leave Italy in order to travel in foreign lands. As Giovanni de' Medici was not rich nor his family any longer of importance in Italian politics, so that he possessed little value as a hostage, the Pontiff consented to this request, whereupon the future Leo X. and the future Clement VII., with ten chosen friends of congenial habits and ideas, departed from Rome on their intended expedition. Having reached Venice, the Cardinal laid aside the signs of his rank, so that the whole party might appear dressed alike, and in this manner the twelve travellers crossed the Alps to seek consolation for the fallen fortunes of the House of Medici in the novel excitement of beholding strange nations and of visiting the famous towns of Northern Europe.

Their first country to sojourn in was Bavaria, where they expressed their delight at the beautiful buildings of Nuremberg and Ratisbon, nor was their pleasure lessened by the terms of perfect equality on which all existed. For every night it was customary amongst them to choose by lot a leader for the ensuing day, whose commands all were obliged to obey without question. And in thus manfully setting at defiance the blows of ill-fortune, the Medici was wont to declare in after years that neither before nor since had he enjoyed so much true freedom of thought and action. At Ulm, however, the identity of this distinguished traveller became recognised, on which the Emperor Maximilian, who had always kept the warmest regard for the memory of the Magnificent Lorenzo, at once summoned his old friend's son to his presence. On hearing from Giovanni's own lips the reason of this pilgrimage, Maximilian's admiration was raised, and after prophesying a brighter future for the Medici, he immediately congratulated his visitor upon his recent decision thus to turn his evil fate to such good account;—far better it was, said he, for a man, however highly placed, to enlarge his mind by the study of men and manners abroad, than to sulk in luxurious idleness at home.[1]

Wending their way up the rich valley of the Rhine with its thriving towns, this band of Italian exiles reached Brussels, where they were hospitably entertained by Don Philip, the Emperor's son, on the strength of his father's warm recommendation. From Brussels Giovanni and his companions proceeded westward till they found themselves at Terouenne near the Flemish coast, at which point a difference of opinion arose as to the advisability of crossing the sea so as to visit England, a project on which the future Leo X. it seems had set his heart. It would indeed have been interesting to be able to record a visit of the Medici to our island, and still more so to learn his impressions of London and its inhabitants, but unfortunately the Cardinal's plan was over-ruled by the majority of the party, who positively refused to embark. Their course was accordingly directed into France, in which country a curious misadventure befel the whole party, for at Rouen the magistrates of that town made them all prisoners in spite of Giovanni's protestations and open disclosure of his rank; nor was it until letters from King Louis had been received that the innocent wanderers were released by the obstinate Frenchmen, whom Giovio consequently describes as hasty and suspicious as a nation. On being at last set at liberty, the Cardinal and his friends

---

[1] Jovius, lib. i.

were allowed to travel unmolested across France, until they reached Marseilles, where they chartered a ship for their conveyance to Italy, for apparently the aspect of the sunny Mediterranean did not appear so alarming to the less adventurous members of the party as the grey waters of the English Channel. But scarcely had they embarked than a succession of inopportune squalls compelled the captain to keep under lee of the Genoese coast, until worn and weakened by the discomforts of their protracted voyage, by an unanimous vote they decided to land at Savona. Here, in the native town of his own humble ancestors, they unexpectedly found Cardinal Giuliano Della Rovere, an exile from Alexander's wrath, who gave a warm welcome to Giovanni and Giulio de' Medici, and at this point Leo's first biographer mentions with proud satisfaction a certain historic meal, whereat there sat down to table the three famous Churchmen, each of them at that moment in evil plight, but each destined later to wear the tiara successively as Julius II., Leo X. and Clement VII. Bidding farewell to Della Rovere, Giovanni de' Medici continued his journey to Genoa, where he remained for some time as the guest of his sister Maddalena, the wife of the peace-loving Francesco Cybò.[1]

With the opening of the new century the political situation in Italy underwent a complete transformation. In the summer of 1503, Alexander expired suddenly at the Vatican, and, as Cæsar Borgia lay helpless on a sick-bed at this critical moment, the conclave was enabled to hold its proceedings without fear of any disturbing influence from that dreaded quarter. On this occasion the most exemplary member of the Sacred College was

---

[1] Jovius, lib. ii.

elected to the vacant throne in the person of Francesco
Piccolomini, who out of compliment to his famous uncle[1]
assumed the title of Pius III.   But the new Pontiff was
already fast sinking to the grave at the very time of the
conclave—a circumstance that perhaps in some degree
prompted the choice of the cardinals.   To the disappointment of all Italy, but scarcely to the surprise of the
Roman court, the new Pope only survived his elevation
twenty-six days, dying on 18th October—"What boots
it to be pious, when an evil Alexander is permitted to
reign for years, and a Pius for scarce a month?" demanded an indignant epigrammatist, when the fatal intelligence was spread abroad.   Once more the conclave
assembled, and as on this occasion Giuliano Della
Rovere, by means of a secret compact with the now
partially recovered Cæsar Borgia, obtained the votes
of the Spanish cardinals, he was finally chosen Pope on
1st November by the name of Julius II.   Nor did
this fateful year draw to its close without producing
one more event of importance to the House of Medici,
for on 28th December, during the rout of the French by
the Spaniards under the celebrated "Gran Capitan,"
Gonsalvo da Cordova, poor Piero de' Medici, who as
usual was serving with the losing army, terminated his
useless existence.   For on trying to cross the swollen
stream of the Garigliano after the battle, the vessel bearing Piero and his cousin Paolo Orsini, together with a
number of refugees and four pieces of artillery, foundered
and sank in deep water.   Piero's body, recovered many
days later in the shallows near the river's mouth, was
conveyed to the great Benedictine abbey of Monte
Cassino hard by, of which his brother the Cardinal was

---

[1] Æneas Sylvius Piccolomini of Siena, Pope Pius II.

titular abbot, and here it was buried with due display of
military honours. Yet nearly fifty years were allowed
to elapse before a monument was erected to the deceased
prince, whose memory was perhaps not held very dear
by his surviving brothers. In 1552, however, the first
Grand-Duke of Tuscany caused a splendid tomb from
the chisel of Francesco Sangallo[1] to be raised in the abbey
church, although it is significant to note that in its accompanying epitaph no mention is made of the unhappy
prince's career save to state the cause of his early death,
and to tell the chance visitor that he was the son of the
Magnificent Lorenzo, the brother of Leo X., and the
cousin-german of Clement VII.

By his wife, Alfonsina Orsini, Piero de' Medici left
two children : a daughter Clarice, who was later married
to the Florentine merchant-prince, Filipppo Strozzi ; and
a son and heir, Lorenzo, afterwards Duke of Urbino,
who had been born two years prior to his father's headlong flight from his capital in 1494. It is a striking but
hardly an inexplicable circumstance that with the premature end of Piero il Pazzo, the fortunes of the depressed
House of Medici began steadily to improve, as the old
Emperor Maximilian had predicted to the despondent
Cardinal during his visit to Germany.

[1] Vasari, *Life of Fr. Sangallo.*

CHAPTER III

RISE TO POWER UNDER JULIUS II

Julius Secundus loquitur.—" I raised the revenue. I invented new offices and sold them. I invented a way to sell bishoprics without simony. . . . I recoined the currency and made a great sum that way. Then I annexed Bologna to the Holy See. I beat the Venetians. I jockeyed the Duke of Ferrara. I defeated the schismatical Council by a sham Council of my own. I drove the French out of Italy, and I would have driven out the Spaniards too, if the Fates had not brought me to death. I have set all the princes of Europe by the ears. I have torn up treaties, and kept large armies in the field. I have covered Rome with palaces, and I have left five million ducats in the treasury behind me. . . . I have done it all myself too. I owe nothing to my birth, for I don't know who my father was ; nothing to learning, for I have none ; nothing to youth, for I was old when I began ; nothing to popularity, for I was hated all round " (*Julius Secundus Exclusus*).

CARDINAL Giovanni de' Medici had tasted enough of the bitter of adversity to appreciate his improved position due to the death of Alexander VI. and the election of Julius II. For the last nine years he had experienced what was practically double exile, being forcibly kept out of his native Florence and at the same time rendered chary of settling permanently in Rome, which was in reality also his rightful abode. Although as a nephew of Sixtus IV. the new Pope looked with no favourable eye upon the political pretensions of the House of Medici, yet Julius was personally at least well-disposed towards the young Cardinal. In any case, through the untimely, or timely, death of Piero, Giovanni de' Medici

had become a personage of increased consequence in
the world of Italian politics.   Piero's only son, Lorenzo,
was but eleven years old when his parent was drowned
in the Garigliano, so that Giovanni now came to be
regarded as the real head of his family, and it was to
the Cardinal that the Medicean party, crushed but still
capable of future action, now turned with renewed hopes
of success.   Living with Giovanni in his Roman palace
(later known as the Palazzo Madama), not far from the
venerable Pantheon in the heart of the mediæval city,
were the cunning Bernardo Dovizi and the ever-faithful
Giulio ; whilst often residing with his elder brother in
Rome was Giuliano de' Medici, one of the most esteemed
princes and most charming personalities of the Italian
Renaissance, "pre-eminent above all other men," quaintly
observes Giovio, "by reason of the perfect harmony of
virtues abiding in his nature and conduct".[1]   This improved position Giovanni was astute enough to strengthen
yet further by trying to obtain the good graces of the
youthful Cardinal Galeotto Franciotto, the Pope's favourite
nephew and papal vice-chancellor.   Although Giovio
states explicitly that this newly formed intimacy between
the Medici and Franciotto had its origin in the diplomatic
aims of the former rather than in any mutual inclination
of the two young men, yet it is certain that ere long
Giovanni grew deeply attached to Galeotto, and that
the sorrow expressed by him at the papal nephew's
sudden and premature death was both genuine and
abiding, for on the testimony of Tommaso Inghirami,
we learn that in after years, when the Cardinal de'
Medici had been transformed into the Pontiff Leo X.,
he could not endure to hear Galeotto's name men-

[1] Jovius, lib. i.

tioned in his presence, and if anyone were so careless as to allude to his passed friend, the Pope would
invariably turn aside his face to hide the tears he was
unable to repress.   And in the Medici's case this instance
of real affection is of peculiar interest, for with the exception of his brother Giuliano, there exists no record of
Leo showing any strong affection towards any one of
his contemporaries save this nephew of Julius II.

With the renewal of public confidence in Rome,
Giovanni prepared to enjoy the pleasant existence of a
prince of the Church, whose personal tastes, derived from
his illustrious father, had early marked him out as a
leading patron of the literature and fine arts of his day,
so that the hospitable Palazzo Medici soon became known
as a prominent literary and artistic centre.   Painters,
sculptors, jewellers, poets and scholars all found a hearty
welcome in the saloons of the Medici, whose natural
delight in music also induced him to encourage singers
and players of instruments, who were engaged to perform
at the many sumptuous banquets that he gave, notwithstanding the dying Lorenzo's earnest counsel to be
moderate in all things.   For in spite of numerous benefices the Cardinal was not nearly so opulent as many of
the colleagues with whom he endeavoured to vie, nor
was his extravagant style of living compensated for by
any aptitude for household management on his part.
Even the prudent Giulio's economy was unable to prevent his cousin from running continually into debt, an
inconvenience which seemed however to sit very lightly
on the easy-going Cardinal, although oftentimes the well-
spread table stood depleted of its choicest silver vases
and goblets, owing to the fact that the plate had been
deposited temporarily with the Roman butchers and fish-
mongers for lack of ready money.   As the Cardinal

preferred to risk his credit rather than to retrench, debts rapidly accumulated, yet he only declared cheerfully that men of mark like himself were specially provided for by Heaven, so that they need never lack long for all that was necessary, if only they kept a lively faith in their predestined good fortune.[1] When the daily audiences were finished, and the last scholar with his poem in manuscript or goldsmith with some graceful design for a ring or chalice had been dismissed, the Cardinal usually rode out into the Campagna to amuse himself with hawking or hunting, for he had inherited his father's love of outdoor sport. This period of daily exercise in the fresh air was of peculiar value in helping to reduce the already bulky frame, which threatened its owner with excessive stoutness at no distant date, unless he made abundant use of the remedies which Lorenzo had suggested long ago in his famous letter. But this pleasant existence, wherein business, sport and culture were so agreeably blended, this daily life of entertaining and of being entertained, of encouraging obsequious scholars who hung intent on his shrewd criticisms, and of examining or buying works of art, could not long continue undisturbed under such a Pontiff as the vigorous old man who had lately ascended the throne of St. Peter.

Julius II. undoubtedly shone as a great statesman, but he was in reality a greater warrior, for much as he busied himself in the finer arts of diplomacy, in his heart he preferred the rough life of the camp to the deliberations of the council-chamber. At the date of his election all Italy was at peace, with the exception of the endless war between Florence and her revolted colony of Pisa. Yet this state of quiescence was but the

---

[1] Jovius, lib. ii.

ominous lull before the approaching storm, for the pontificate of Julius was fated to be remembered as the most
turbulent and bloody in the annals of the Papacy, a circumstance for which the ambitious policy of Julius himself was mainly responsible. At his accession the French
were firmly established in the Milanese; the Spaniards
were masters of Naples; Venice was busily engaged in
annexing one by one the various towns of the Romagna,
which had recently formed part of Cæsar Borgia's
short-lived duchy, whilst she was also strengthening her
position along the seaboard of the Adriatic. Such a
situation was bound to lead to mischief in the near future,
and although the presence of two sets of invaders constituted at once a menace and a disgrace to Italy as a
whole, yet it was the growing predominance of Venice
amongst the Italian states that most of all excited the
alarm of Julius, whose aim was now directed to prevent
the Venetian Republic from becoming the dictator of
Italy, in reality her only possible means of salvation from
the designs of these foreigners. In the first place to
humble and cripple Venice, and in so doing to extend
the boundaries of the Holy See; then to rouse the whole
Italian nation and by one united effort to free Italian
soil from the polluting presence of the "Barbarians";[1]—
such was the ardent desire of Julius, which like many
another grandiose conception was entirely local and selfish in its main object, and patriotic only in a secondary
sense.

In the military expeditions and deep-laid schemes of

---

[1] The contemptuous epithet of "Barbarian" is fiercely repudiated
by the author of the *Julius Exclusus*, who lays stress on the mongrel
pedigree of the Italian people, "who are but a conglomerate of all the
barbarous nations in the world, a mere heap of dirt, yet they are
absurd enough to call everyone not born in Italy a barbarian!"

JULIUS II, CARDINAL DE' MEDICI AND OTHERS

this Pope, the Cardinal de' Medici had for the first time
an opportunity to display his inherent diplomatic ability
both in humouring the irascible Julius and in silently
building up the collapsed fortunes of his own House.
That the utmost caution and dissimulation had always
to be practised by the young Cardinal will appear obvious
at once to those who care to study the characters of the
two men, for it would be well-nigh impossible to name
two great historical types more diverse from every point
of view than the reigning Pontiff and the future Leo X.
Thus the Medici was a young man barely thirty
years of age, just beginning to creep warily into that
treacherous sea of Italian statecraft; Julius, on the other
hand, had many years behind him of varied political experience, whilst he was considered venerable in having
passed his sixtieth year in an age wherein medical at-
tentions often proved more disastrous than disease itself.
Julius was violent, arrogant and ill-tempered; the
Cardinal was always calm, suave and credited with a
remarkable mildness of disposition, upon which all contemporary writers emphatically dwell. The Pope, sprung
from a plebeian stock, the grandson of a Genoese fisherman, with a peasant's coarseness and garrulity ; Medici,
a cultured Florentine scholar with a Roman princess for
his mother, ever scrupulously courteous even under severe
provocation and with a complete mastery over that unruly member, the tongue. The Pope was fond of an
active military life, loving camps and sieges, not refusing
to partake of the coarse fare of his soldiers nor even
objecting to use their oaths under stress of excitement ;
whilst the fastidious Cardinal had a perfect horror of
martial savagery and bloodshed, and undoubtedly held
opinions, which were none the less strong because they
had to be kept secret, concerning the propriety of a Roman

Pontiff taking the field in person like a general. Julius, although he gave commissions to Raphael and Michelangelo, had no real sympathy with art, which he regarded solely as an useful means of recording his own prowess ; he was notoriously unlearned, and at times did not hesitate to express his contempt for the classical literature wherewith his own court was so deeply engrossed : " Put a sword in my hand, not a book, for I am no schoolman ! " had replied the plain-spoken Pontiff to Michelangelo, when the sculptor asked him to suggest a fit emblem for the Pope's bronze statue to be erected in Bologna. Of the Medici's true understanding of art and letters, it is needless to speak here. In outward appearance, as in age, the two Churchmen offered the strongest contrast ; Julius spare, bearded—he was the first Pontiff to wear hair on his chin—alert in defiance of his years ; the Cardinal, corpulent despite his youth, slow in his movements and constantly requiring spectacles or spy-glass to aid his feeble vision. Nevertheless, although the two men differed in appearance, aims, ideas, age, learning, manners and morals, it was now the manifest duty of the younger man to pay court to the reigning Pope, in order to obtain the full amount of sympathy and confidence necessary for the intended restoration of the Medici to Florence, which at this period of his career formed without doubt the overwhelming desire of the future Leo X.

In the height of the summer of 1507, Cardinal de' Medici received a foretaste of Julius' methods of campaigning, when he accompanied his master on the expedition to reduce Perugia and Bologna, both cities being nominally fiefs of the Church. Twenty-four cardinals in all swelled the papal train, yet only 500 men-at-arms were engaged for their protection, so that it speaks elo-

quently for the intense terror which the name of Julius
had already inspired throughout Italy, that on the Pope
reaching Orvieto, Gian-Paolo Baglioni, tyrant of Perugia,
should have hastened to come in person to make his submission.   Julius received this treacherous vassal of the
Church with lofty condescension, and without waiting to
collect an adequate army, pressed forward to seize the
surrendered city : a piece of wilful rashness, which aroused
the wonder, or rather the deep disappointment of
Machiavelli, who has criticised this hasty action of the
Pope and the cowardly complaisance of Baglioni in one
of the most famous passages of the *Discorsi*.   There
could be no question that Julius ran the gravest risk in
thus placing himself and all his court at the mercy of one
who was in reality an aristocratic brigand with a small
but well-trained army.   The defenceless condition of the
Pontiff and his cardinals, together with the vast amount of
treasure in their luxurious trains, must have been apparent
to the greedy eyes of the Umbrian tyrant ; nevertheless,
he shrank from committing a sacrilegious crime on so
grand a scale, and for his omission thus to purchase an
undying reputation for good or ill, Machiavelli has censured the hesitating Baglioni in the bitter language of
which he was an acknowledged master, and in terms
clearly expressive of his own detestation of the methods
of the warrior Pope :—

" Men know not either how to be splendidly wicked
or wholly good, and they shrink in consequence from
such crimes as are stamped with an inherent greatness
or disclose a nobility of nature.   For which reason
Giovanpagolo, who thought nothing of incurring the guilt
of incest or of murdering his kinsmen, could not, or more
truly durst not avail himself of a fair occasion to do a
deed which all would have admired ; which would have

won for him a deathless fame as the first to teach the prelates how little those who live and reign as they do are to be esteemed, and which would have displayed a greatness far transcending any infamy or danger that could attach to it."[1]

From Perugia the papal army and its followers crossed the Apennines by way of Gubbio to the plains of the Romagna, not resting till they reached Cesena, at which place the Pope had arranged to meet with the Cardinal d' Amboise, the all-powerful minister of Louis XII., who in return for sundry favours to himself and his nephews, was prepared to withhold French aid from threatened Bologna. Having thus bribed France to complaisance, Julius now launched one of his bulls of excommunication against Giovanni Bentivoglio, who promptly fled from the city to the French camp, all ignorant of the shameless bargain lately concluded between the Pope and the French cardinal. This open display of rank cowardice on the part of the old tyrant of Bologna must have afforded some measure of satisfaction to Giovanni de' Medici, who had certainly not forgotten Bentivoglio's ill-timed merry-making over the misfortunes of Piero and himself some thirteen years before, when the Medici had been forcibly driven from Florence. On 11th November, Julius entered the city of Bologna in state, where, as befel every Italian conqueror in that era of perpetual change of masters, the indifferent populace greeted the victorious Pope as a liberator and benefactor, as a second and a more glorious Julius Cæsar. Amidst waving of kerchiefs and showers of late-blooming roses, the self-satisfied Pontiff proceeded towards the vast church of San Petronio, nor was he aware that in the midst of the

----

[1] *Discorsi*, book i., chap. xxvii.

applauding crowds stood a sharp-eyed observant traveller
from the north with fur collar well tucked up to his ears,
who was watching narrowly the passing procession.   For
by a curious chance Erasmus of Rotterdam happened
to be visiting Bologna at the very moment of Bentivoglio's flight and the Pope's triumphal entry into the
city, so that to feelings outraged by such a spectacle of
worldliness may have been due the production of that
striking satire called the *Julius Exclusus*—Pope Julius
excluded from Paradise—which has ever been attributed
to the pen of the great Humanist in spite of his repeated
denials.   " Would that you could have seen me carried
in state at Bologna, and afterwards in Rome ! " the boast-
ful Pontiff is made to exclaim to the indignant Apostle
at the gate of Heaven.   " Carriages and horses, troops
under arms, generals prancing and galloping, handsome
pages, torches flaming, dishes steaming, pomp of bishops,
glory of cardinals, trophies, spoils, shouts that rent the
heavens, trumpets blaring, cannon thundering, largesse
scattered among the mob, and I borne aloft, the head and
author of it all ! Scipio and Cæsar were nothing in
comparison with me ! "[1]   In any case it is certain that
Erasmus was an interested eye-witness of the strange
scene which is described so vividly in the Pope's apology
for his life to the Janitor of Heaven.

So far the cardinals, whom their militant master had
turned into lieutenants of his warlike enterprise, had not
suffered greatly during this autumn campaign.   True,
they had endured some degree of misery from the bites
of the rapacious mosquitoes infesting the marshes of the
Romagna, to which their disfigured faces bore ample

[1] *Julius Exclusus.* A Dialogue in the form of a drama performed
in Paris in 1514. A translation of this amusing work is included in
Froude's *Life and Letters of Erasmus*, Appendix to Lecture VIII.

testimony,[1] but the ease with which an almost unarmed
Pope could reduce in so short a space of time and
practically without carnage two of the most important
towns in central Italy must have given intense satisfaction to those members of the Sacred College who shared
their Pontiff's views. But this opening campaign, which
seemed little short of a triumphal procession with none
of the horrors and scarcely any of the hardships of war,
was destined to be succeeded by many stern experiences.
Towards the close of December, 1508, the celebrated
League of Cambrai, the most cherished object of the
papal diplomacy, was concluded between France, Spain,
the Empire and the Papacy, for the admitted purpose of
stripping Venice of all her dominions on the mainland :
a political combination against which the Republic of St.
Mark made a most feeble show of resistance. Defeated
by the French troops at Vaila and despoiled of her
colonies, the humiliated state was ere long only too
thankful to implore for the Pope's mercy and the blessing of an alliance with the Holy See.   Having thus
reduced to impotence the sole Italian state which seemed
capable of resisting the foreign invasion, and having got
the towns of the Romagna into his own hands, Julius
realised that the primary object of his detestable and
unpatriotic policy had been secured, and now that the
might of Venice was hopelessly broken for the sake of
a few miserable fortresses, he was anxious to obtain
Venetian co-operation in striking a severe blow at French
influence in Lombardy.   A reconciliation was easily
effected, whereupon the Pope promptly seceded from
the League of Cambrai, even boasting that by such a
piece of perfidy " he was thrusting a dagger into the

[1] Adriano da Castello, Creighton, vol. v., p. 102, note 1.

side of the French King". At the same time he made
arrangements for a number of Swiss mercenaries to
descend upon Milan under the direction of his devoted
agent, the Cardinal Matthew Schinner of Sion in the
Valais, who had lately supplied Julius with that historic
bodyguard of picked mountaineers, the Swiss Guard,
who in their quaint parti-coloured livery have continued
for nearly four centuries to keep watch and ward at the
portals of the Vatican.

Of Julius' endless troubles, secular and ecclesiastical,
of his wars and sieges, of his marches and counter-
marches, of his massacres and excommunications, we
have no space to speak in a work which is wholly concerned with the career and character of his successors.
But on 13th May, 1511, Bologna, "the Jewel of the
Pope's crown," was retaken with French assistance by
Alfonso d' Este, Duke of Ferrara, who signalised his
contempt for the spiritual fulminations of Julius by removing from the façade of San Petronio the fine bronze
statue of the militant Pontiff, a justly admired work of
the divine Michelangelo. Reserving the head of the
figure to add to his stock of curiosities in the ducal
museum at Ferrara, the dauntless prince had a large
piece of artillery cast from the component bronze, which
in mockery he christened " Giulio," and concerning
which he was wont to indulge in many a coarse jest.
But a far more serious incident than this open insult to
the Pope succeeded the fall of Bologna : an incident
which, there is good reason to believe, made an indelible
impression on the mind of Cardinal de' Medici, now held
in the highest favour by Julius and recently invested
with the important see of Amalfi. The late capitulation
of Bologna had not taken place without manifest signs
of treachery on the part of its Cardinal-Legate, the

worthless Francesco Alidosi, Bishop of Pavia, detested by all decent men but adored for some mysterious reason by the Pontiff, who placed absolute confidence in Alidosi's good faith and personal devotion towards himself. After the recapture of the city, which was on all sides attributed to the venal aims of this papal minion, the Cardinal-Legate proceeded to Ravenna, where on entering into the Pope's apartment, he threw himself at his indulgent master's feet and openly accused Julius' own nephew, Francesco-Maria Della Rovere, Duke of Urbino, of having been the cause of the late catastrophe. So deep-rooted was the Pope's infatuation for Alidosi, that he at once turned upon the duke, who was standing beside his throne, and with threats and curses—and Julius was ever an adept at foul invective—drove the young man, his own nephew and heir, from his presence on the mere word of one who was commonly reported a liar and a villain. Successful in his mission and more confident than ever of the papal protection, Alidosi quitted the palace in high spirits to return to his castle of Rivo, when at an evil moment in one of the streets of Ravenna he chanced to meet with the retiring Duke of Urbino. With ill-timed levity the triumphant Legate must needs jeer at the crestfallen prince, whereupon, infuriated beyond all control by this last insult, Della Rovere leaped from his horse and with naked sword rushed upon his traducer, flinging him off his mule and raining blow after blow upon the defenceless Churchman as he lay writhing and screaming in the mire of the street. " Take that, you traitor ! and that, and that, and that for your deserts ! " cried the duke, until having dealt his prostrate foe some half-dozen strokes on the head and body, he left the corpse to be hacked to pieces by some of his attendants. " A favourite has no friends,"

—particularly a favourite of the type of Alidosi—so that many persons, including the Legate's own servants, looked on unconcernedly upon this murder of an unpopular Churchman in broad daylight.   Having completed the foul deed, the living secular tyrant fled with his train towards the lofty citadel of Urbino, leaving the dead ecclesiastical tyrant a shapeless blood-stained mass in the mean lane of Ravenna.   Even in those days of universal violence and crime such an act of combined sacrilege and brutal revenge stands without parallel, so that it is highly probable that Leo's subsequent hatred of Alidosi's murderer arose originally from his feelings of horror at this assassination of one who, however vile and unscrupulous, was yet a Cardinal-Legate and a bishop.   But of this matter we intend to speak more fully in a later chapter.   It is enough to state here that the sympathies of the common people lay as usual with the aggressor, and that the cry was raised on all sides, " Blessed be the Duke of Urbino ! Blessed is the death of his victim ! Blessed be the name of God, from Whom all good things do proceed ! " [1]   In fact, Julius alone of all men expressed grief at the news of the wretched Alidosi's fate ; he beat his breast, he refused food, and as he was being conveyed that night towards Rimini from Ravenna—a place now grown hateful to him in his bereavement—his attendants could hear loud. cries of impotent rage and deep groans of sorrow issuing from the curtained litter of this extraordinary old man.   When the violence of his grief had somewhat spent itself, Julius appointed a committee of four cardinals, amongst them being Giovanni de' Medici, to make a full inquiry into the conduct of the Duke of Urbino ; nor was it until

[1] *Diary of Paris de Grassis,* Creighton, vol. v., Appendix, pp. 309-311.

many months had elapsed that the Pope, at last convinced of Alidosi's acts of treachery in the past, finally
consented to receive his heir back into favour.

At the close of this same year 1511, the Holy League
between Spain, Venice, England and the Holy See, another political creation of the Pope's fertile brain, was inaugurated with the expressed object of driving the French
out of Italy. A new papal army, composed chiefly of
Spanish infantry under Raymond de Cardona, viceroy of
Naples, and of Italian cavalry under Fabrizio Colonna, was
now formed to re-conquer the lost cities of the Romagna,
and of this mixed force Cardinal de' Medici was named
Legate : an appointment clearly showing how successful
had been Lorenzo's son in his supreme efforts to win the
complete confidence of a Pope who was originally chary
of trusting a Medici. Early in the new year the papal
forces advanced to the siege of Bologna, now held by the
re-instated Bentivogli with the aid of French troops under
Lautrec and Yves d'Allègre. In order to effect a breach
in the walls, the Spanish engineer, Pedro Navarro, laid
his mines at a certain point of the rampart which was
dominated by a chapel of the Virgin, consequently known
as La Madonna del Barbacane. The attempt was successful in its initial stage, for on the fuse being ignited, the
Cardinal and the besieging army saw the fragment of
wall blown high into the air, and then to their amazement
and terror (so Jovius gravely informs his readers) they
beheld wall and chapel descend uninjured and fit themselves again into the breach made by Navarro's explosion.[1]
The spectacle of this military miracle caused a profound
impression both amongst the soldiers of the papal army
and the defenders of the city ; and whatsoever phenomenon

[1] Jovius, lib. ii.

may have happened on this occasion, it is evident that
some curious incident, ascribed by all present to Divine
interposition, raised the spirits of the besieged and depressed those of their assailants at a most critical moment.
In any case, the delivery of the beleaguered town was
close at hand, for the famous Gaston de Foix, a prince of
the royal House of Navarre, who flashes for a brief moment
like some brilliant meteor across the troubled sky of the
Italian wars, suddenly appeared within sight of the towers
of Bologna. The timely arrival of Gaston and his victorious troops, fresh from the sack of unhappy Brescia,
was the signal for the immediate retirement of the army
of the Holy League. Having relieved Bologna, Gaston
next pressed on to Ravenna, which was stubbornly held
against his attack by the Colonnas and their Roman
followers. Meanwhile the Cardinal-Legate, in duty
bound to succour Ravenna, decided to advance, and to
encamp about three miles from the town, at a spot in the
neighbourhood of the famous basilica of Sant' Apollinare
in Classe. The united forces of France and of Ferrara
had already taken up a strong position midway between
the streams of the Montone and the Ronco, which join at
Ponte dell' Asse, about a mile and a half to the south of
Ravenna. The numbers on both sides were fairly equal,
but the advantage of generalship lay obviously with the
French, who possessed Gaston himself, Alfonso of Ferrara,
Yves d'Allègre, La Pallice and a host of other accomplished leaders. On the part of the League, Fabrizio
Colonna, the cavalry commander, was reputed to be headstrong, whilst Raymond de Cardona, in the elegant words
of Jovius, "shone more in civil life than on the battlefield ".[1]

Blood-red uprose the sun upon that memorable

[1] Jovius, lib. ii.

Easter morning, which fell on 11th April, 1512, and the superstitious soldiers in either camp declared that the flushed skies denoted the coming death of a generalissimo, although whether of Gaston or of Cardona remained to be seen.   Each army possessed its cardinal in attendance, for with the French was Federigo Sanseverino, one of Julius' most bitter opponents and a leading supporter of the schismatic Council of Pisa, whose gigantic form encased in mail was prominent on a huge charger, as he rode about the French camp performing the regular duties of an officer.   Very different were the aspect and behaviour of the orthodox legate.   Habited in his flowing robes of scarlet and wearing the broad-brimmed tasselled hat, the full panoply of his exalted office, Giovanni de' Medici made a conspicuous figure, as bestriding a white palfrey and with silver cross borne before him,[1] he passed along the ranks of the Italians and Spaniards, exhorting the soldiers to acts of valour and offering up prayers for victory.   His naturally peaceful disposition made the prospect of a bloody and confused engagement singularly distasteful to him, yet the position of legate in his master's army forbade him to retire from the scene of expected massacre, although in any case his defective eyesight rendered his presence on the battlefield useless in victory and a cause of anxiety in the event of defeat.

The fight opened with a duel of artillery, for which the level nature of the battlefield gave full scope, and which proved all to the advantage of the French, since Alfonso of Ferrara had long been paying special attention to this branch of warfare, so that his guns were the best constructed and most ably served in all Italy.   Colonna's cavalry suffered severely from this heavy and well-

---

[1] He is so represented in the famous Tapestries of Raphael, see chapter ix.

directed cannonade, but the Spanish infantry, reputed
the best foot-soldiers in Europe, escaped almost un-
scathed owing to the foresight of the capable Navarro,
who bade his men lie prone upon the flat surface of the
plain, so long as the murderous hail of bullets from across
the intervening Ronco continued. Colonna, however,
maddened by the havoc wrought by Duke Alfonso's
artillery and disgusted with what he deemed the cowardice
of the Spaniards, now charged headlong towards the
river, compelling the Spanish infantry to follow his lead.
Along the banks of the Ronco raged the battle with
almost unparalleled ferocity, for in this case hatred and
jealousy of race were added to the ordinary lust of
fighting.   Richly clad in a mantle distinguished by the
heraldic devices of the royal House of Navarre and
with right arm left bare for the fleshing, rode hither and
thither that splendid youth, Gaston de Foix, swearing he
would never quit the field save as victor and urging the
troops of France to pursue the hard-pressed Spaniards,
who were slowly retiring in good order long after
Colonna's cavalry had been scattered to the four winds.
But at the very moment when the battle of Ravenna
was actually won, and the enemy's camp already captured, Gaston de Foix, forgetting in the supreme hour of
triumph that it is the first duty of every capable general
to safeguard his own life, must needs lose everything by
a piece of boyish folly. Streaming with sweat and
bespattered with human brains and blood, the young
leader, flushed with victory and already beholding
visions of the coveted Neapolitan crown before his
dazzled eyes, spurred in person after Cardona's retreating
battalions.   In mid-career a stray bullet knocked the
prince headlong from his charger to the ground, whence
mortally wounded he rolled down the steep bank into

the turbid waters of the Ronco. In vain did the unhappy youth cry aloud for quarter, shouting to the savage
Spanish soldiery above him that he was the brother
of their own queen; little did they reck at such a
moment of their victim's birth and honours. Pierced
with a hundred wounds in every portion of his body,
Gaston de Foix lost at once the hard-won fruits of
his victory and also his young life at the precise moment
when he seemed to hold all Italy in his eager and
ambitious grasp.

Death was busy amongst the leaders in both armies,
but especially in that of the French, during this historic
engagement, wherein at least 20,000 men are said to
have perished. Amidst the universal din and confusion,
which in this case were not a little increased by the
slaughter of so many generals on either side, young
Giulio de' Medici, as usual in attendance upon his
illustrious cousin, was enabled to escape in the mass
of terror-stricken fugitives to Cesena; but the Cardinal-
Legate, impeded by his blindness yet showing commendable pluck and coolness in a situation of extreme peril,
remained on the battlefield, deeply absorbed in performing
the last sad offices for the dead and dying. He was
engaged in this truly Christian task, when he was perceived by some common soldiers of the victorious army,
who, recking nothing of the sanctity of a cardinal's robe
and person, hastened to lay violent hands upon so
glorious a prize as the papal legate. The would-be
assailants of the Medici, however, were opportunely struck
down by a gentleman of Bologna, named Piatese, who
for his better protection handed the Legate over to
Federigo Gonzaga, of the noble House of Mantua.
Gonzaga immediately led the captive Cardinal into the
presence of Sanseverino, by whom his Florentine col-

league was received with every mark of respect.   On
the strength of his old friend's kindness, the cunning
Medici now ventured to ask as a special favour that his
cousin Giulio might be allowed to proceed under a safe-
conduct to the French camp.   To this seemingly innocent request Sanseverino, too much engrossed in
quarrelling with the new French commander, La Pallice,
to reflect upon any possible ill consequences of his
complaisance, at once consented, so that Giulio was able
to reach Ravenna before many hours were past.   By
means of his cousin the shrewd Cardinal-Legate obtained
the desired opportunity of sending to Rome an authentic
report of the late battle, and also an exact appreciation
of the present strength of the French army.   For the
Cardinal had already perceived clearly that, although the
forces of King Louis had indeed gained a stupendous
victory, yet the consequences of such a success had been
greatly impaired, if not altogether destroyed by the loss
of Gaston de Foix, on whose able strategy and far-
reaching aims all future policy depended.   Hurrying
from Ravenna with the Legate's minute instructions,
Giulio arrived in Rome at a most critical juncture.
Already stragglers from the defeated army had reached
the Eternal City, where by the exaggerated language
which all bearers of evil tidings are so prone to employ,
they had spread consternation amongst Julius and his
cardinals attendant, whilst Pompeo Colonna and the
Roman barons were already preparing to rouse the
populace in favour of an expected French army.   The
fortunes of Julius had now sunk to their lowest ebb, and
so intense was his alarm that an escape by sea from
Ostia had even been seriously suggested.   To the scared
Pontiff and his court Giulio truly brought most welcome
relief, for he was able to explain by means of his cousin's

careful instructions that the dreaded Gaston was no more; that the Duke of Ferrara had returned to his capital; that La Pallice and Sanseverino were on terms of open rivalry; and that, in short, there was little fear of the conquerors now descending upon Rome. Time was all that was needed for repairing the shattered fortunes of the League, since the delays and quarrels of the new French leaders were likely to continue indefinitely, so that in contriving to despatch so able a messenger to Rome with such speed, the captive Cardinal-Legate had indeed performed a signal service to the Pope and the Holy See. Thus reassured, Julius recovered his wonted presence of mind and again began to treat with the French King. A master-stroke, also suited to the exigencies of the moment, was the Pope's decision to summon a general Council to meet with all convenient despatch at the Lateran, an action almost certain to counteract the dreaded influence of the schismatic Council, or *conciliabulo*, which had recently transferred its sittings from Pisa to Milan. Possibly this ingenious idea of calling a Council in Rome itself as an antidote may have originated with the Cardinal-Legate, for the very notion of holding such an assembly had always been highly repugnant to the arrogant Julius; at any rate, it is remarkable that this announcement followed close upon Medici's lucid explanation of the general situation in Italy after the battle of Ravenna.

In the meantime the Legate had been escorted in honourable durance to Bologna, where the unfeeling citizens came in crowds to gibe at the captive prince of the Church and at his fellow-prisoner, Pedro Navarro. The Bentivogli, however, treated Giovanni with consideration, as did likewise Bianca Rangone at Modena, whither he was next transferred. This lady, a daughter of the

House of Bentivoglio, actually stripped herself of all her
jewels in order to provide properly for the Cardinal's
immediate necessities, and it is pleasant to be able to record that this act of kindness shown him in an hour of
distress was not allowed to pass unnoticed in the days of
prosperity and power that were now so close at hand, for
Leo X. granted many favours to the fortunate children
of the Lady Bianca.   From Modena the Cardinal was
taken to Milan, where he was honourably lodged in the
house of Sanseverino, whilst many of the leading Milanese citizens came to pay him court in spite of his being
a French prisoner of war.   In fact, the situation in Milan
was most extraordinary, seeing that here was the schismatic
Council under the presidency of Carvajal and Sanseverino
holding its sittings and anathematising the Roman Pontiff,
whose captive legate meanwhile was being treated with
marked deference by the Milanese themselves, who
scarcely tried to hide their contempt for the Council in
their midst; indeed, the ambitious Carvajal was continually assailed in the streets and mocked by the children
as "Pope Carvajal".   Hither a little later arrived the
indefatigable Giulio, armed with letters from the Pope,
granting to his legate plenary powers to give absolution
to all and sundry at his discretion; whereupon so many
applications were made to the orthodox legate that the
Medici's secretaries were kept busily employed day and
night in preparing the necessary forms.   Numbers of the
French officers even openly asked for letters of absolution for their late crime in opposing the arms of His
Holiness at Ravenna and Bologna; nor was any attention paid by the governor of Milan to the indignant protests of Carvajal and his colleagues, who complained
bitterly of Medici's honourable treatment and his manifest
influence.   The final withdrawal of the French troops

from Milan before the advancing Swiss at the close of May, 1512, at last compelled the Council, now utterly discredited in the eyes of all men, to retire with the French forces, intending, so it was declared, to select some safe spot in France for its further proceedings. As a hostage the Cardinal-Legate of Bologna undoubtedly possessed no small value in the estimation of King Louis, and accordingly Medici was constrained to follow in the retreating army under a strong escort. Ideas of escape had already suggested themselves to the Cardinal, who was firmly resolved not to be carried a prisoner beyond the Alps without making a desperate effort to regain his liberty. The attempt, carefully matured beforehand, was arranged to take place at the village of Cairo on the banks of the Po, at which spot the French army had decided to cross the river. Closely guarded and watched, the Cardinal by feigning illness was yet allowed to spend the night at the humble house of the parish-priest of Cairo, whilst the French ecclesiastics of the Council were embarking in the barges that were ready to bear themselves and their attendants to Bassignano across the stream. That night a certain priest named Bengallo, who was in Medici's train and was the guiding spirit of the whole plan, went secretly to implore a country gentleman of the neighbourhood, one Rinaldo Zazzi, to act as his assistant in the matter of the Cardinal's escape. Zazzi was at first unwilling to join in so hazardous a scheme, even though the good priest begged him with tears in his eyes to rescue the Pope's legate out of the hands of the discomfited barbarians, yet a last appeal to the ever-potent memory of Lorenzo the Magnificent was successful in inducing the hesitating Piedmontese squire to give a reluctant promise of aid, but only on the condition that a local nobleman, by name Ottaviano Isimbardi, should likewise be admitted into their confidence. The disappointed priest had perforce to agree, whereupon Isimbardi was sought and after additional promises and pleadings was gained over to the cause. Zazzi and Isimbardi now arranged to collect a number of peasants from off their estates to compass the rescue of the Cardinal, whose person was to be seized on the following morning at the river's bank, at the precise moment when he was preparing to step into the barge. The whole scheme, concocted with such care and at such risk by Bengallo and his new accomplices, was however nearly frustrated by an error of Zazzi's messenger, who addressed himself to the French priest in charge of Medici by mistake for Bengallo; and although the servant had the wit to invent a reasonable explanation of his strange blunder, the Frenchman's suspicions were aroused, so that he gave the order of embarkation sooner than was anticipated. By a series of pretended delays, however, some little time was gained, with the result that as the Cardinal, who managed to be almost the last person left on the river-bank, was about to step into the boat prepared for him, Zazzi and Isimbardi suddenly appeared on the scene with a band of armed men, who quickly drove back the startled Frenchmen and conveyed Medici to a temporary hiding-place. But the Legate's troubles were as yet by no means finished, in spite of this successful beginning, for the French, furious at losing a valuable hostage by so simple a device, set to work to scour the surrounding country, though happily not before the Cardinal had been able to don military attire—a most unsuitable disguise, it would seem, for one of his bulky figure and elegant manners—and to flee in an opposite direction. Under the circumstances Isimbardi, who accompanied the il-lustrious fugitive, thought it best to seek the protection of a relative, one Bernardo Malespina, although he was known to sympathise with the French faction. To the dismay of the poor Cardinal and to the genuine surprise of Isimbardi, Malespina however not only declined to assist the refugee's flight, but insisted on keeping Medici a close prisoner, until he had communicated with the French general, the celebrated Gian-Giorgio Trivulzi. Shut up under lock and key in a dark and dirty pigeon-house, the Legate had ample time to bewail his evil fate, for there was every reason to suppose that Trivulzi, though an Italian by birth, would insist on his being handed over to the French. But to the unbounded joy and relief both of the Cardinal and of Isimbardi, the general's reply was all in favour of the fugitive; for Trivulzi informed Malespina that he might liberate the Cardinal, if he were so minded, seeing that fortune had so far helped him to elude his late captors. Malespina had sworn to his kinsman to abide by Trivulzi's decision, and although refusing actively to help in the matter of escape, he had no objection to leaving ajar the door of the dove-cote, as though by accident. Issuing thus from his undignified place of restraint in Malespina's castle, the Cardinal hastened in disguise to Voghiera and thence to Mantua, where he was hospitably entertained by the Marquis and his consort, the famous Isabella d' Este of Ferrara. Such are the bare outlines of the story of Leo's escape, and for its sequel we must add that according to his usual, if not invariable custom, on succeeding to the Papacy he did not fail to remember and reward all those devoted friends who had assisted in his rescue. The brave and resourceful Bengallo was nominated bishop of Nepi; titles and estates were bestowed on Zazzi and Isimbardi; whilst the over-cautious Malespina must have lived to regret bitterly his harsh treatment of the poor wanderer imprisoned in his fowl-house. As a memorial of this interesting and by no means unimportant episode in the career of the first Medicean Pope, the Marchese Isimbardi caused the walls of the chief saloon of his villa at Cairo to be adorned with a series of frescoes illustrating the story of the Pontiff's flight, beneath which he added a personal inscription, containing the words : "O Ottaviano Isimbardi! to thy efforts of a truth doth Florence owe a Medicean Prince, Italy a Hero, and the world a Leo the Tenth!" Modesty was not a common attribute of the noblemen of the Italian Renaissance, nor self-glorification a rare one.

The real political importance of the Medici's escape from the French army at this exact moment must not be overlooked. Had he not attempted, and with success, to break away from his captors, he would undoubtedly have been borne away to France and been kept there as a hostage, at least until the death of Julius II. In that case the restoration of the Medici in Florence—an event of which we intend to speak presently—would certainly never have occurred, whilst without this increased influence in Italian politics, which the recovery of Florence gave to him, would he ever have been elected Pope, particularly if he were remaining a prisoner—honourably treated, no doubt, but a prisoner none the less—on alien soil. Nor, seeing how this extraordinary piece of good fortune befel the Cardinal within a few weeks of his triumphal entry into Florence and within a few months of his ascending the pontifical throne, can we wonder that both Jovius and Egidius of Viterbo should allude to this event as miraculous in an age which attributed all good or evil to the direct intervention of a watchful Providence. "It was the act of God," says the latter chronicler, "and before all other things that have been done in past ages, is it marvellous in our eyes!"[1]

[1] Cavaliere Rosmini, *Istoria del Magno Trivulzio;* Jovius, lib. ii. ; Roscoe, vol. i., pp. 322-324, and p. 324, note 10.

CHAPTER IV

RETURN OF THE MEDICI TO FLORENCE

Let no man scheme to make himself supreme in Florence who is not of the line of the Medici, and backed besides by the power of the Church. None else, be he who he may, has such influence or following that he can hope to reach this height, unless indeed he be carried to it by the free voice of the people in search of a constitutional chief, as happened to Piero Soderini. If any therefore aspire to such honours, not being of the House of Medici, let him affect the popular cause (F. Guicciardini, *Counsels and Reflections*).

THE discomfiture of the French had been so complete, that soon after the evacuation of Milan there were remaining to them scarcely half a dozen fortresses of all their late conquests in Lombardy. Once more the expelled Sforza were installed in Milan; Bologna was again in the hands of Julius II., whose fury against the unfortunate Bentivogli burned so fierce that he threatened to raze the whole city and transplant its fickle inhabitants to the town of Cento; Parma and Piacenza were likewise seized by the ambitious but not self-seeking Pontiff, who claimed these important towns for the Church as forming outlying portions of the ancient exarchate of Ravenna; Venice, now supported by her new friend and former foe, the Pope, was preparing to annex Brescia and Cremona, which were still held by French garrisons; whilst the vacillating Emperor and the shrewd Ferdinand of Spain were silently working to obtain some substantial advantage out of the recent failure of the French arms. To settle the affairs of Italy and to apportion the spoils amongst the component members of the League, a conference had been called at Mantua in the summer of 1512. But a more important matter than the pacification of Northern Italy to be discussed at this meeting was the question of dealing with the only independent state of consequence which had been openly hostile to the victorious League, for throughout the late campaign Florence had remained an acknowledged, if not a very active ally of the French King. The collapse of the late invasion had indeed imperilled the actual existence of the Florentine Republic, now guided by Piero Soderini, who in 1503 had been duly elected Gonfalionere for life and endowed with powers somewhat akin to those enjoyed by a Venetian doge. Soderini, who was an eminently honest but not very able public magistrate, had for some time past regarded this French alliance with serious misgiving, but partly from a natural indecision of character and partly from a high-minded sense of loyalty to the pact made with King Louis, he had taken no definite step to dissociate the Republic from an union which was singularly distasteful to the Pope, whose hatred of the French amounted to a veritable passion. To pursue a middle course under these circumstances proved a fatal mistake, and Soderini's recent conduct in affording shelter to the refugees of both armies after the battle of Ravenna had only exasperated the French without winning the gratitude of the League. Now, with the invaders practically swept out of the country, Soderini found himself and the Florentine Republic completely isolated, so that it is not difficult to understand the feelings of grave alarm wherewith the Gonfalionere and his adherents were regarding this coming conference at Mantua. In order to propitiate the heads of the League, therefore, the perplexed ruler of Florence despatched to Mantua his brother, Gian-Vittorio Soderini, a person "more learned in the laws than in the higher arts of diplomacy," to treat on behalf of the recalcitrant Republic.

Conspicuous amongst the representatives of the various powers convened at Mantua was the Emperor's plenipotentiary, the haughty Matthew Lang, bishop of Gurck, who was ready to offer his master's good-will to the highest bidder. The Medicean interests were in the hands of Giuliano de' Medici in the absence of the Cardinal, who was engaged in restoring order in Bologna. Giuliano, acting under the advice of his elder brother, was naturally lavish of his promises both to Lang and to Cardona, the leader of Ferdinand's army ; but all such promises, however tempting they might seem, were necessarily contingent on the restoration of the Medici, who were still exiles. Had Piero Soderini invested his brother with fuller powers to pledge the credit of the Florentine state to an unlimited extent, he might possibly have succeeded in buying off the representatives of both King and Emperor, for without the Spanish army of Cardona, Julius would in all probability have been unable to carry out his open project to overthrow the existing government of Soderini and to replace it by the rule of the Medici. For, thanks to the years of loyal service and his recent misfortunes in his master's cause, the Cardinal had completely succeeded in winning the papal confidence and favour, and had been actually marked out by Julius as a proper instrument for the chastisement of obstinate Florence, which had not only made an unholy alliance with the detested French, but had also granted hospitality to the late schismatical Council at Pisa. But although the anxious Soderini must have been fully

aware that, in order to avert the papal vengeance and to
placate the enmity of the League, there was absolute
necessity for other and more subtle methods than mere
appeals to fair-play and common-sense, he shrank from
bribery on the required scale, allowing the promises of
Giuliano de' Medici to transcend in value his own more
frugal offers.

Meanwhile, the Cardinal, his brother Giuliano, their
cousin Giulio and Bernardo Dovizi da Bibbiena, with all
their friends, were busily employed in furthering the
restoration of the Medicean family in Florence, whether
as acknowledged rulers or as private citizens ; the actual
form of their re-entry seemed of little consequence at the
moment.   Julius now willingly invested the Cardinal
with legatine authority in Tuscany, whilst there was
placed at his disposal the Spanish army under Cardona,
which was encamped near Bologna.   Yet Giovanni, who
fully realised that the precise moment for a vigorous
effort to regain Florence had in very truth arrived, still
met with many difficulties in his path, in spite too of the
warm support of the Pope and the League.   Cardona
himself regarded with indifference, if not with dislike,
this proposed descent upon Tuscany, and the Spanish
general's aversion had to be overcome by such sums of
money as the impoverished Cardinal could scrape together.   Even more serious and exasperating than
Cardona's reluctance was the strong opposition of the
papal nephew, Francesco Della Rovere, Duke of Urbino,
who stoutly refused to second his uncle's scheme against
Florence in this emergency ; denied artillery to the
Spanish army ; and even forbade the Vitelli and Orsini,
cousins of the Medici and eager upholders of their cause,
to quit the force, which as Captain-General of the Church
he himself was then commanding.   Whether the duke

PANORAMA OF FLORENCE IN THE YEAR 1529

had been secretly bribed, or was acting thus out of a
personal dislike of the Cardinal, who had sat as one of his
judges in the late enquiry concerning Alidosi's murder,
it is impossible to say; but certain it is that his unseason-
able attitude of sharp hostility to the Medici was one
which he had every reason ere long to deplore under the
Medicean pontificate, which he little dreamed was so
near at hand.   But the energy and tact of the Cardinal
were sufficient to surmount all initial difficulties.   It was
he who contrived to purchase two pieces of the much-
needed artillery, and during the passage of the Apennines
it was his personal influence with the mountaineers that
secured pack-horses and food for the ill-equipped army.
At the village of Barberino, on the confines of the Republic's territory, arrived an embassy from the city of
Florence, offering terms to which Cardona might have
been tempted to accede, had it not been for the presence
of the Cardinal, who insisted before all things upon the
acceptance of the League's late resolution—a resolution
naturally of the first importance to the struggling Medici
—that the exiled members of the family should be permitted to return to Florence as private citizens.   Upon
this vital question the negotiating parties were quite
unable to agree, the Gonfalionere boldly stating his
preference for an appeal to arms rather than for any
arrangement which might include a restoration of the
Medici; and to this grave determination Soderini had
been urged not a little by the arguments of Niccolò
Machiavelli, his secretary-of-state, who had now served
the Florentine Republic with devoted skill for the past
fourteen years.   Acting under Machiavelli's advice,
Soderini now permitted the enrolment of a force of local
militia, and also gave orders for the strengthening of all
fortresses, whilst he boldly thrust into prison some twenty-

five prominent supporters of the Medicean faction, who were already agitating noisily for the return of their patrons.   Having taken measures so decided and alert, the Gonfalionere, convoking the Grand Council of the city, amidst breathless silence addressed his fellow-citizens in a speech, which for pure patriotism, sound reasoning and personal unselfishness must ever confer honour upon the speaker, and to some extent redeem his fixed reputation for incompetence and sloth.   After expressing his readiness to resign the office of Gonfalionere, Soderini warned all loyal upholders of the Republic against re-admitting the Medici within their walls, even in the guise of private citizens.   For true citizens they could no longer be, he clearly explained, since after so many years of absence from civic life and of residence in foreign courts, they had been transformed into princes, even assuming they had been private persons at the time of their expulsion nearly twenty years before.   And this remark would apply with special force to the young Lorenzo de' Medici, the heir of the family, who, having been an infant at that date, could not therefore possibly remember any of the traditions of his House, but would of necessity behave like a tyrant of the type of a Benti-voglio or a Gonzaga, relying not upon the public love and acquiescence in his rule, but upon force of arms and the support of the Papacy, which his uncle the Cardinal could be trusted to obtain.   The Gonfalionere ended his oration by solemnly warning his hearers that the times and government of Lorenzo il Magnifico, "who was ever anxious to cover his real prerogative with a mantle of private equality rather than to make an ostentatious display of his power," would be reckoned as a golden age compared with the open tyranny which his sons and grandsons would inaugurate, were they admitted into the city. "It therefore becomes your duty," were his last words, "now to decide, whether I am to resign my office (which I shall cheerfully do at your bidding), or whether I am to attend vigorously to the defence of our fatherland, if you desire me to remain."[1]

The patriotic and sensible arguments used by Soderini were received with enthusiasm by his audience, and even by the mass of the citizens, who were distinctly averse to a Medicean restoration. For a time the united determination of the Florentines to resist any attempt at invasion was manifest and genuine, whilst the work of defence, already begun in the early summer, was being pushed forward with feverish alacrity, chiefly under the supervision of Machiavelli. But although Machiavelli was perhaps the greatest genius of his age and whole-hearted in his endeavours to defend his fatherland, yet his talents shone rather in the theoretical than in the practical art of warfare. He could give excellent advice on paper as to strategy and training, but as a civilian pure and simple he was scarcely competent to undertake those more laborious tasks, which necessarily belong to the peculiar province of skilled generals and engineers. Unlike his great fellow-citizen Michelangelo, who was destined seventeen years later to erect the fortifications of San Miniato during the siege of Florence, Machiavelli was neither architect nor mechanician ; yet it is of interest to recall the plain circumstance that on two momentous occasions Florence was prepared for defence by the devoted efforts of this pair of her most illustrious sons.

.   .   .   .

The town of Prato with its crumbling brown walls

---

[1] Guicciardini, *Storia d' Italia*, lib. xi.

and its black and white striped cathedral-tower, which rises so prominent a feature of the fertile and populous Val d' Arno, stands on the right bank of the rushing Bisenzio, and at no great distance from the western slopes of Monte Morello. Even to-day Prato retains much of its mediæval appearance, whilst its works of art by Donatello and the Robbias, and also Lippo Lippi's glorious frescoes in the cathedral-choir, attract yearly many visitors to the prosperous little city that stands in the midst of a fruitful Tuscan landscape. Situated within eight miles of Florence, this place had long shared the political fortunes of its more important neighbour, and it was familiar to Giovanni de' Medici, who in the past had been its *proposto*, or nominal protector, although his first visit hither, undertaken nearly twenty years ago, had been attended by a melancholy accident of a type common enough in those days of elaborate pageants. A triumphal arch, placed above the Florence gate of the town and intended to represent some allegorical scene, had suddenly collapsed on the young Cardinal's approach, so that two pretty children, dressed as welcoming angels, fell to the ground and perished miserably in the wreckage : an unforeseen catastrophe which quickly changed the festal aspect of the town into one of universal mourning.[1] The Pratesi now, on hearing of the advance of Cardona's army bearing in its ranks their late protector, their " Dolce Pastore," as certain poets had designated him, recalled to mind this long-passed event, and drew an evil augury from the near presence of the Cardinal. Nor were the good people deceived in their dismal prognostications, although the Florentine Signory had hastened to pour thousands of troops within their walls,

---

[1] Nardi, *Istorie Fiorentine*, lib. v.

since it was openly known that Cardona, deeming his
artillery too weak and his men too exhausted to attack
Florence itself, was meditating an assault upon Prato,
where he could at least obtain the means of victualling
his famished troops.   The first effort of the Spaniards
resulted in complete failure, due rather to a lack of
cannon than to any skill on the part of Luca Savelli,
the Florentine commander ; but the second assault,
made from the direction of Campi on the afternoon of
29th August, succeeded with an ease which astonished all
who witnessed the operations.   Battering down with
the Cardinal's two pieces of cannon a portion of the
wall near the Mercatale gate, the Spaniards rushed into
the breach almost unopposed ; the Tuscan militia bands, a
mere rabble of armed peasants that Machiavelli had levied
for the defence, flying like frightened sheep before the
onslaught of Cardona's veterans.   Thereupon followed
an indescribable scene of confusion, plunder and massacre,
the awful effects of which have not been forgotten to
this day in unhappy Prato, "where, rightly or wrongly,
the name and memory of Giovanni de' Medici, Pope
Leo X. will for ever be associated with the blood
and tears of its citizens ".[1]   For nearly two days the
Sack of Prato of impious recollection raged unchecked.
Neither age nor sex was spared by the ferocious soldiery,
who were said, though probably without truth, to have
included a large number of Moslem mercenaries.   No
quarter was granted either to peaceful merchant or to
fleeing peasant ; priests were struck down at the altar ;
the crucifix, and even the Host were insulted ; the
churches were plundered ; and the famous shrine of
the *Cintola*, the Madonna's girdle, which is the historic

---

[1] Baldanzi, *Storia della Chiesa Cattedrale di Prato.*

relic of Prato, is said to have escaped depredation only by means of a timely miracle that terrified its would-be devastators.[1] Monasteries were set on fire, and their inmates stabbed or beaten ; the very convents were invaded by the licentious soldiery. " It was not a struggle, but sheer butchery," comments the historian Nardi ; " it was an appalling spectacle of horrors," declares the unemotional Machiavelli, whose hastily-levied militia had in no small degree contributed by cowardice and inexperience to the disaster itself. To add to the terrors of the scene, a fearful thunderstorm with torrents of rain raged all night over the town, so that the fiendish work of destruction and outrage was rendered yet more easy, and any attempt at keeping order was thereby rendered impossible. " The place was a veritable pool of blood," writes a contemporary chronicler ; and indeed, when we take into account the small area of the town and the mass of soldiery suddenly admitted within the narrow compass of its walls, it becomes easy to understand so terrible, if exaggerated a description, especially on hearing that the number of those who perished in the sack of Prato has been estimated at so high a figure as 5000 persons.

With the dawn of 30th August, the work of massacre and rapine was continued with renewed force. By the clearer light of day persons of every rank in life and of either sex were dragged from sanctuary or hiding-place, and after the application of rough and ready forms of torture (said to be a characteristic of the Spanish troopers) to enable their captors to discover the whereabouts of their supposed hoards, the unhappy victims were brutally slain and their bodies stripped before being flung into the

[1] *Archivio Storico Italiano*, vol. i. : " Il Miserando Sacco di Prato," di Messer Jacopo Modesti.

streets.   Every well in the town was choked with naked corpses, and the walls of the Cathedral still bear to-day an inscription alluding to this horrible phase of the sack of Prato.   After a day and a night of unsurpassed carnage and cruelty, the Viceroy Cardona made his state entry into the town, and at once gave the order for the booty to be sold at public auction ;—" O Dio ! O Dio ! O Dio ! che crudeltà ! " is the dismal comment of an eye-witness, one Pistofilo, a secretary in the train of Ippolito d' Este.[1]

The part played by the Cardinal and his brother in the events leading up to the sack of Prato has been censured in the severest terms by a modern Italian historian.   "The Medici," declares with indignation the late Cesare Guasti, "descended upon the confines of their own fatherland (shameful to relate!) in the rear of a foreign army ; whilst the Cardinal, making use of his legatine powers, actually obtained at Bologna for this force the very cannon which were to open the fatal breach in the walls of Prato.   As Cardinal-Legate he tolerated all the horrors committed at the sack of the town, even the very outrages upon persons and places devoted to religion."[2]   That the Medici were responsible for this invasion of Florentine territory by a foreign force, there can be no question of doubt, for, as we have already shown, Cardona was loth to move southward, and but for the Cardinal's gold and arguments would never have done so at all.   To this extent, it may be at once frankly admitted, the Medici were directly answerable for the ensuing capture and sack of Prato, which had refused to capitulate at the joint request of the Cardinal-Legate and

---

[1] *Il Sacco di Prato e il Ritorno dei Medici in Firenze nel MDXII.*
A collection of documents and poems edited by Cesare Guasti
(Bologna, 1880).
[2] *Ibid.*, Prefazione.

of Cardona, or even to supply the invading army with the provisions which were so badly needed.   But it is unreasonable to accuse the Cardinal of directly instigating or approving the subsequent sack of the place with its attendant brutalities.   As a Tuscan, as a prince of the Church, and as a human being naturally inclined to methods of mercy, it seems inconceivable that Giovanni de' Medici could have witnessed otherwise than with feelings of shame and indignation the cruel treatment of the little city which was itself almost a suburb of his native Florence.   His real responsibility lay in his having raised a tempest, the fury of which he himself failed to foresee, and the progress of which he was absolutely powerless to check or even mitigate.   But it appears illogical to brand as a crime this forcible attempt of the exiled Medici to return to their native land, even under cover of an alien army, when we take into consideration the previous expulsion of the Cardinal and his brothers from Florence, their outlawry, the seizure of their private estates and the blood-money set on their heads by a hostile government.

" This day (29th August), at sixteen of the clock, the town was sacked, not without some bloodshed, such as could not be avoided. . . . The capture of Prato, so speedily and cruelly, although it has given me pain, will at least have the good effect of serving as an example and a deterrent to the others."[1]   Thus writes the Cardinal to the Pope on the very day that saw the seizure of the town and certain unpleasant features of the sack ; but it is evident from the writer's tone that the worst excesses had not yet been committed, when Giovanni de' Medici was inditing his despatch to Julius II.   The pro-

[1] Villari, vol. ii., p. 13, note 2.

bability is that the Cardinal and his brother Giuliano, on hearing of the continuance of the sack and of the abominable acts of cruelty and sacrilege in the captured town, hastened to do what was possible to save the women and children from further outrage and the convents from spoliation. On the authority of Jovius, the Cardinal, his brother and his cousin Giulio did their utmost, "with prayers and even with tears," to compel Cardona and his officers to safeguard the women and unarmed citizens, so that it was due to their frenzied efforts that the Cathedral, which was packed with terrified refugees, was protected from the fury of the lawless soldiery. In the various accounts of contemporary writers, all of them with Medicean sympathies, the part played by the Cardinal in thus endeavouring to save the honour of the women and the lives of the inoffensive burghers, is constantly insisted on, and although the phrases used are often grossly flattering and the account of the Cardinal's tears sounds somewhat unctuous, yet it appears evident that the Medici did all they could to alleviate the evils of the town, which had thus been made the scapegoat of the whole Florentine state for the past ill-treatment of the exiled family that was now returning to power and prosperity.

> Di lagrime si bagnia el viso e 'l petto
> El nostro Monsignore, anche il fratello.
> E poi diceva ; "O Cristo benedetto,
> Di rafrenar ti piaccia tal fragello !
> O Prato mio, da me tanto diletto,
> Come ti veggo far tanto macello ! "[1]

And another poet actually goes so far as to speak with a dismal pun of the presence of the Medici as being *medicina* to the ills of the unhappy Pratesi ! Certainly, after his election to the papal throne, Leo X. received in

---

[1] *Il Sacco di Prato*, p. 87.

Rome a deputation from Prato with encouraging words
of sympathy and expressions of favour, but such promises
were for one reason or another never carried into effect,
so that we can scarcely marvel at the evil reputation
borne by Leo X. and the Medici even at this distance of
time in the little city that suffered so terribly at the return of Lorenzo's two surviving sons.

The heart-rending reports of the excesses perpetrated
by the Spanish soldiers, " more cruel than the Devil himself," [1] and of the rank cowardice displayed by the Tuscan
regiments, upon which Soderini and the sanguine Machiavelli had relied to preserve the city from invasion, had
the immediate effect of bringing the Florentines to a full
sense of their imminent peril.   A sack of Prato repeated
on a gigantic scale in Florence itself was a possible catastrophe to be averted at any price, no matter how costly
or humiliating to the Republic.   With the popular consent, therefore, the faction of the *Palleschi*, led by the
Albizzi, the Strozzi, the Salviati and other families
favourable to the Medicean cause, was requested to
arrange for an armistice with the Viceroy Cardona, whose
bloodthirsty troops were hourly expected to appear at the
city gates.   The terms that had been so scornfully rejected at Barberino were promptly accepted, the Signory
expressing its willingness to renounce the French alliance ;
to pay a large indemnity to the Viceroy ; to dismiss
Soderini from the official post he had held for the past
nine years ; and—most important concession of all—to
re-admit the exiled Medici without reserve.   Piero
Soderini himself, on being approached by the Medicean
leaders, at once stated his intention of retiring ; whereupon he was escorted under a safe-conduct to Siena,

[1] Landucci, p. 323.

whence a little later he wisely fled over-sea to Ragusa, in order to avoid the clutches of the revengeful Julius. In spite of his nerveless rule and mistaken policy, it is impossible not to admire poor Soderini's candour and un-selfishness ; yet the very qualities on which our modern appreciation is based are those which aroused the fierce contempt of his brilliant lieutenant, Machiavelli :—a lasting contempt which found its utterance in the heart-less epigram composed in after years at the death of his master, the deposed Gonfalionere of Florence, whose childlike simplicity seemed only in Machiavelli's eyes to render his departed soul worthy to abide in Limbo, the bourne of unbaptised infants:—

> La notte che mori Pier Soderini,
> L' alma n' andò nell' Inferno alla bocca.
> E Pluto le grido : " Anima sciocca,
> Che Inferno?   Va nel Limbo dei bambini ! " [1]

It is pathetic to reflect that this cruel verse is far better known than the stately epitaph upon Soderini's beautiful tomb by the Tuscan sculptor Benedetto da Rovezzano, in the choir of the Carmelite church in his own Florence, which stands but a few yards distant from the little chapel that the frescoes of Masaccio have rendered famous for all time.

With the hurried departure of Soderini and the signing of the treaty with Cardona, the city was once more thrown open to the triumphant Medici after an enforced absence of nearly eighteen years.   Nor were portents lacking in that superstitious age to give timely warning of the return of the Magnificent Lorenzo's sons and grandson.   Men noted that the French King's shield with the golden lilies—the lilies of France that Savonarola

---

[1] (Died Soderini, and that very night
Down to Hell's portals flew his simple soul ;
Where Pluto cried : " Not here, O foolish sprite,
Canst thou remain.   Of babes we take no toll ! ")

always wished to unite with the crimson *gigli* of Florence [1]
—had mysteriously fallen to ground during the night-
time, and that a thunderbolt had struck the crest of the
palace of the Signory, passing through the very chamber
of the Gonfalionere and finally burying itself in the pavement near the foot of the grand staircase.[2]   The heavens
themselves seemed to be fighting on behalf of the illustrious wanderers, who were now daily expected to return
to the city, which their presence alone appeared likely to
save from the ruin that had lately overtaken little Prato.
Already masons and painters were busily engaged in restoring the escutcheons of the family that had been
pulled down by the mob in 1494, or in erasing the crimson
cross, the heraldic emblem of the Florentine people, which
had in certain instances replaced the familiar coat of gold
with its red pellets, the historic *palle* of the Medicean
House.   And the sight of this hasty transformation of
the Cardinal's armorial bearings on the old palace in Via
Larga so affected a worthy citizen belonging to the
faction of the *Palleschi*, by the name of Gian-Andrea
Cellini, that, being of a poetical turn of mind although
only an *ebanista* or inlayer of ivory and wood by profession, he set himself to compose a quatrain suitable to
the occasion, which, so we learn on the authority of his
son Benvenuto, was quoted by the whole of Florence :—

> Quest' arme, che sepolta è stata tanto
> Sotto la Santa Croce mansueta,
> Mostra or la faccia gloriosa e lieta,
> Aspettando di Pietro il sacro ammanto.[3]

[1] " Gigli con gigli sempre devono fiorire."
[2] Jovius, lib. ii.
[3] *Vita di Benvenuto Cellini*, lib. i., cap. i.
(This glorious shield, concealed for many a year
Beneath the sacred Cross, that symbol meet,
Raises once more a joyful face to greet
Peter's successor, who approaches near.)

The gist of this simple little epigram must have appeared obvious to all its readers. The father of the prince of jewellers, then a lad in his twelfth year, thus artlessly predicts the supreme honour which in the near future awaits the Cardinal Giovanni de' Medici, now tarrying outside the gates of the city before advancing to occupy again the grand old mansion that had been his birthplace.

Meanwhile Giuliano had already passed the walls on 1st September and taken up his abode in the house of Messer Francesco degli Albizzi, one of his keenest supporters. Nevertheless, deeming that as a matter of course he had returned to the old palace in Via Larga, the fickle Florentine crowd must needs parade the broad space before the palace doors to cry aloud, *Palle! Palle!* in the hope of attracting the attention and gaining a glimpse of the returned prince. Giuliano, however, on his part appeared most anxious to avoid all such public manifestations, for he proceeded to walk with his friends unguarded about the streets, after first donning the *lucco* or long citizen's hood and shaving off beard and moustache in accordance with Florentine taste. So far as he was personally concerned, Giuliano was willing and even desirous to settle down as a private individual in his native city, where his courteous manners and innate modesty soon won him the affection of all save the more ardent members of his own party. But his liberal views were by no means shared by his elder brother, the Cardinal, who was absolutely determined to secure the re-instatement of the Medici in Florence beyond the possibility of another expulsion similar to that of 1494. Prompt measures, the Cardinal was convinced, must be taken at the present moment, when the support of Cardona's army lay at his back ; for, realising Giuliano's

pliable nature and the young Lorenzo's utter inexperience, he was fully aware that this unique opportunity
might yet be wasted, and the proud position held in succession by his father, his grandfather and his great-grandfather, might again be wrested from his House on the
coming retirement of the Spaniards. Amidst wild scenes
of enthusiasm, therefore, on the part of the more eager of
the *Palleschi*, who were quick to recognise their true
leader in the Cardinal-Legate rather than in the gracious
and liberal-minded Giuliano, the second son of the
Magnificent Lorenzo entered the city by the Faenza
Gate with 400 Spanish lances and 1000 foot-soldiers,
under the command of Ramazotto, a roving captain for
whose head the Florentine Signory had only a few
weeks before offered blood-money merely on account of
his seeking service under the Medici.[1] Taking possession in state of his former residence at Sant' Antonio,
which the rabble had pillaged and whence as a boy of
eighteen he had fled for his life in the dingy garb of a
friar, thus did Giovanni de' Medici once more re-enter
Florence as her undisputed master and the arbiter of
her fate. "The city was reduced to the point of help-
lessness save by the will of the Cardinal de' Medici, and
his method was the method of complete tyranny," wails
Francesco Vettori, when two days after his arrival at
Sant' Antonio, Giovanni, making an ingenious use of the
attendant Spanish army, contrived to replace the late
system of administration by a *Balià*, or executive
council, consisting of forty-five members all chosen by
the Cardinal and all therefore devoted adherents of the
Medici. Skilled in the peculiar diplomacy of his father
and well versed in the traditions of his House, which

[1] Landucci, p. 321.

always sought the substance rather than the pomp of power, the Cardinal was yet able to accomplish this internal revolution without bloodshed and without flagrant violation of the old republican forms ; and thus the Balià, arranged and erected by Giovanni de' Medici, continued the true source of political power in Florence until the third and last exodus of the Medicean family in 1527. Nor did the victorious Cardinal disdain to make use of the smaller arts in winning popular applause and acquiescence in his restored rule, for he organised costly masquerades to tickle the people's fancy, causing the old Carnival ditties, against which Savonarola had waged so fierce a war, to be sung once more in the streets, as in the long-past days of the Magnificent Lorenzo. These efforts to revive the dormant spirit of Florentine merriment were chiefly carried out under the auspices of the two newly established societies of the *Diamond* and the *Broncone*, or *Bough*, so named from the emblems assumed respectively by Giuliano and Lorenzo de' Medici. Emblematic heraldry being the fashion of the day, the prudent Giovanni himself did not despise the use of a personal badge, which might afford all men a clue to his intentions and ideas, and accordingly he selected the device of an ox-yoke inscribed with the single word *Suave*, in allusion to the significant circumstance that, however firmly fixed his rule might be over the Florentines, yet " his yoke was easy and his burden was light ".[1] But it is impossible to dwell further on the numberless incidents that mark the restoration of the Medici in 1512, a most important episode in Florentine history, of which the future Leo X. is at once the presiding genius and the picturesque figure-head.   For, apart from the diplomatic

---

[1] Scipione Ammirato, *Ritratti de' Medici* (Opuscoli, vol. iii.).

skill exhibited by him throughout this critical period and
the careful steps whereby he secured the political triumph
of his House without seriously offending public opinion,
it is necessary also to record the remarkable clemency
which as conqueror he displayed towards the city that
had so ignominiously, not to say unjustly, expelled and
outlawed him in his youth.   Such mild treatment goes
to prove, if any further proof were needed, the real affection which Leo X. bore towards Florence, as well as his
natural inclination to mercy, a quality of which his contemporaries so often speak with admiration.   And when
we reflect upon the all-pervading spirit of fury and vengeance of those times, and call to mind the innumerable
acts of bloody retribution wrought in that same spirit, it
becomes impossible for any impartial person to withhold
praise for the forbearance, the patience and the kindli-
ness of a prince who had at last regained possession of
a rebellious and ungrateful city after so many years spent
in undeserved poverty and exile.

As the actual, though not officially recognised head
of the Florentine state, the Cardinal now gave audience
to the papal datary, Lorenzo Pucci, and to other ambassadors, including the powerful Bishop Lang, whom
he entertained at the family villa of Caffagiolo, where so
much of his own childhood had been spent.   But fate
did not intend the Cardinal's personal guardianship of
Florence to be of long duration, for shortly after the exposure of Boscoli's abortive plot, which only served to
rivet yet more firmly the new-forged Medicean fetters,
there arrived in February, 1513, news first of the illness
and then of the death of Pope Julius, who expired on the
twentieth day of that month.   Despite the fact that he
was suffering severely from a constitutional malady and
in consequence appeared unequal to bear the fatigues of

the tedious journey to Rome, the Cardinal hastily made arrangements for the government of the city in his absence, and was then conveyed southward in a litter in order to assist at the coming conclave.   Men nodded their heads and speculated as to the prospects of the Florentine Cardinal's election, for notwithstanding his comparative youth and his precarious health, Giovanni de' Medici had by sheer force of talent combined with patient statecraft already won back Florence ; and now that the Medicean star was once again in the ascendant, not a few persons were ready to predict that as one of the ablest, the noblest born and the most popular members of the Sacred College, the second son of Lorenzo the Magnificent owned an excellent chance of obtaining the supreme honour of Christendom, so as to complete the recent triumph of his illustrious House, which had at last recovered its old prestige and importance in the polity of Italy.

CHAPTER V

LEO DECIMUS PONTIFEX MAXIMUS

Cette Europe des premières années de la XVIme siècle, labourée par la guerre, decimée par la peste, ou toutes les nationalités de l'Europe intermédiare s'agitent en cherchant leur assiette sous l'unité apparent de la monarchie universelle de l'Espagne ; ou l'on voit d'un même coup d'œil des querelles réligieuses et des batailles, une mêlée inouïe des hommes et des choses, une religion naissante en lutte de violence avec la réligion établie, l'ignorance de l'Europe occidentale se debattant contre la lumière de l'Italie : l'antiquité qui sort de son tombeau, les langues mortes qui renaissent, la grandé tradition littéraire qui vient rendre le sens des choses de l'esprit à des intelligences perverties par les raffinements de la dialectique religeuse ; du fracas partout ; du silence nulle part : les hommes vivant comme les pélerins et cherchant leur patrie cà et là ; une republique littéraire et chrétienne de tous les esprits élevés, réunis par la langue Latine, cette langue qui faisait encore toutes les grandes affaires de l'Europe à cette époque ; d'épouvantables barbaries à côté d'un précoce élégance des moeurs ; une immense mêlée militaire, réligieuse, philosophique, monacale (M. Nisard, *Renaissance et Reforme*).

IT affords some satisfaction to recall that the last days of Pope Julius were marked by edifying conduct, and that he prepared for his approaching end with a calm dignity well befitting the august office he held. Summoning the Consistory to assemble a few days prior to his agony, the aged Pontiff, stretched on the sick-bed whence he was fated never to rise, despatched a peremptory message to his cardinals to refrain from all simony or bribery at the coming election of his own successor ; he lamented the defection of the rebellious Carvajal and Sanseverino, yet as a man he would not refuse them his final blessing, although as Pontiff he was denouncing their late secession in terms of withering hate ; he spoke also of Christ's Church, with complacency designating himself a miserable sinner and an unworthy vice-regent, who had however consistently striven for the true interests of the Holy See.   To the last the dying Pope continued to utter imprecations against the French and the obdurate Alfonso of Ferrara, whose fall he had been so anxious to accomplish ; the cry of " Fuori ! Fuori ! Barbari ! " (Out of Italy, ye Barbarians !) still issued from the cracking lips in the frequent attacks of feverish delirium, and his wondering attendants sometimes imagined that these half-conscious threats were levelled not only at the discomfited Gaul, but also at the favoured Spaniard, whose sword the bellicose Pontiff had not scrupled to utilise in his late campaigns.   At length the constant flow of hazy invective ceased, and the old man passed away peacefully, the news of his death provoking an outburst of genuine grief in Rome, the like of which had not been seen within the memory of living man, and which seems to have astonished the decorous Paris de Grassis, the papal master of ceremonies, to whom Julius had long since given explicit instructions as to the decent disposal of his corpse.   Loud were the lamentations of the Roman populace, which was traditionally expected to curse a pontiff when dead, however much it may have cringed to him during life ; tears were falling on all sides ; women with dishevelled hair were weeping like children at the gates of the Vatican ; the crowd struggled fiercely to kiss the papal feet which according to ancient custom were made to protrude outside the enclosing grille of the mortuary chapel.   *Uomo terribile*, Julius was vaguely accounted a patriot by the short-sighted Italians, who totally failed to recognise in this papal scourge of the hated foreigner the true consolidator of the temporal power of the Papacy. No, it was the grand Pontiff, now lying in state before them, who had chased the invading French back across the Alps ; that was all men cared to remember at the last hour of Julius.

Considered solely as a secular prince and judged by the standard of his own turbulent age, Julius certainly shines as a monarch who was guided by definite and high-minded principles rather than by pure self-interest for himself or for some less worthy brother or nephew. He had continued the policy of the Borgia, it is true, but all his exertions had been made to strengthen the Holy See, of which he had always deemed himself but the temporary guardian, and not to found a principality for some kinsman. For with the sole exception of the little town of Pesaro, all the hard-won conquests of the late Pope had gone to swell that papal empire, which Julius considered absolutely essential for the proper maintenance and autonomy of himself and his successors. So far then as he is the acknowledged founder of the States of the Church, Julius appears as a disinterested and even patriotic conqueror. But if, on the other hand, we turn to criticise his career from a moral standpoint, regarding him (as he doubtless regarded himself) as the Vicar of Christ, the vice-regent of the Prince of Peace, what language can be found adequate to convey an opinion of the violent old man who deliberately embroiled all the princes of Europe, and deluged his own unhappy country with blood, all for the sake of a few coveted towns and fortresses ? Fire and sword, rapine and starvation, these are the characteristics of the reign of Julius II., who nevertheless expired perfectly contented with the results of his blood-stained pontificate and utterly unconscious of the mischief he had wrought or the

GIULIANO DELLA ROVERE (JULIUS II)

Divine laws he had broken.   " He was so great that he might be accounted an Emperor rather than a Pope ! " remarks the half-admiring Francesco Vettori; whilst Guicciardini, the Livy of his age, who after Machiavelli ranks as its pervading genius, expresses more forcibly his private opinion concerning the famous Warrior-Pope. " Only those who have abandoned the art of plain speaking and have lost the habit of right thinking extol this Pontiff's memory above that of his predecessors.   It is such persons who declare it to be the Pope's duty to add territory to the Apostolic See by force of arms and spilling of Christian blood, rather than to occupy himself in setting a good example, in correcting the general decay of morals and in trying to save the souls for whose sake Christ has made him His vicar on earth." [1]   But far more illuminating than a score of dissertations upon the morality and aims of Julius II. is an inspection of Raphael's splendid portrait of this Pope,[2] which hangs in the Pitti Palace at Florence.[3]   The Umbrian artist, it is needless to relate, has depicted his subject in a most favourable attitude.   Exhausted and anxious, the old man sits wearily in the broad high-backed chair, his bejewelled hands clinging for support to the framework and his bearded chin sunk languidly upon his breast. Physically he is resting, but his quick mind, the painter clearly shows us, is still at work, for the Pope's brain was ever teeming with the many grandiose schemes which only the natural term of years forbade him to accomplish. It is a moment of necessary repose, but merely the repose

[1] *Storia d' Italia*, lib. xi.

[2] The original cartoon, of more interest than the painting itself, is preserved in the Corsini Palace in Florence.

[3] The National Gallery of London possesses a fine replica of this celebrated portrait.

of a quiescent volcano that is ready at any minute to burst into fierce flames of passion or invective. Perhaps this fascinating likeness has performed better service to the memory of the irascible Julius than all the arguments of his apologists. The venerable countenance, distinguished by "the natural foliage of the face" (as the courtly Valeriano named this novelty of a papal beard), the nervous supple hands, the crimson velvet vestments, the air of profound reflection, all appeal strongly to posterity on behalf of the Warrior-Pope, for they produce an undeniable effect of real majesty and of lofty meditation. Julius was not without his virtues, but these, as we have tried to explain, were more than balanced by his defects ; yet here in Raphael's admirable picture of the Pontiff, the virtues alone are apparent, the vices are not perceptible. The unrestrained temper, the vulgar peasant's suspicion, the coarseness, the indifference to suffering are not suggested on the canvas : only the grandeur of the Pope's conceptions and his stately presence are exhibited to our scrutiny. Magnificent as it undoubtedly is as a masterpiece of the great painter, yet Raphael's portrait of Julius II. does not afford so perfect a mirror of the mind as does his likeness of Leo X., which also adorns the collection of the Pitti Palace. Strange it is that both these glorious portraits of the two greatest of the Popes of the Renaissance, who represent respectively the selfish violence and the pagan culture of that brilliant epoch, should thus finally be placed side by side in a Florentine gallery, where "all the world in circle" can pass by and draw its own conclusions of the character and worth of each from the pictures of the divine artist of Urbino.

There were only twenty-four cardinals in Rome ready to assemble in the ensuing conclave. On the morning of 4th March, therefore, all these attended the customary mass of the Holy Spirit, which owing to the dilapidated state of St. Peter's had to be sung in the adjacent chapel of St. Andrew instead of at the high altar.   Through the chinks and crevices of the tottering walls the stormy winds of March shrieked and wailed, whilst the acolytes were kept busily employed in relighting the tapers on the altar, which the tempest would not permit to burn steadily.   After this ceremony, of necessity shorn of its usual splendour, the cardinals entered the building, which according to the prescribed rule had every door locked and every window hermetically sealed, so that it is easy for us to comprehend how dreaded an ordeal a conclave always seemed to the older and feebler members of the Sacred College.

Giovanni de' Medici, who on account of a terrible ulcer had been compelled to travel in a litter all the way from Florence to Rome, did not reach the conclave until 6th March, arriving in such a state of pain and exhaustion that it was evident to all that the immediate attendance of a surgeon was imperative.   A certain Giacomo of Brescia,[1] who had gained a high reputation for his medical skill, chanced to be in Rome at this moment, and he was accordingly admitted within the carefully guarded portals of the building, where he operated with success upon the suffering Cardinal, who for some days remained too ill to leave his bed, whilst his colleagues were still wrangling and scheming over their choice of a new Pope. At length on the seventh day of discussion, the guardians of the conclave, in order to bring to a point the deliberations of the cardinals, decided to reduce the daily meal of the princes of the Church to one solitary dish, and this

[1] His house, a good specimen of Renaissance architecture, is still standing in the Borgo Nuovo near St. Peter's.

parsimonious diet combined with the stifling air of their present abode at last produced an universal desire in the imprisoned members of the College to select a Pontiff speedily, if only as a means of escape from the foul atmosphere and the scanty supply of food. The elder members of the conclave had now tired of their persistent but unavailing efforts on behalf of Cardinal Alborese, whilst the younger faction was joined by Raffaele Riario, cousin of the late Pope, who had originally aspired to the tiara himself but was beginning to realise the hopelessness of his secret ambition. Meanwhile the younger cardinals, and especially a clique formed of such as belonged to reigning houses, like Louis of Aragon, Ghismondo Gonzaga of Mantua, Ippolito d' Este of Ferrara and Alfonso Petrucci of Siena, were most eager to elect one of their own rank and ideas. They were heartily sick of the late Pontiff's savage wars with their attendant horrors and fatigues; they were still smarting from the sharp reproofs and lectures of the rough Ligurian peasant who had been their master; and they were consequently most anxious to obtain a Pope who should appear in every way the exact opposite of Julius II. in birth, manners and principles. Now, there was no one of their number answering better to this description than Giovanni de' Medici, who was the son of a sovereign, was a cultured man of letters and was credited with peaceful proclivities. Medici was likewise the most popular member of the Sacred College, wherein he did not possess a single enemy, if we except Francesco Soderini, brother of the recently expelled Gonfalionere of Florence, yet even in this solitary instance of real enmity, opposition was removed through the tactful machinations of Bernardo Dovizi, now serving as Medici's secretary in the conclave, who contrived to placate the hostile Florentine Cardinal by hinting at a possible matrimonial alliance between the young Lorenzo de' Medici and a daughter of the rival House of Soderini. Those engaging manners and studied efforts to please, which Medici had always culti-vated so assiduously, had in fact endeared him to all his companions in the College, whereof, though com-paratively still a young man, he had been a member for twenty-four years and had participated in four papal elections. The proposal of Medici's name therefore as being *papabile*, or worthy of the tiara, was received with general satisfaction, and now that the adhesion of both Riario and Soderini had been gained by the young Cardinal's supporters, his election became a foregone con-clusion. On 11th March the formal scrutiny took place, whereat Medici himself, as senior Deacon, had to record and count the votes cast into the urn. A true son of Lorenzo the Magnificent, the Pontiff elect showed in his face and manner no trace of triumph or pleasure whilst thus employed : a circumstance which afforded great satis-faction to his colleagues. With perfect calm the new Pope received the proffered homage of his late peers, and on being requested to announce the pontifical title which he intended to assume, Medici replied with modest hesitation that he would prefer to be known as Leo X., provided the Sacred College approved of this selection of a name. The title indeed caused some surprise, as coming from one to whom the epithet *clemens* or *pius* might have been deemed more appropriate ; nevertheless, the cardinals, who were doubtless ignorant of Medici's hidden reason for preferring so vigorous a title,[1] declared their consent, and even went so far as to call it an ideal name, which they themselves would have chosen had

[1] See chapter i.

similar luck befallen them. The formal preliminaries of an election being concluded, Alessandro Farnese now broke the seals laid upon the shuttered windows over-looking the piazza, and thrusting his head through the aperture, in a loud voice announced the welcome intelli-gence to the expectant crowd below in the usual set terms:—"Gaudium magnum nuntio vobis! Papam habemus, Reverendissimum Dominum Johannem de Medicis, Diaconum Cardinalem Sanctae Mariae in Domenica, qui vocatur Leo Decimus!" (I bring you tidings of great joy! We have a Pope, the most Reverend Lord, Giovanni de' Medici, Cardinal Deacon of Santa Maria in Domenica, who is called Leo X.!)

Thus at the remarkably early age of thirty-seven was Giovanni, second son of Lorenzo de' Medici, late tyrant of Florence, elevated under the happiest of auspices to the highest dignity in all Christendom. For although the conclave of 1513 cannot be accounted free from in-trigue, yet it appears in striking contrast with most of the papal elections that had preceded it. Nor was there any suspicion of bribery in Medici's case, unless Bibbiena's successful attempt to win over the reluctant Soderini can be considered as such; broadly speaking, the choice made was spontaneous, and one that relied solely on the merits and position of the person selected. Malicious rumour certainly hinted that the support of Riario and the older cardinals had been gained in their full belief that Medici, despite his youthful years, was not likely to survive his newly acquired dignity any great length of time, since he was in obvious ill-health and suffering, even in the conclave, from a painful malady, concerning which the accurate Paris de Grassis presents us with a mass of minute and revolting details.[1] This prejudiced

[1] Creighton, vol. v.

view did not, however, reflect the general opinion of the time, nor has it been endorsed by modern historians, who are inclined to follow the more kindly criticism of Francesco Guicciardini :—

"Almost all Christendom heard with the greatest joy of the election of Leo the Tenth, and on all sides men were firmly persuaded that at last they had obtained a Pontiff distinguished above all others by the gifts of mind he had inherited from a noble father, and by the reports of his generosity and clemency that resounded from all quarters. He was esteemed chaste ; his morals were excellent ; and men trusted to find in him, as in his parent's case, a lover of literature and all the fine arts. And these hopes waxed all the stronger, seeing that his election had taken place properly, without simony or suspicion of any irregularity." [1]

In Rome itself the election of Leo X. was hailed with unfeigned satisfaction, and with exuberant joy in that world of letters and culture whereof the late Cardinal de' Medici had for many years been regarded as a munificent patron. But the expressions of content in the Eternal City were mild in comparison with the frantic outburst of popular rejoicing, which was now witnessed in Florence, the place of the new Pontiff's birth. The momentous news from Rome arrived in Florence at two of the clock on the Friday following the scrutiny, and when the report was officially confirmed, the ecstacy of the *Palleschi*, now of course the ruling party, knew no bounds of reason or restraint. The bells were rung madly ; fireworks were exploded ; artillery was fired ; and in all the streets bon-fires were raised of tar-barrels and brushwood, supplemented in many cases by the household furniture of unfortunate citizens suspected of hostility to the Medici.

[1] *Storia dell' Italia*, lib. xi.

The shops and dwellings of the poor *Piagnoni*, the puritan
followers of Savonarola, were on all sides plundered,
while in not a few instances the roofs were set alight by
crowds of Medicean partisans, drunken with wine or
enthusiasm, and shouting aloud *Palle !* and *Papa Leone !*
at the top of their raucous Tuscan voices.   The din was
terrific, and the disorder finally grew so serious, that the
Florentine Council of Eight, alarmed for the public
safety, was compelled to issue an order threatening with
the gallows all persons caught in the act of robbery or
arson.   This Medicean orgy—*questa pestilenzia*, as the
republican Landucci styles these proceedings—endured
for four days, during which time the whole town resounded
with festal explosions and reeked with the pungent smoke
of the bonfires, which the revellers kindled daily before
the Palazzo Vecchio or in front of the Medicean mansion.
Other adherents of the Medici regaled the eager crowds
with sweet wine drawn out of gilded barrels, that had
been set in rows upon the historic *Ringhiera*[1] of the
civic palace.   As a final proof of the city's intense joy
and proud content, a deputation of prominent officials
fetched from Impruneta the famous statue of the Madonna,
the *palladium* of the Florentines, and with the effigy
gorgeously arrayed in nine new mantles of cloth-of-gold,
the procession halted before the portals of Casa Medici
in Via Larga, where food and wine were provided and
crackers exploded.   But in the midst of this bout of
unrestrained carnival over the novel honour that had
befallen the city, there were not lacking some sober
spirits, who were able to discern the dubious advantages
of a Florentine Pope.   "I am not surprised," remarked
to certain bystanders the shrewd Lomellino, the

[1] A stone platform extending along the northern side of the
palace, long since removed

historian of Genoa, who was an amused spectator of these scenes of popular rejoicing, "at your present satisfaction, since your city has never yet produced a Pope, but when you have once gained this experience, as has been our case in Genoa, you will grow to realise a Pontiff's dealings with his native land and the price his fellow-citizens have to pay for the honour."[1]

Giovanni de' Medici was, as we have already said, only in his thirty-eighth year when he attained to the supreme dignity, which one of his father's courtiers, the poet Philomus, had predicted for him nearly a quarter of a century before;—"What joy," had cried the far-seeing bard, "will so high an honour afford your beloved parent, and what verses will Apollo inspire me to write in commemoration of the event!"[2]

> Eximiumque caput sacra redimire thyara
> Pontificis summi ; proh gaudia quanta parenti
> Tum dabis, et quantis mihi tum spirabit Apollo !

In outward appearance the new Pontiff was tall with a dignified carriage, despite a stout and unwieldy frame. His head was disproportionately large ; his smooth-shaven countenance was flushed and unhealthy in hue ; whilst his great prominent eyes were so feeble of vision that in order to perceive any person or object, no matter how familiar, the Pope was obliged to use continually a spy-glass, which was rarely absent from his hand. He had a short fleshy neck with a pronounced double chin, a broad chest and an enormous paunch, with which his spindling legs made a curious contrast. His only claim to physical beauty lay in his hands, of which their owner was inordinately proud and was frequently to be observed examining with artless satisfaction ; they were plump,

[1] Bacciotti, *Firenze Illustrata*, vol. i., p. 78.
[2] Roscoe, Appendix IX.

white and shapely, and usually adorned with rare and splendid gems.[1] Unlike his father, whose speech was always rasping and singularly unpleasing to the ear, Leo was the happy possessor of a soft, persuasive and well-modulated voice; his manner was almost invariably courteous and genial, and he had sedulously trained his natural gift of tact to the highest degree of perfection, so that he could always appear deferential towards his elders, and jocular, or even boisterous in the society of younger men. As may be gathered from this description, the youthful Pope did not enjoy robust health.[2] From his early years he had been the victim of a chronic infirmity which the ignorant quacks of that age could neither cure nor alleviate, and which not only caused him perpetual inconvenience and frequent attacks of pain, but also at certain times rendered the poor sufferer's presence most unpleasant to the friends around him. It speaks eloquently for Leo's natural good-nature and his acquired habit of self-control, that he never allowed this constant source of annoyance to affect his temper, which seems to have remained even and suave to the last.

Since Giovanni de' Medici was but a deacon in the conclave whence he issued as Pope, with all convenient despatch he was ordained priest on 15th March, and consecrated bishop two days later, whilst on 19th March he was formally enthroned and crowned, the Cardinals

[1] *Vita Anonyma Leonis X.*, Bossi-Roscoe, Appendix CCXVIII.; Jovius, lib. iv.; Scipione Ammirato, *Rittrati de' Medici*, etc.

[2] Quod ad valetudinem attinet, ulcere quodam quod fistulam vocant in inferiore parte corporis quae plurime carne contecta est laborabat, eoque interdum graviter cruciabatur; nam cum intercluderetur plerumque sanies retentaque fluere solita erat, eum ita perturbabat; atque ita de valetudine dejiciebat, ut praeter ulceris dolorem febre etiam corriperetur, sed ea brevi solvebatur (*Vita Anonyma Leonis X.*)

Farnese and Louis of Aragon placing the heavy triple diadem on his head. For this purpose a pavilion had been specially erected on the steps of the dilapidated basilica of St. Peter, the façade of which bore in large letters of gold an inscription in honour of " Leo the Tenth, Supreme Pontiff, Protector of the Arts and Patron of Good Works". The usual ritual of a papal coronation was duly carried out in this meagre temporary building, and Paris de Grassis describes in his Diary how, as master of the ceremonies, he bore in accordance with ancient custom to the foot of the throne a rod decorated with a bunch of tow, which he ignited with a burning taper, and then, whilst the dry flax was being rapidly consumed in a sheet of bright flame, addressed the time-honoured warning : " Holy Father, thus passeth away the glory of this world ! " And again, " Thou shalt never see the years of Peter," whose traditional reign as first Pontiff is said to have endured for twenty-five years.[1] And yet Leo was but thirty-seven, so that, if he were to attain to the ordinary human age-limit of threescore years and ten, he would then have exceeded by eight summers the great Apostle's tenure of the dignity ; nevertheless, the young Pope's indifferent state of health rendered such an admonition a salutary warning in the midst of all this pomp and worship.

By ancient precedent it was permitted to the cardinals assisting at a papal coronation to present petitions to the new master who had been their late colleague, and on this occasion Medici's reputation for lavish generosity and his dislike of refusal had the effect of giving rise to

---

[1] Of the Roman Pontiffs, Pius IX. (1846-1878) has exceeded "the Years of Peter," as he has himself proudly recorded above the Apostle's statue in the nave of the Basilica. Also Leo XIII., whose reign occupied twenty-five years (1878-1903).

an extraordinary number of requests from the cardinals on behalf of themselves, their relations and their innumerable dependants.   So boundless were the extent and variety of their demands that Leo, half-amused and half-disgusted at the audacity of many of their pleas, rebuked the unseemly greed of the Sacred College with a mild but satirical reproof: "Take my tiara," exclaimed the Pontiff to his importunate suppliants, "and act as if each one of you were Pope himself!   Agree among yourselves on what you desire, and take your fill."[1]

For the late ceremonies in the derelict basilica of St. Peter there had been small time for preparation and smaller scope for splendour.   The festivities of Holy Week were also close at hand, and in consequence Leo was forced to defer the elaborate procession and act of public rejoicing on which his heart was set, until the occasion of his formal occupation of the historic church and palace of the Lateran.   The date of this impending event therefore the Pope fixed not without secret satisfaction for 11th April, the first anniversary of the battle of Ravenna, which had seen the papal army scattered and the present Pontiff a prisoner of the French King. This decision afforded Leo an unique opportunity for indulging in his inherited taste for splendid pageantry, since not only had he the overflowing treasury of the thrifty Julius at his disposal, but likewise, as he soon perceived, the Roman court and the Roman people were setting to work with feverish activity upon preparations, which were destined to make of Leo's triumphal progress across the city of the Cæsars and the Popes the greatest spectacle of pomp and beauty which even that era could produce.   But before proceeding to de-

---

[1] *Diary of Paris de Grassis*, Bossi-Roscoe, lib. iv., cap. iv., p. 18.

scribe in detail this most famous pageant, which marks
the opening of the Leonine Age, it will be proper for us
in the first place to give a brief description of the Eternal
City as it appeared in the year that witnessed the elevation of the Cardinal de' Medici to the pontifical
throne.

If the Florence of our own days has preserved intact
no small portion of its ancient character, the Rome of
King Victor-Emmanuel owns few features that were
prominent within its walls at the date of Leo's election.
Looking down from the carefully tended gardens of the
Pincian Hill upon the city spread beneath us, we can
perceive scarcely a single object which must have been
familiar to the eyes of the Medicean Pope nearly four
centuries ago.   And yet within the memory of many
persons living the Eternal City has undergone an almost
complete transformation of aspect, for the Rome of Pius IX.
was itself a totally different place from the modern
capital of United Italy ; so many an ancient landmark
has been recently swept away, so many obtruding public
edifices have arisen, and so many hundreds of brand-new
streets on a stereotyped Parisian model have been
constructed on all sides.   Rome, like a palimpsest, is
perpetually changing her character, and it is curious to
reflect that the great spreading capital of to-day could
hardly appear less strange or bewildering to the contemporaries of Leo X. than would the old papal seat of
Pio Nono, which so many still love to recall with its
stately air of repose and its picturesque scenes of ecclesiastical life.   Only the Pantheon with its low dome and
lofty colonnade, the vast circle of the Colosseum and
certain of the ruined Thermæ (and these not a little
altered or curtailed) survive from one century to another,
linking the Rome of the Middle Ages, the Rome of the

sovereign Pontiffs and the Rome of the Italian Kings with the imperial city of Augustus and the Antonines.

A very small portion of the immense area enclosed by the irregular ring of mouldering walls was occupied by houses in the year 1513, the remainder being covered with vineyards, gardens, groves and even with thickets of brier and myrtle, so dense that deer and wild boar occasionally sought shelter within their recesses. Out of this bosky expanse peeped forth at various points the forms of ancient churches with delicate arched *campanili* of red brick beside them; whilst here and there were conspicuous huge masses of tawny ruins draped with ivy or eglantine that harboured myriads of pigeons, which the sportsmen of the city would sometimes shoot or snare in idle hours. The classic Forum, known by the humble appellation of the Cattle Market (Campo Vacchino); stretched as a long marshy scrub-covered expanse, wherein a few shafts of antique temples still rose aloft, but the Via Sacra and the foundations marking the heart of the proud city lay hidden beneath a crust, some thirty feet in depth, of superincumbent soil and rubbish. Beyond the utter desolation of the Roman Forum towered the gigantic bulk of the Flavian Amphitheatre, inexpressibly grand in its lonely magnificence and with its fabric practically intact, for the evil days of Roman vandalism had scarcely begun in earnest. The Palatine, the Coelian and the Aventine were but wooded hills, dotted with a few farms and convents, or with decayed heaps of ancient buildings, which were now forming convenient quarries for the architects of the new palaces and churches springing up on all sides. The Capitol itself with its tall towers and forked battlements resting on the Titanic sub-structures of antiquity still retained the aspect of a mediæval fortress which had been bestowed upon it two centuries before by Boniface VIII., but the Tarpeian Rock beside it was but a barren cliff, as its local name of Monte Caprino—the Goat's Hill—implied. The population of Rome, computed at various figures but probably numbering about 60,000 souls, was chiefly huddled into the narrow space lying between the Capitol and the Tiber and into the trans-pontine quarter of Trastevere, the denizens of which have always affected to boast a pure descent from the ancient Romans themselves—*gli Romani di Roma.* These two districts together constituted the mediæval town, which was still a maze of dark filthy alleys, inter-spersed by churches or palaces. Around the Vatican itself was rising a new and splendid quarter of the city, with residences for the princes of the Church or for the numerous envoys to the papal court, but in the main Rome still kept its mean appearance of the Middle Ages. The older houses, many of them overhanging the muddy Tiber and often entered by means of boats, were mostly distinguished by exterior stairways and by tall stone turrets, of which a few specimens survive to-day. On all sides the fortified ruins, including the arches of Constantine, Titus and Severus, bore ample testimony to the unsettled and lawless conditions of the past, and to the old-time feuds of Orsini and Colonna, of Frangipani and Gaetani.

Standing on the Pincio, then clothed with vines and olives, the stranger would at once become aware of the absence of that world-famous group of buildings, which constitutes the most prominent object in Papal Rome. In the room of the great domed church and the far-spreading courts of the modern Vatican, there uprose to view only the façade of old St. Peter's, and beside it the tall form of the Sistine chapel and the Torre Borgia,

for Alexander VI. had embellished the papal residence,
and had strengthened the neighbouring Castle of Sant'
Angelo,[1] which he had joined to the Vatican itself by
means of a stone gallery of communication, that was
doomed to play a conspicuous part on more than one
occasion in the later annals of the secular Papacy.   But
the glittering exterior of the venerable basilica merely
masked what was in reality a naked ruin, whilst the
completed portion of the palace was surrounded by a
trampled wilderness littered with hewn and unhewn
blocks of stone or marble, and with fine antique columns
pilfered from the pagan fanes : evidences of the late
Pontiff's work of demolition and his earnest desire to
erect a Christian temple, or rather a mausoleum for
himself, which should exceed in size and splendour every
structure the world had hitherto beheld.   At the extreme
point east of St. Peter's within the circumference of the
city walls, rose the second papal palace and the vast
church of St. John's Lateran, the true cathedral of
Rome, "the mother and head of all churches on the
face of the earth," with the famous Baptistery beside it,
wherein the Emperor Constantine had been made a
Christian by Pope Sylvester.   Once the seat of power
and magnificence under such Pontiffs as Innocent III.
and Urban IV., the Lateran had long been abandoned
as a residence by their successors, who now only cared
to concentrate their energy and expend their wealth
upon the rival palace across the Tiber.   Yet the
neglected Lateran still owned a special sanctity and importance, so that a new Pope's formal procession thither

[1] The Municipality of Rome—whether in a fit of moral zeal or
of childish vandalism, we leave the reader to decide—has recently
effaced all their heraldic bearings from the escutcheons of the Borgia
Pope on the face of the Castle of Sant' Angelo.

was always made the occasion for a solemn display of pontifical majesty. At this particular moment also an additional interest was afforded by the circumstance that the council, recently convoked by Julius and regarded with so many brave hopes by the would-be reformers of the Church, was now holding its sittings within these very walls, so that Leo's coming visit possessed even more significance in men's minds than was usually attached to this papal ceremony of the *Sacro Possesso*, or formal entry into the Lateran.

It was in truth a brilliant opening to the Leonine Age, which was fated to prevail in Rome for fourteen years with one short interval, and when we contrast the scenes of popular delight and extravagance of 1513 with the awful yet inevitable catastrophe of 1527, we grow to comprehend dimly the close connection between the golden days of Leo's reign and the period of shame and outrage which was to terminate that glorious epoch under the unhappy Clement. Yet no sadness of impending disaster, no premonition of future destruction hung over the expectant city or the genial Pope, who ever since his coronation had been taking an almost child-like interest in every detail of the projected pageant, which the anxious Paris de Grassis was superintending. At length the desired morning broke, warm, sunny and balmy, as only a Roman spring-tide can produce, an ideal day for an open-air festival, of which the programme was arranged and developed on so grandiose a scale "that this spectacular representation of the secular Papacy in 1513 has afforded us also the most perfect picture of its established splendour".[1] And a truly marvellous sight did the Eternal City present on this

---

[1] F. Gregorovius, vol. vii.

occasion, with every house on the line of procession
decked with wreaths of laurel and ilex, and with every
casement displaying rich brocades or velvets of all shades
of colour, arranged with an exquisite taste for general
effect.   Triumphal arches, many of them real works of
art in themselves and the invention of the leading
painters and architects in Rome, had been erected to
span the streets at various points, for the wealthy
merchants, headed by the famous Sienese banker,
Agostino Chigi, were all vying to attract the notice and
win the praise of their new ruler.   Priceless antique
statues of the pagan gods and goddesses, the prized·
treasures of many a choice collection, had been set in
niches of these arches, often in incongruous proximity to
the effigies of Christian martyrs or divinities, amongst
whom the favourite Medicean saints, St. John the
Baptist, St. Lawrence and the Arab physicians Cosmo
and Damiano naturally appeared conspicuous.   On all
sides were to be observed inscriptions, mostly in Latin,
applauding the new Pontiff and calling down blessing on
his head ; and fulsome as were many of these eulogies,
yet there can be no question but that the city of Rome
was as delighted with Leo at this early period, as the
Pope himself was overjoyed at the display of all this
adulation and festal magnificence.   Of the numerous
arches, trophies and obelisks, most people adjudged the
palm of merit to that reared by Agostino Chigi, whose
vast income seemed to place him at an advantage over
other private persons.   A wholly unconscious critic of
his own times, Chigi had likewise placed in letters of
gold upon the frieze of his eight-columned arch an elegiac
couplet, comparing the coming reign of the Medicean
Pontiff to that of Minerva, and naming Leo's two predecessors as votaries respectively of Venus and Mars :—

Olim habuit Cypris sua tempora; tempora Mavors
Olim habuit; sua nunc tempora Pallas habet.[1]

To counterbalance Chigi's prophecy of this approaching
intellectual millenium, the goldsmith Antonio da San
Marco had either by accident or design inscribed below
a statue of Aphrodite, an exquisite production of some
Grecian chisel with which he had adorned his trophy, a
solitary pentameter, that must have greatly tickled Leo's
exuberant sense of humour:—

Mars fuit; est Pallas; Cypria semper ero.[2]

Many were the flattering sentiments conveyed thus
to the first Medicean Pope, and many were the anxious
hopes expressed for a coming period of peace and prosperity.—"Live according to your established piety! O
live for ever, according to your deserts!" announced
another of these inscriptions; whilst on Cardinal Sauli's
portico were to be seen verses alluding to the Pontiff's
supposed horror of the bloodshed wherewith the late
reign had been so disgracefully stained :—

Non de coesorum numero fusoque cruore,
Sed de sperata pace trophaea damus.[3]

The entrance to the Capitol bore a motto with a deeper
and more spiritual meaning:—

Genus humanum mortuos parit, quos Ecclesia vivificat;

which served to remind the fortunate Medici of the
boundless powers conferred by the great Apostle of the
gold and silver keys upon all his successors.   Another
arch, reared by the delighted Florentine residents of

---

[1] Venus has fled, and now the War-God's arms
    At last have yielded to Minerva's charms.
[2] Mars is fled, and Pallas reigns,
    Yet Venus still our queen remains!
[3] Not for slain victims nor for shedding blood
    We rear these trophies, but for future peace.

Rome in grateful honour of their illustrious countryman, was distinguished by a medley of Medicean emblems and heraldic devices—the ring and ostrich plumes of the Magnificent Lorenzo, the ox-yoke of the reigning Pontiff, the burning branch of the youthful heir of Piero de' Medici and the diamond of Giuliano, whilst the address upon its architrave recorded the respectful homage of his fellow-citizens to "the Ambassador of Heaven". In addition to these triumphal erections, the streets had been strewn with sprigs of box and myrtle; improvised altars had been set up at several corners, and every doorway was festooned with verdant wreaths. The populace was wearing festal attire, and in sign of the general quiet and sense of security all private persons were forbidden to wear swords. Some of the public fountains had been made to run with wine instead of water, and the whole city prepared itself to enjoy the coming procession with a zest and good-humour that had ever been denied to the late Pope's set triumphs after his vigorous campaigns.

First to quit the broad piazza before the Vatican, where the huge train was being marshalled, were the men-at-arms followed by the households of the cardinals and prelates of the court, all richly clad in scarlet. These were succeeded by a number of standard-bearers, including the captains of the *Rioni*, or historic divisions of Rome, and after them thundered the cavalcade of the five *Gonfalonieri*, wielders of the more important banners connected with the Holy See, conspicuous in their number being Giulio de' Medici in the robes and insignia of a knight of Rhodes. Behind this group of horsemen with their fluttering ensigns was led a string of milk-white mules from the papal stables, housed in gorgeous trappings, whilst behind them walked over one hundred equerries of the court, all of noble birth and clad in gala

robes of red fringed with ermine, the hindmost four bearing
the papal crowns and jewelled mitres upon short staves
of office.   These gave place to a second cavalcade composed of a hundred Roman barons with historic names,
each noble being followed by an armed escort of servants
dressed in their master's livery, prominent amongst them
being Fabrizio Colonna and Giulio Orsini, who rode
side by side with clasped hands in sign of present amity
and of past discord.   The notables of Rome were in their
turn succeeded by a company of the chief citizens of
Florence—Tornabuoni, Salviati, Ridolfi, Pucci, Strozzi
and the like—many of them being related to the Supreme Pontiff, in whose honour all this elaborate pageant
had been planned.   Amidst the gay trains of the Italian
and foreign ambassadors, pursuing on the heels of the
Florentine merchant-princes, appeared the form and retinue of the late Pope's nephew, Francesco Della Rovere,
Duke of Urbino, all decorously apparelled in deep
mourning and making thereby a curious streak of sable
amidst the glowing uniforms around them.   The laity
having all passed, the clergy now made their appearance
in due order, escorted by a host of sacristans and pages
in crimson velvet with silver wands, some of whom
directed the paces of the palfrey that bore on its back the
Sacrament in a glittering monstrance, above which Roman
citizens upheld a canopy of cloth-of-gold.   Hundreds of
priests, lawyers and clerks in flowing robes of scarlet,
black or violet next passed in review, preparing the way
for the bishops and abbots to the number of two hundred
and fifty, after whom advanced the cardinals, each prince
of the Church bestriding a beautiful steed with trailing
white draperies and each supported by eight chamberlains.   At the head of the Sacred College ambled the
handsome and haughty Alfonso Petrucci, Cardinal of

Siena, little dreaming in his youthful pride of the ignominious fate lying in store for him at no distant date ; whilst
beside the last cardinal rode the bluff Alfonso d' Este,
Duke of Ferrara, husband of Lucrezia Borgia and the
undaunted opponent of the terrible Julius, but now
obviously an eager suppliant for the good graces of his
successor.   Behind the cardinals and their equipages
walked discreetly the Conservators of Rome, humble
representatives of the ancient senators of the former
Mistress of the World, and close upon their footsteps
tramped Julius' Swiss body-guard,[1] two hundred strong,
a corps of picked mountaineers armed with halberds and
clothed in parti-coloured uniforms of green, white and
yellow.   Last of all rode the Supreme Pontiff himself,
the author and object of all this magnificence, mounted
on the white Arab stallion he had ridden on the fatal
field of Ravenna, which until its death was always regarded by its owner with a degree of affection almost
amounting to superstitious awe.[2]   Draped in snowy
housings, the beautiful creature, after its paces were
first tried by the haughty Duke of Ferrara in person, had
been led by the Duke of Urbino, as Prefect of Rome,
to the fountain in the centre of the space before St. Peter's,
where His Holiness with the assistance of his nephew
Lorenzo de' Medici was adroitly lifted into the saddle.
Above horse and rider eight Roman citizens of patrician
rank bore aloft a *baldacchino* or canopy of embroidered
silk in order to shield the Sovereign Pontiff from the
envious rays of the Sun-God, with whom not a few poets
and courtiers were already beginning to compare the

[1] The present uniform of the Swiss Guard at the Vatican—said on
doubtful authority to have been designed by Michelangelo—is composed of stripes in equal parts of red, yellow and black.
[2] Jovius, lib. iii.

LEO X RIDING IN STATE

fortunate, the resplendent Leo X. Sinking beneath the weight of triple tiara and of jewelled cope, the Pontiff was nevertheless sustained throughout the tedious length of his public progress across the city by the deep sense of exalted satisfaction, that was reflected in his broad purple face, from which the perspiration ran in streams as the result of the unusual exertion beneath a hot April sun. With hands in perfumed gloves sewn with pearls, the Pontiff continued to bestow blessings at regular intervals to the cheering crowds, which perhaps appreciated even more than the papal benedictions the silver coins flung ceaselessly by a pair of chamberlains, who carried well-filled money-bags. Led on his favourite white steed, with dukes and nobles beside him esteeming it a privilege to touch his bridle, Leo proceeded slowly in an ecstacy of gratified pride from the piazza of St. Peter's towards the bridge of Sant' Angelo. At this point, according to the usual custom, the Jews of Rome were assembled in order to request in all humility the permission to reside in the Holy City and also to present a copy of the Law; and as the gorgeous figure in shining crown and robes approached, the rabbi meekly stepped forward to give the prescribed greeting and to offer the volume. "We confirm your privileges," replied the Pope, opening the proffered scroll, "but we reject your faith!" (Confirmamus sed non consentimus!) and then allowed the book of the Law to fall like an accursed thing to the ground.

Turning aside gladly from the group of supplicating Hebrews, Leo continued his course towards the Lateran along the historic *Via Papale*, the Pope's Way, doling out largesse and giving endless benisons, whilst the whole air rung with prolonged cries of *Leone ! Leone ! Palle ! Palle !* From time to time the Pope's features were

seen to relax into a broad smile, as his attendants explained to him the gist of certain of the welcoming inscriptions, which his purblind eyes could not decipher ;
and fatiguing though this prolonged ceremonial must
have been to one in Leo's indifferent state of health, yet
the distance between St. Peter's and the Lateran did
not appear too lengthy to the admiring and admired
Pontiff, who was thus taking his fill of all the pomps and
vanities of his age in their most entrancing form, and
tasting that sweet but seductive draught of popular
adulation which has affected many a strong brain.

Arrived before the pile of the Lateran, the Pope dismounted beside the equestrian statue of the Emperor
Marcus Aurelius, which then adorned this part of the city.[1]
Tired physically with his late efforts and excitement but
still unsated with the homage paid him, Leo took formal
possession of that ancient seat of power, which was so
intimately connected with the deeds of many illustrious
predecessors. After the due performance of the rites
incidental to the *Sacro Possesso*, there followed a banquet
in the great hall of the palace, served with all the ostentatious luxury of which the Italian Renaissance was
capable. The meal ended, the glittering train prepared
to start homewards in the glowing atmosphere of an
April sunset. More shouts of applause, more benedictions, more largesse out of the savings of the frugal Julius
flung to the expectant rabble, yet when the gloaming
fell upon the scene and began to dim the brilliant hues of
the vestments and uniforms, the long papal procession
had scarcely reached the Campo de' Fiori. Torches and

---

[1] This famous statue now occupies the most prominent position
on the Roman Capitol, whither it was moved by Michelangelo under
Paul III., not without opposition from its owners, the canons of the
Lateran.

tapers now began to twinkle in every window of the city, eclipsing the starlight of the spring evening, and producing a weird but lovely effect upon the returning cavalcade. At last even Leo had grown exhausted, so that on reaching the gateway of the castle of Sant' Angelo, whose vast circular form loomed out black and distinct against the star-lit sky, he dismounted to enter the castle portals as the guest of young Alfonso Petrucci, who was doomed four years later to be strangled by his affectionate host's command in a noisome vault below the gilded and painted chamber wherein he was now entertaining his master. " In thinking over all the pomp and lofty magnificence I had just witnessed," naïvely records the simple Florentine physician Gian-Giacomo Penni in his lengthy account of the ceremony which he had evidently watched with envious eyes, "I experienced so violent a desire to become Pope myself, that I was unable to obtain a wink of sleep or any repose all that night. No longer do I marvel at these prelates desiring so ardently to procure this dignity, and I verily believe every lacquey would sooner be made a Pope than a Prince!"[1]

Thus terminated the supreme pageant that marked the happy accession of the first Medicean Pontiff and inaugurated with such a burst of splendour those golden days of culture and patronage, of license and extravagance, to which in after years the poets and scholars, who had participated in their delights, were wont to refer with affectionate regret; even exaggerating the bountiful

[1] The chief account of the *Sacro Possesso* of Leo X. is derived from this letter of Gian-Giacomo Penni, directed to Contessina Ridolfi, the Pope's sister, in Florence. *Chronicha delle magnifiche et honorate pompe fatte in Roma per la creatione et incoronatione di Papa Leone X.* (Bossi-Roscoe, lib. v., pp. 189-231). For another and shorter account, see Aless. Luzio, Appendix, Doc. 2.

condescension bestowed upon arts and letters by this Papal Mæcenas, to those less fortunate aspirants to fame and fortune, who had never tasted the joys of the Eternal City during the all-too-rapid passing of the Leonine Age.

CHAPTER VI

MEDICEAN AMBITION

Cette grande force de François Ier n'était pas seulement de circonstance et de situation; elle était aussi personelle. Tout réussit à la jeunesse, tout lui sourit. . . . Ni Charles VIII., ni Louis XII., les sauveurs prédits par Savonarola, n'avaient répondu aux exigences de l'imagination populaire; l'un petit, mal bâti, difforme par sa grosse tête; l'autre cacochyme, bourgeois, Roi des bourgeois. Celui-ci au contraire, beau de race, de fleur de jeunesse, plus beau de sa victoire, trouvant pour tous par sa langue facile des mots de grâce et d'espérance, n'était il pas enfin, pour l'Italie et pour le monde, ce Messie promis, attendu? (J. Michelet, *La Renaissance*).

SPECULATION was rife throughout Europe as to the public policy the first Medicean Pope was likely to pursue, although it was no difficult matter for such as had followed his past career as a Cardinal under Julius II. to make a shrewd guess at Leo's probable attitude towards the movements and questions of the day, both domestic and foreign. That he had a strong personal dislike to France would be a natural conclusion of such observers, seeing that the French King had supported the late Florentine Republic, and that Leo himself only a year before had endured in the French camp some months of captivity, which had not been wholly without discomfort and indignity. On the other hand, Leo had every reason to favour the Spaniards, whose lances had helped him to win back his native city for himself and the Medici. His late remarkable display of clemency in Florence led men to expect a Pontiff averse to war and

strife ; his moral reputation aroused the high hopes of all
those who were anxious to reform and purify the Church ;
his affability invited men to look for a ruler more reasonable and kindly than Julius ; whilst his manifest devotion
to literature provoked the Humanists to prepare for a return of the golden age of Roman letters under Augustus,
and to find in Leo X. a veritable Papal Mæcenas and a
perfect patron.

"It is my opinion," so writes Count Alberto Pio to
his master the Emperor, "that the Pontiff will be gentle
(*mitis*) as a lamb rather than fierce as a lion. He will
cultivate peace and not war. He will observe all his
vows and engagements most scrupulously. He will certainly be no friend to the French, yet on the other hand
he will not prove himself their implacable foe, like Julius.
He dreams of honour and glory. He will patronise men
of letters, at least *improvvisatori*, poets and musicians.
He will erect palaces. He will perform with care the
sacred offices, and will not neglect any ecclesiastical duty.
He will not rush into any war, except a crusade against
the Turks, unless much provoked or absolutely compelled
thereto. He will try to finish whatsoever he has undertaken. He will be unassuming in manner, and easily
prevailed on. These are my prognostications concerning Leo, but men change from hour to hour, and the
Divine power often plays tricks with our human calcula-
tions."[1]

Although Pio's general estimate of character and fore-
cast of Leo's policy sound fairly accurate, yet in the letter
just quoted the writer evidently does not lay sufficient
stress on the new Pontiff's overweening but carefully hidden
ambition, the existence of which was little suspected by
the world at large, or even by his own intimates who had

[1] Roscoe, vol. i., p. 352, note 13.

elected him Pope.   As the son of a ruler who had purposely instilled into his children's minds his own principles
of statecraft from their earliest years, Leo possessed advantages above most of his predecessors in that he had
been familiar from a tender age with the subtle methods
of a tyranny which concealed the most selfish aims under
a beneficent guise.   During the years of ignominious exile
under Alexander VI. and of hard service under Julius II.
the Cardinal de' Medici had been digesting the paternal
advice he had received in his youth, whilst his late experiences of poverty and insignificance had only served
to whet his natural appetite for pomp and power.
Throughout this period of nearly twenty years he had
found ample opportunity for the cultivation of those arts
of dissimulation, whereof his father was acknowledged so
able an exponent, and of which Leo himself was destined
to become a yet more perfect master.   As the Magnificent Lorenzo had ever masked the machinery of his relentless tyranny by genial manners and by a wise rejection of all the outward attributes of majesty, so Giovanni
de' Medici had learned to hide his most cherished schemes
in the event of future success under an aspect of careless
gaiety, and even of idleness.   But at last the wheel of
Fortune had turned; at last the hour for putting into
practice the theories privately formulated in past years
had arrived.   In the spring of 1512 we find Giovanni
de' Medici poor, an exile and even a prisoner ; twelve
months later he is Supreme Pontiff with boundless wealth
and undisputed master once more of the city of his
ancestors.

As scion of a ruling house which had held in kindly
but undoubted thraldom for four generations one of the
richest states of Italy, the new Pope's position was far
superior to that of a plebeian Della Rovere, desiring

only the glory of the States of the Church, of which he had been elected ruler for life ; still less was it comparable with the newly acquired sovereignty of an aristocratic adventurer like the Borgia, who had endeavoured to utilise the Papacy as a means of founding in Italy a new reigning dynasty. Nevertheless, Leo X. had undoubtedly absorbed not a little of the polity of both his predecessors, for from Julius he obtained the grandiose idea of freeing Italy from the presence of the foreigner, whilst Alexander's open intention to weld Central Italy into one important state strongly appealed to the personal ambition of the Medici. In Italian politics therefore Leo X., following the more private aim of raising his House to a height hitherto undreamed of, had set his heart upon forming the duchies of Ferrara and Urbino together with the towns of Parma, Piacenza and Modena into a new compact realm, of which the papal nephew or brother was to become sovereign under Leo's own guidance. But this ambitious attempt to create a brand-new state was intended only as a step towards a far wider and more patriotic policy. The French, already discomfited at the time of Leo's election, and now by the recent battle of Novara driven altogether out of Italy, might yet in course of time be made useful instruments for expelling the victorious Spanish forces from the Milanese and the kingdom of Naples. It was in truth a dangerous game, this proposed setting of the two leading European powers against each other by means of a delicate but unscrupulous diplomacy, which was based on the Pope's fixed intention of making an ,open pact with one party and of intriguing with the other. Indeed, Leo X. has not without reason been credited with the invention of the maxim recommending this tortuous practice, which was bound to produce ultimate disaster for its followers ; a result that was achieved, not indeed in Leo's reign, but in that of his successor and faithful pupil, Pope Clement VII.   Julius then having scattered the French by means of the Spaniards, and Leo in his turn having removed the conquering Spanish forces by the subsequent aid of France, it was secretly hoped that Italy would by this date be sufficiently consolidated to prevent any further encroachment from either nation ; and thus the whole country would be definitely and for ever relieved of the presence of the " barbarian," and the House of Medici with Leo at its head would become paramount throughout the whole peninsula.   With all the might and resources of Italy concentrated thus in his own family and holding the keys of St. Peter in his hands, Leo began to indulge in the hope of being able some day to dictate terms to princes beyond the Alps, and even perhaps to bring the Empire itself beneath the dominion of the Church, as had actually come to pass in the reign of his great predecessor and fellow-countryman, the monk Hildebrand, Pope Gregory VII.   Without stopping to criticise this attractive conception of a great Medicean supremacy, based alike on secular and ecclesiastical power, or to expose the many weak places in this magnificent fabric of future policy, we must acknowledge that such a scheme offered a singularly brilliant and alluring prospect ; and that it was not altogether impossible of attainment may be gathered from the views and suggestions concerning an universal Medicean despotism in Italy set forth by Machiavelli in the pages of the *Prince*.

It was Leo's particular opportunity or misfortune that his election had taken place at a most critical moment, when Europe was not only affected by the various wars and intrigues of her rulers, but was likely to be still further disturbed by great impending changes in the near future. Henry VII. had died three years before Leo's accession, and the English throne was now occupied by a talented but restless young prince; whilst it must have appeared evident to the more thoughtful that the sickly Louis XII. of France, the aged Emperor and the cunning old Ferdinand the Catholic of Spain must ere long be replaced in the course of nature by youthful heirs. It was upon the young princes therefore rather than upon the old and passing sovereigns that the leading statesmen of the day looked with feelings of anxiety and hope; their attention being engrossed by a contemplation of the youthful Henry Tudor, of the stripling cousin of the French King, and more particularly of the Archduke Charles, in whom a disproportionate amount of European sovereignty seemed likely to centre at no distant date. The uncertainties of the present and the possibilities of the future presented therefore a wide field of operations to a Pontiff, who was eager to turn every combination and every chance in the outside world to the immediate advantage of his own family and to the eventual solidarity of Italy by means of the unique powers wherewith he had recently been invested. "The vigorous policy of Julius II.," remarks Bishop Creighton, "was now abandoned for one more in the temper of the age. Leo X., with a genial smile upon his face, pursued his ends by an elaborate system of mine and countermine." [1]

In accordance with this deep-laid plan of family aggrandisement, which during the next six years gives the key-note to all his policy both at home and abroad, Leo's first step was to create the easy-going Giuliano de' Medici Gonfalionere of the Church, and to nominate his young nephew Lorenzo governor of Florence in

[1] Creighton, vol. v., p. 229.

Giuliano's stead. For the education and guidance of this youth of twenty summers there had recently been drawn up a manual of statecraft, based on the well-known tenets of the Magnificent and approved, if indeed it were not actually composed, by the Pontiff himself, so as to teach the heir of the family all the devices necessary to the proper maintenance of a Medicean despotism in the city without offering open violence to the old republican forms. Giuliano, however, the Pope evidently preferred to keep near his own person in Rome, partly out of the genuine affection he bore to his younger brother, but partly also, perhaps, because he had good reason to fear the possible effects of Giuliano's liberal views and simple nature in his dealings with the fickle and turbulent population of Florence. At the suggestion of Leo himself the city of Rome now proposed to do honour to the Pope's brother, and arrangements on a most lavish scale were made to promote him to the honorary rank of a Roman patrician in September, 1513. For this purpose the palace of the Capitol had been decorated in the most elaborate manner with a series of pictures designed by Baldassare Peruzzi, who had therein portrayed numerous scenes illustrating the historical connection between Ancient Etruria and the city of Rome. The whole ceremony, which had been planned in detail by Gian-Giorgio Cesarini, Gonfalionere or standard-bearer of the Roman Senate and People, included a procession from the Vatican to the Capitol, endless addresses of welcome to the Medicean prince from every public body in Rome, long-winded Latin orations from ambitious poets, and finally a banquet of barbaric profusion which lasted for six hours. The feast was in its turn succeeded by a pastoral eclogue, wherein the actors, after bestowing the most fulsome praise on Leo, did not scruple to poke the

broadest fun at the late Pope's foibles ; a piece of bad
taste which convulsed the whole audience with laughter.
The masque was followed by a series of allegorical scenes,
including one in which a beautiful woman, robed in cloth-
of-gold and intended to personify the city of Rome, was
borne on the shoulders of a giant to Giuliano's chair to
thank him for the gracious condescension wherewith he
had accepted the late homage of the imperial city. After
other conceits of this nature, the entertainment was made
to conclude with a significant representation of Florence
weeping for the loss of her Medicean progeny and being
comforted by Cybele, the mother of all the gods, who
united the two female figures of Rome and Florence and
suggested that henceforth both cities should dwell in
mutual concord and happiness under the rule of that
family, which loved each with an equal devotion. Next
day a broad Latin comedy, the *Poenulus* of Plautus, was
presented in an improvised theatre "with such elegance
that it is scarcely credible that even in the days of
Plautus himself his play could have been performed
better ".[1] In grateful appreciation of his brother's reception by the city, the Pontiff granted various privileges, even reducing the tax upon salt—always a most
jealously-guarded source of revenue in those days,—whilst
again in return for Leo's generosity the citizens of Rome
caused a marble effigy of the Pope, the work of Giacomo
del Duca, one of Michelangelo's pupils, to be placed upon
the Capitol with the brief laudatory inscription, *Optimi
Liberalissimique Pontificis Memoriae S.P.Q.R.*[2]

The festivities held at the Capitol in honour of Giuli-

---

[1] Creighton, vol. v., pp. 226, 227. Lanciani, pp. 96-98. L. Pas-
qualucci, *Giuliano de' Medici eletto cittadino Romano in* 1513
(Roma, 1881).

[2] This statue of Leo X., a very feeble work, still adorns the
palace of the Conservatori on the Capitol.

ano de' Medici and expressive of the new union between
Rome and Florence, were succeeded two months later
by the submission of the French King, who now repudiated the schismatic Council, that had given so much
offence to the autocratic Julius. Since the disaster of
Novara, Louis had lost every foothold in Northern Italy,
besides being crippled by the defeat of Guinegatte, or
the Battle of the Spurs, at the hands of the united English
and Imperial forces ; whilst the hereditary ally of France
and foe of England had recently been crushed on the
fatal field of Flodden in this very year. Now that the
humiliated Frenchmen had been expelled from Italian
soil, Leo did not intend to pursue them with the unreason-
ing rancour of his fiery predecessor ; on the contrary,
the Pope was secretly meditating to make some use of
the defeated nation for his cherished object of ridding
Italy equally of the favoured Spaniards. Smooth and
pious words were accordingly addressed to the hesitating
Louis, and every effort was made to clear the path of
obstacles in the way of his coming submission. The
newly restored Maximilian Sforza, Duke of Milan, was
urged to treat with leniency and even with generosity
those of his subjects who had accepted the late French
rule ; the Emperor was admonished likewise on the
duties of mercy and forgiveness in a Christian prince ;
and even in his congratulatory letter to Henry VIII. on
his successful repulse at Flodden of James IV. of Scotland, Leo cannot refrain from remarking that "it was
certainly very distressing for me to hear of so much
shedding of Christian blood, of the destruction of such
numbers of those who are dear to Our Universal Lord,
and especially of the evil fate of an illustrious and valiant
Christian monarch, the husband of thine own sister".[1]

[1] *Leonis X. Litterae,* Roscoe, Appendix XXVII.

With the Pope thus posing openly as a public peace-maker and exhorting the sovereigns of Europe to acts of Christian charity and forgiveness by means of letters couched in the elegant Latin of his secretary, the erudite Bembo, the year 1514 was everywhere marked by a cessation of open warfare and by an increase of diplo-matic intrigue.   Marriages with Leo's approval were likewise planned with the object of ending hereditary feuds amongst the reigning families of Europe ; nor was the Medicean House itself forgotten in these undertakings of political matrimony, for the Pope obtained no small amount of satisfaction from the union of his brother Giuliano with the Princess Filiberta of Savoy, a sister of the widowed Duchess of Orleans and consequently aunt to the future Francis I. of France.   The news of this alliance, a brilliant one for the quasi-royal House of Medici, was warmly received at the Roman court, where the bride's arrival was awaited with im-patience as the one thing needful to complete the perfec-tion of that ecclesiastical paradise, which alone required the permanent presence of a princess in its midst : " God be praised ! " writes the delighted Cardinal da Bibbiena to the expected bridegroom, " for here in Rome we lack nothing but a court with ladies ! "   But this period of comparative peace and repose was ere long rudely disturbed by the occurrence of one of those events which all far-seeing men must long have anticipated. On New Year's Day, 1515, expired Louis XII. worn out by the gaiety and high spirits of his young bride, the Princess Mary of England,[1] and his sudden demise raised to the throne of France the ever-famous King Francis I.   This ambitious youth had long conceived an unbounded admiration for the aims and personality

---

[1] Sister of Henry VIII. and afterwards Duchess of Brandon.

of the brilliant but short-lived Gaston de Foix, so
that, taking the ill-fated victor of Ravenna for his model,
Francis now burned to revenge the late French de-
feats in Italy and to win back that sovereignty
which Charles VIII. had enjoyed for so brief a space.
Except that he was youthful and vain-glorious, the new
King of France possessed no feature either mental or
bodily in common with the little caricature of a man,
who had been crowned at Naples twenty years before
and had been hailed as saviour of Italy and regenerator
of the Church by the impassioned Savonarola. To a
generous and heroic disposition and a shrewd if unripe
understanding Francis added also remarkable beauty of
form, for he was of commanding stature and owned an
attractive face, which was distinguished rather than
marred by a long but shapely nose, the nose that Aretino
once celebrated in a comical yet complimentary ode.
In short, Francis was the ideal young warrior-prince of
his age ; handsome in person, brave in the battle-field,
highly gifted in intellect as became a grandson of the
poet Duke of Orleans, courteous to all in the days of
prosperity and destined to prove himself patient and
dignified in that hour of humiliation which lay in waiting
for him in the distant and as yet unforeseen future. His
adoring sister, Margaret of Valois, "la Perle des
Valois, la Marguerite des Marguerites," hastening to
rescue her darling, her brother, her king after the fatal
catastrophe of Pavia, has described Francis of France
for us in simple yet living verses of her own composition :—

> " C'est Luy qui a de tout la connoissance. . . .
> De sa beauté il est blanc et vermeil,
> Les cheveux bruns, de grande et belle taille,
> En terre il est comme au ciel le soleil.
> Hardi, vaillant, sage, et preux en bataille,

Il est bénin, doux, humble en sa grandeur,
Fort et puissant, et plein de patience,
Soit en prison, en tristesse et malheur. . . .
Il a de Dieu le parfait science. . . .
Bref, Luy tout seul est digne d'être Roi." [1]

Such is the picture drawn by Margaret of Valois of
her sovereign and brother, who now in his twenty-first
year declared his intention to invade Italy and to succeed
or perish in the attempt.

With a well-equipped army of 60,000 infantry,
30,000 cavalry and 72 pieces of artillery, Francis, accompanied by the veteran Milanese general Trivulzi,
the young Constable of Bourbon and that skilful Spanish
engineer, Pedro Navarro, whom his master Ferdinand
of Spain had been too mean to ransom after the battle
of Ravenna, crossed the Alps despite all obstacles human
and natural, and entered the plain of Saluzzo in Pied-
mont in the early autumn of 1515.   The forces of the
Pope, the Emperor and the Duke of Milan, who had
lately convened a league "for the defence and deliverance
of Italy" against the new French aggression, were
astounded and disheartened by this unexpected and
marvellous strategy.   Nor was it long before the two
armies found themselves encamped opposite each other
at Marignano, some few miles from Milan, the joint
forces of the confederates consisting of the Spanish army
under Cardona; of a vast array of Swiss mercenaries in
the pay of Pope and Emperor and controlled by the
warlike Matthew Schinner, Cardinal of Sion; and last,
of Leo's own army commanded by his nephew, Lorenzo
de' Medici, who had been given the title of "Captain
of the Church and of the Florentines".   We are at this
point offered a typical example of Leo's crooked policy
in the circumstance that Lorenzo, who had been ap-

[1] J. Michelet, *La Renaissance.*

pointed to fill this post owing to the illness of his uncle
Giuliano, had received explicit but private instructions
from the Pope that the troops under his command were
to be led into the fray only after the issue of the engagement had been definitely decided. But although determined to safeguard his own interests in the event of
a possible French victory, yet so anxious was Leo for
the defeat of the invaders, that he likewise sent secret
orders to Schinner to urge forward the Swiss and to
allow no chance of their defection by means of French
gold. Following his instructions from Rome, therefore,
Schinner addressed the 30,000 Switzers before the
citadel of Milan, bidding them in passionate phrases to
defend the cause of Holy Church and of the Keys of
St. Peter by annihilating the barbarian host now encamped at Marignano: "Would that I were permitted
to wash my hands in the Frenchmen's blood!" is
the concluding sentence of the fierce harangue that
Guicciardini puts into the militant cardinal's mouth.

After some vicissitudes in the field the great battle
of Marignano ended in a decisive victory for the French,
who thus destroyed for ever the overweening reputation
of that Swiss infantry, upon which Leo had calculated
with such confidence. Unhappy Milan at once opened
her gates to the conqueror, whilst her Sforza Duke,
weary of being the puppet alternately of Pope, Emperor
and French King, gladly agreed to accept a pension
from the magnanimous Francis, who now assumed the
sovereignty of the whole Milanese. Meanwhile, before
the tide of success had turned definitely in favour of the
French, the impetuous Schinner had hastily despatched
a messenger to Rome, telling of the expected victory of
the confederate army, and this welcome report was received at the Roman court with such transports of open

delight, that the Cardinal Bibbiena actually gave orders
for a public illumination.   But that very evening, whilst
the city was sparkling with the festal lights of supposed
triumph, Marino Giorgi, the Venetian envoy, whose
state was once more in close alliance with the invading
French, obtained authentic information as to the true
result of the recent battle near Milan.   Early the following morning, therefore, Giorgi presented himself at the
Vatican to request an immediate audience of the Pope.
Generally unpunctual in his habits, Leo was ever a late
riser from bed, and accordingly had to be awakened on
so important an occasion by his chamberlain.   Half-
dressed and still heavy with sleep, the Pope anxiously
hurried into the hall of audience.   Taking a malicious
but concealed pleasure in the Pontiff's obvious agitation
and pretending to assume that Leo's equanimity would
in no wise be affected by his news, the unfeeling Giorgi
much enjoyed the delivery of his unwelcome message.
"Holy Father, yesterday Your Holiness gave me bad
news, which turned out to be false; but to-day I can
offer you information which is not only good, but also
true.   The Swiss are utterly routed!"   Glancing at the
accompanying despatch, Leo, with the habitual smile
for once absent from a woe-begone and terrified countenance, forgot for a brief moment his accustomed arts of
almost oriental dissimulation.   Clasping his hands he
cried aloud with the genuine alarm of a trickster unmasked, "What, then, will become of us, and also of
you?"[1]   "So far as we are concerned, all will be well,"
replied the unconcerned ambassador, "seeing that we
are the Most Christian King's own allies, nor is Your

[1] "Quid ergo erit de nobis, et quid de vobis?" (J. Michelet, *La
Renaissance*, p. 369)—"Notre victoire le pressait en flagrant délit de
duplicité."

Holiness likely to suffer any hurt at his hands"; and
leaving Leo thus a prey to the alarm he had neglected
to hide, Giorgi, highly gratified with his late diplomatic
encounter, returned to his own house, where a barrel of
wine was broached for himself and his companions to
drink to the late victory and to the memory of the slain
at Marignano. On the following day Giorgi was summoned to the Vatican, where he was angrily accused by
Leo of having openly rejoiced at the late intelligence, to
which the envoy replied with an air of astonished
innocence: "Holy Father, the rejoicings were confined
to your own palace the other evening, there were none
in my house!" "It was all the fault of the Cardinal of
Santa Maria in Portico (Bibbiena)," retorted the Pope,
"and he acted without my knowledge in the matter.
But, my lord ambassador of Venice, we shall now see
what the Most Christian King will do, for we shall place
ourselves in his hands and at his mercy." "Holy
Father," replied Giorgi, who was thoroughly enjoying
Leo's discomfiture, "neither Your Holiness nor the Holy
See will obtain the least hurt, for is not the Most
Christian King a son of the Church?"[1]

Having decided to seek the mercy of the Most
Christian King, Leo proceeded without further delay,
in spite of the alarm and opposition of the Roman court,
to arrange for a conference with Francis who, although
fully aware of the Pope's treachery at Marignano, was
most anxious for various reasons to gain the latter's
good-will and alliance. Late in November, therefore,
Leo arrived with an immense retinue outside the walls
of Florence on his way northward towards Bologna, the
fixed trysting-place of King and Pontiff, but at the

[1] Albéri, *Relazioni Venete*, serie 2da, vol. iii., p. 44; Creighton,
vol. v., p. 244.

special request of the Signory, he consented to tarry
awhile at the Gianfigliazzi villa in the suburb of
Marignolle, whilst the city was busily preparing a public
reception worthy of one who was its first citizen as well
as its spiritual chief.   It was the Medici's first entrance
into his birthplace as Supreme Pontiff, and even his
unbounded craving for adulation and pageantry must
have been appeased by the sight of the triumphal arches,
the elaborate artistic surprises and the applauding crowds
of his own countrymen, for whom Leo with all his faults
and selfishness bore a sincere affection.   The Pope with
eighteen cardinals and accompanied by hundreds of
nobles and men-at-arms made his state-entry into the
city by the Porta Romana, which still bears on its brown
weather-stained face a broad marble tablet telling posterity of this auspicious event and of the honour conferred
thereby on the Florentines.   So vast was the papal
train that the authorities had first removed the outer
courtyard of the gate itself, through which the brilliant
slow-moving throng passed on St. Andrew's Day, 30th
November, 1515.   At the church of San Felice below
the Pitti Palace, through Leo's spy-glass was perceived
the first of the many triumphal erections; this at San
Felice bearing on its crest a bust of the Magnificent
Lorenzo with the legend borrowed from Holy Writ,
"This is my beloved Son" (*Hic est Filius meus dilectus*),
the sight of which made the emotional Pontiff fall into
tears.   Down the broad street of Via Maggio with its
stately but gloomy palaces, across the old bridge of
Santa Trinità backed by the huge form of the Spini
mansion, and thence through the Porta Rossa, the New
Market and the narrow Via Vaccereccia into the great
square of the Signoria below the frowning civic palace
wound the long papal procession, with Leo himself in

LEO X'S STATE ENTRY INTO FLORENCE

tiara and glittering cope bestowing numberless benedictions upon his fellow-citizens to the accompaniment of a
continuous shower of broad silver pieces amongst the
bystanders.   Beneath the wide arches of the Loggia de'
Lanzi a huge figure of gilded wood representing Hercules
with his club, the work of Baccio Bandinelli, had been
erected, overtopping Donatello's group of Judith slaying
Holofernes, which this same city of Florence had placed
in Orcagna's beautiful arcade at the time of the expulsion
of the Medici some twenty years before, to serve as a
solemn warning to tyrants, as its terse inscription testifies
to-day.[1] Sweeping past the Loggia and the historic
statue of the Florentine *Marzocco*, that placid lion clasping the emblem of the City of the Lily in his paws, the
cavalcade proceeded by way of the frowning mass of
the Bargello towards the gigantic form of the Duomo,
the Pope meanwhile surveying through his monocle the
cheering crowds of townsmen and peasants and stopping
ever and anon to admire the many festal surprises, or to
read their flattering inscriptions.   Possibly this enthusiastic reception in his native Florence may have seemed
even more agreeable and satisfying to the fortunate Leo
than those splendid pageants which had marked his
progress from St. Peter's to the Lateran, less than three
years before ; but it was evident that the popular rejoicings were equally sincere and spontaneous in both cities.
On reaching the Cathedral steps Leo must have expressed his astonishment at the remarkable transformation of its naked and unsightly front through the skill of
the architect, Jacopo Sansovino, aided by the ready
brush of Andrea del Sarto, then a rising young Florentine
painter.   For from the crest of the roof to the level of

[1] *Exemplum Sal. Pub. Cives. Pos. Mccccxcv.*

the ground a temporary façade adorned with columns, cornices, architraves and portals, all fashioned out of wood and plaster so as to imitate rare and antique marbles, had been hastily erected, with statues in its niches and with its flat spaces covered in chiaroscuro in "the Perfect Painter's" most graceful and attractive manner. "Everybody," says Landucci, "was filled with amazement at its pictures and ornaments; saying it ought to serve as a model for a new façade to the Cathedral, since all were so pleased at its noble and stately appearance;—indeed, we were all distressed to see it dismantled and removed."[1] Within the spacious nave of the church itself a narrow but lofty platform had been constructed on trestles, whereby the Pontiff and his companions might advance unimpeded to the high altar, whilst the immense crowd below could secure a better view of the illustrious guest. On reaching the altar, His Holiness doffed jewelled tiara and gorgeous cope, appearing to public gaze clad in the rochet of white brocade, the crimson *mozzetta* or cape, and the loose skull-cap, also of crimson velvet, in which Raphael has depicted Leo X. for us in his most famous portrait. Thus arrayed, the Pontiff, after offering up prayers and making some splendid gifts to the Cathedral treasury, pursued his course amid renewed applause towards the great Dominican convent of Santa Maria Novella, where a set of rooms, magnificently appointed, had been prepared for his reception. Luxurious quarters had likewise been provided for the eighteen cardinals, and for such distinguished guests as the poet Sannazzaro, the chamberlain Serapica, the papal secretaries Bembo and Sadoleto and others who had swelled the train of

[1] Landucci, p. 356. Vásari, *Vita di Andrea del Sarto.*

Leo on this occasion. Of the efforts thus made by the richest city in Italy to do honour to Pope Leo, her own citizen, Landucci mentions fifteen arches, trophies, obelisks, statues or emblematic figures placed at various points of the Pope's line of procession ; nor does he omit to mention the wholesale destruction of dwelling-houses that were thought to interfere with the pleasing effects aimed at by the Florentine artists, who had been entrusted by the Signory with the general scheme of decoration. Over two thousand workmen had been kept busily employed night and day for the space of a full month, making use of the churches themselves as temporary workshops, whilst the expenses entailed amounted to no less a sum than 70,000 florins, a piece of civic extravagance which caused no little regret to the frugal Landucci, who laments this squandering of the city's wealth upon "such flimsy conceits, which passed away like a shadow," although he affects to rejoice at the benefits conferred thereby on the carpenters and artisans of Florence.[1]

On the following day, however, the Pope exchanged his apartments at Santa Maria Novella for the famous suite of rooms in the Palazzo Vecchio, still known as "the Quarter of Pope Leo X.," which in later years were adorned with an interesting series of frescoes from the brush of Vasari, who on the walls and ceilings of these chambers has commemorated Leo's principal achievements, as well as those of other members of the senior branch of the Medicean House. Although this gallery of historical incidents in the careers of Leo X., Clement VII. and their immediate ancestors is not the work of a contemporaneous artist (for Vasari was but an infant at

[1] Landucci, p. 359.

the date of Leo's official entry into Florence), yet these beautiful and well-preserved frescoes in the so-called *Quartiere di Leone Decimo* of the old Florentine public palace are deserving of more attention than is usually paid to them.   In particular, the large composition depicting the papal procession just described, with its interesting view of the Piazza della Signoria in Vasari's time and with its curious representation of Leo's eighteen scarlet-clad.cardinals on mule-back, of the Pope himself borne aloft in his chair of state, and of the papal train, which includes portraits of Bembo, Aretino, Serapica, Lorenzo de' Medici and of half the notabilities of the Leonine Age, is especially worthy of careful inspection by those who wish to study the gayer and more pleasing aspect of the life of the Italian Renaissance.[1]

But Leo's first visit to his native town was of necessity curtailed, for he was most anxious to reach his true destination, Bologna.   After kneeling beside the tomb of his father in San Lorenzo, where to the edification of the impressed bystanders he made his orisons with tears streaming down his cheeks, and after spending some hours with the ailing Giuliano in the old mansion of his family, Leo prepared to leave Florence on 3rd December for Bologna, which city the Pope had prudently selected as his place of meeting with King Francis, whom naturally he was anxious to avoid receiving in Rome whilst flushed with his recent victory.   The main features of the coming conference had already been arranged as early as 15th October, between the French chancellor, Duprat, and Ludovico da Canossa, bishop of Tricarico, who was perhaps Leo's ablest diplomatic agent.   Broadly speaking, by this suggested treaty the Pope was to re-

[1] Bacciotti, *Firenze Illustrata*, vol. i.

pudiate his former alliance with the Emperor (with whom, it is probably needless to remark, Leo was still in constant communication); he was to surrender those coveted cities of Parma and Piacenza to the King of France, as conqueror of the Milanese; and he was also required to restore for a fixed sum the towns of Reggio and Modena, which he had lately acquired from the Emperor, to their rightful owner, Alfonso of Ferrara, who was Francis' ally. In return for these concessions, Francis swore to protect the States of the Church and the Medicean realm of Florence, and also to bestow revenues and commands upon the papal nephew and brother; whilst the long-standing dispute concerning the privileges of the Gallican Church was to be settled to suit the mutual convenience of King and Pope, without reference to the French people or clergy. Under the circumstances, it cannot be denied that this proposed compact, which was mainly due to the arts and blandishments of the insinuating Canossa, was highly favourable to the Pontiff, who hoped moreover to secure even better terms than these as the result of a personal interview with the youthful King.

The Pope's reception by the Bolognese, many of whom were still regretting the expulsion of their late Bentivoglio rulers, offered a striking contrast with the late civic greetings in Florence. Neither cheering crowds nor triumphal arches met the eyes of the entering cavalcade as it threaded its way through the arcaded streets of the town towards the great Palazzo Pubblico, where the leading citizens received their papal master with black looks and in a sulky silence, which was even broken once or twice by the raising of the old cry of *Sega!* *Sega!* of the departed Bentivogli.[1] But Leo was deter-

---

[1] *Sega*, "a saw"; the heraldic emblem of the House of Bentivoglio.

mined to show himself gracious on this occasion, and
therefore only reproved the indignant Paris de Grassis,
when the latter pointed out to him that the authorities
were treating His Holiness with scant respect, since only
one canopy of silk and another of shabby stained cloth
had been provided by the city to afford the customary
shelter for the Sacrament and for the person of the
Supreme Pontiff.[1]   Yet Leo's good humour was proof
even against conduct so dastardly as this, so that he
merely gave orders for the silken *baldacchino* to be borne
above the Host, whilst he himself dispensed altogether
with this particular emblem of state.   Under these de-
pressing conditions of manifest disloyalty and dislike, the
Pope formally convoked the consistory in a hall of the
palace, where twenty cardinals were now collected, the
most prominent absentee of the College being Francesco
Soderini, whom Leo had left behind in Rome to act as
legate, not out of any special confidence in the Florentine
Cardinal's powers, but because he deemed his presence
in Florence or Bologna as likely to excite intrigue.

On 11th December Francis was met in state by
Giulio de' Medici at the city gates, but in spite of the
exhortations of Paris de Grassis, the King positively refused to be made the central figure of an organised
pageant, declaring bluntly that "he cared not a whit for
processions".[2]   Plainly habited, the young monarch made
his way through the pressing and staring throng of
citizens towards the Palazzo Pubblico, where he was
most cordially received by the Supreme Pontiff.   Although the marplot of all his far-reaching schemes in
Italy, Leo, who had a keen appreciation of youthful grace
and beauty, could not but regard with interest, or even

[1] *Diary of Paris de Grassis*, Creighton, vol. v.
[2] Fabroni, Appendix XLIV.

with paternal affection this young Prince Charming, who
was now ushered bare-headed into his presence.   Kneeling at the pontifical feet, the French King made solemn
profession in his native tongue of his intense devotion
towards the Holy See and naïvely expressed his pleasure
at thus beholding face to face for the first time "the Pope,
the Vicar of Our Lord Jesus Christ".   To this ingenuous
greeting, Leo, who was perfectly versed in the art of
public oratory, "replied in the most excellent manner,
for fair speech was always customary with him".   The
formal ceremonies of the meeting concluded, a private
conference between Pope and King was next arranged,
whereat Leo without doubt made full use of every
Medicean art to threaten or cajole the prince into re-
laxing some of the terms already agreed upon.   But
upon the point of Leo's surrender of Parma, Piacenza
and Modena, the King, despite his youthful years and
his expressed veneration for the person of the Pontiff,
remained obdurate.   Leo, therefore, much exasperated
at this failure of the usual methods of Medicean diplomacy,
refused on his part to listen to Francis' earnest appeal
for the pardon of the Duke of Urbino, whose ruin the
Pope was then certainly contemplating.   Leo likewise
received very coldly the proposal for the King's investiture of the realm of Naples, which he declared it would
be impossible for him to grant during the lifetime of
Ferdinand of Spain ; and it was the Medici's undoubted
diplomatic skill that alone prevented the young King,
elated by his recent success at Marignano and supported
by a splendid army, from advancing southward and
forcibly seizing that coveted kingdom, which His Holiness
was so unwilling to bestow.   On the treatment of the
defenceless Gallican Church, in the suppression of whose
ancient liberties both Pope and King had a special in-

terest, Leo and Francis soon came to terms; nor were
they parsimonious in their mutual promises of honours
and titles ;—Leo bestowing a scarlet hat upon Adrian de
Boissy, the king's ,tutor, and Francis creating Giuliano
de' Medici Duke of Nemours.   The main result of this
conference, therefore, proved not particularly satisfactory
to either party, for the King had failed to obtain his
chief object, the investiture of the kingdom of Naples ;
whilst Leo was greatly irritated at the enforced surrender
of Parma and Modena.   And although Alfonso of
Ferrara had good reason to congratulate himself on the
Pope's unwilling consent to give up Modena, yet his
brother vassal of the Church, the Della Rovere Duke of
Urbino, must have foreseen his inevitable overthrow in
the King's failure to avert the impending vengeance of
the angry Pope.

Francis of France tarried altogether only four days
at Bologna, but his brief visit was naturally distinguished
by every variety of pageant and ceremony, including a
Mass said by Leo in person at the high altar of the great
church of San Petronio, on which occasion the French
monarch did not hesitate to serve the Pontiff in his holy
office by bearing in his own royal hands the basin with
the water at the *Lavabo*.   In public a good deal was
said on both sides concerning the virtue of Christian
peace and charity, as also of the dire necessity of an
universal campaign of Christendom against the Turks.
Duprat, the French chancellor, even made an impassioned appeal to the successor of the Fisherman to
guide the barque of Christ's Church into the haven of
perfect peace ; in short, both parties seem to have exhausted themselves in insincere professions of friendship
and confidence.   For nobody was deceived by these fine
sentiments and edifying speeches ; on the contrary, all

men present knew of the royal and papal ambitions, nor
was anyone ignorant of the punishment that was shortly
to fall on the erring Duke of Urbino.

It is impossible to dwell further on the many events
incident to this famous but indecisive conference at
Bologna, which has been commemorated for us in one
of Raphael's splendid frescoes in the Vatican—the Coronation of Charlemagne, wherein the Frankish emperor,
represented with the clear-cut features, the lank black
hair, and the pallid complexion of the youthful Francis
of France, receives the imperial diadem at the hands of
Pope Leo III., in the guise of his namesake and successor Leo X.; whilst the little Ippolito de' Medici,
Giuliano's bastard son, in the livery of a page upholds
the kneeling emperor's mantle. There was of course
the customary interchange of gifts between King and
Pope, His Holiness presenting Francis with a fine diamond and a golden reliquary containing a piece of the
True Cross. The French monarch, however, the future
patron of Andrea del Sarto and of Benvenuto Cellini,
who already prided himself upon his knowledge of modern
and antique art, appeared not a little disappointed at the
papal presents. Assuming Leo to be the possessor of
an abundant store of ancient statuary in Rome, the
young prince coolly expressed to His Holiness an overwhelming desire to possess that marble group of the
Laocöon, of whose beauties he had heard such glowing
accounts. This masterpiece of classical art, which still
remains one of the chief treasures of the Vatican galleries,
had been excavated almost intact about seven years
previously by the lucky owner of a vineyard on the site
of the Baths of Titus. The finder, a certain Felice de'
Fredis, had promptly sold his treasure-trove to the late
Pope, but in the epitaph upon his tomb in a Roman

church Felice proudly asserts' his claim to popular remembrance and gratitude as the discoverer of "this
breathing group in marble" (*respirans simulacrum*).[1]
The present owner of the Laocöon, Pope Leo, must
have been indeed startled at the French King's audaci-
ous request, but although, in the words of an unkind
modern critic, he would sooner have surrendered up
the genuine head of an Apostle than this cherished
block of marble, the Pontiff managed to keep his countenance, graciously declaring his readiness to despatch the
desired object to France.   Nevertheless, having gained
the King's warm thanks for such generosity, it is said that
Leo merely sent instructions to that mediocre Florentine
sculptor, Baccio Bandinelli, whose copies of the antique
were known to be far superior to his original productions,
to prepare a replica of the Laocöon with all speed, wherewith to satisfy this importunate young conqueror.

On 15th December Francis quitted Bologna, not
over-pleased with the results of the late conference,
whilst three days later the Pope himself, only tolerably
satisfied with the French King's concessions, set out for
Florence, arriving there on 22nd December and remaining eight weeks.   This, Leo's last visit to his birthplace, afforded small pleasure either to the Pope or to
the Florentines, for the city was suffering from a scarcity
of provisions, so that the starving populace was much
scandalised at the daily spectacle of thoughtless luxury

---

[1] The epitaph is quoted by Duppa (*Life of Michelangelo*, p. 50) :—
    Felici de Fredis,
    Qui ob proprias virtutes,
    Et repertum Laocöontis divinum quod
    In Vaticano cernes fere
    Respirans simulacrum,
    Im mortalitatem meruit
    Anno Domini MDXXVIII.

and extravagance in a season of dearth, which was openly
exhibited by the younger cardinals, such as Sauli and
Petrucci. In addition to the shortage of corn and disastrous floods in the Arno, the Pope was a prey to the
deepest anxiety concerning the deplorable condition of
his brother Giuliano, who was rapidly sinking into an
early grave. All the males of the House of Medici
seem to have been delicate and short-lived, and Giuliano
was now in the last stages of a galloping consumption,
"appearing utterly shrunken and spent like an expiring
candle," says the historian Cambi, who adds that the
ailing prince bore his distressing malady with exemplary
patience and that the whole city was filled with compassion for his sufferings. Removed for change of air from
the Medicean palace to the abbey below Fiesole, the
dying prince was frequently visited by the Pontiff, of
whose presence at Fiesole there still exists a memorial
in the papal escutcheon that adorns the steep rocky path-
way leading upward from San Domenico. Nor were
these meetings between the two brothers rendered easier
or less melancholy by Giuliano's constant anxiety concerning Leo's open intention to deprive Francesco Della
Rovere of his dominions and to create the young Lorenzo
Duke of Urbino in his stead. The past hospitality he
had accepted at the court of Urbino and a personal attachment to the reigning duke and the Duchess Elisa-
betta made the generous Giuliano most eager to appease
his brother's wrath, but though as a dying man he implored Leo again and again to forgive Della Rovere for
his manifest disobedience and hostility, he could obtain
no satisfactory answer to his constant plea. "Think
first upon getting well, my Giuliano, for this is no meet
time to vex thyself with politics," was ever the evasive
reply of the Pontiff, who besides being filled with an in-

creasing rancour against the duke was likewise importuned
ceaselessly by his sister-in-law, the restless Alfonsina,
to proclaim her only son a sovereign prince in Urbino.
On 19th February, Leo, recalled to Rome by news of
the death of the aged Ferdinand of Spain, quitted for
ever Florence and his unhappy brother, who expired a
month later on 17th March at the abbey of Fiesole in
the thirty-eighth year of his age, childless save for one
illegitimate son, Ippolito de' Medici, the celebrated
Cardinal of a later period. Four days after his death
the body of Giuliano was interred in San Lorenzo with
the utmost pomp and amidst the general grief of the
citizens, for the handsome and liberal-minded if somewhat languid and extravagant prince was undeniably the
most popular with the Florentines of the Magnificent
Lorenzo's three sons. He had always shown moreover
a genuine aversion to all tyranny and double dealing,
and these rare qualities together with his deep sense of
gratitude towards those who had befriended him in days
of poverty and exile mark him as worthy of special praise
in an age of savage violence and selfish cunning. Altogether, despite many moral shortcomings, "Giuliano il
Buono," at once the perfect courtier and judicious patron
of letters, the intimate friend of Castiglione and Bembo,
the handsome prince who was by choice a plain Florentine burgher in the citizen's cloak, appears to us one of
the most attractive personalities the Italian Renaissance
can claim to have produced.[1] And although vexed at
his younger brother's lack of ambition and his simplicity
of character, Leo loved him dearly, so that his death,
though long imminent, was severely felt by the Pontiff,
who—perhaps rightly—had refused to grant a favourite

---

[1] Giuliano's curious emblem—a triangle containing the letters
G.L.O.V.I.S.—is mentioned by Scipione Ammirato (*Opuscoli*, vol. iii.).

TOMB OF GIULIANO DE' MEDICI

brother's dying request. For it had been to Giuliano
that Leo in the first flush of gratified ambition had
spoken those famous words, which have never been dis-
proved—"Since God has given us the Papacy, my
Giuliano, let us enjoy it"; and now half his expected enjoyment had been removed by Giuliano's untimely
end. It was a double blow, alike to Leo's private
affections and to his political dreams, for undoubtedly
the Pope did not bear the same regard towards his
nephew Lorenzo, who through his uncle's death had
now become the sole surviving layman of his House.
There was of course a great display of public mourning
in Rome, but Leo himself was plainly admonished by
that papal Polonius, his own master of the ceremonies,
to control his natural feelings and to show no visible
sign of grief to those around him, "since the Supreme
Pontiff is not a man, but a demi-god, and ought therefore always to exhibit a serene and smiling countenance
on all occasions to the people".[1]

. . . .

It is wholly beyond the scope of the present work to
penetrate within the maze of European politics which
followed upon the death of Ferdinand of Spain and the
peaceful succession of the youthful Archduke Charles to
the thrones of Castile and Naples. Close upon this
momentous event came the treaty of Noyon and the subsequent settlement whereby the series of wars inaugurated
by the League of Cambrai and originally directed against
the republic of Venice was at last terminated, leaving
Venice herself intact indeed in territory but weakened
by the long conflict since the evil day of Vaila. All
Italy was therefore once more permitted to enjoy an in-

[1] *Diary of Paris de Grassis.*

terval of precious peace with the exception of the state of Urbino, which Leo, now secure from French intervention, was preparing to crush with all the military and spiritual weapons at his disposal.   Three definite charges were first formulated against the trembling duke, who shortly after Giuliano's death was cited to Rome to answer in person before the pontifical throne.   Firstly, Francesco-Maria Della Rovere was reminded of his assassination of Cardinal Alidosi four years before : a crime which rendered him unfit to remain a vassal and true protector of Holy Church ; secondly, he was accused of disobedience to Julius' command to assist the return of the Medici to Florence in 1512, and also of intriguing with the French on several occasions ; and thirdly, he was admonished concerning his refusal to serve in the papal army commanded by Lorenzo de' Medici before Milan in the autumn of the previous year.   All these charges were unanswerable, although it was true that Julius had eventually condoned his nephew's murder of Alidosi, and that the duke's real crime in Leo's eyes did not consist so much in his past treachery towards the Church as in his obvious hostility to the House of Medici and its interests.   Nevertheless, it is certain that on two recent occasions Della Rovere had deliberately refused to obey the legitimate orders of his suzerain, the Supreme Pontiff, and it becomes difficult, therefore, to understand why so many historians have set themselves with such ardour to blame Leo for his action in expelling so undesirable a vassal of the Church from the ancient patrimony of the Montefeltre, to which the Della Rovere duke could plead no real hereditary title.   That Leo nursed a personal grudge against the duke and also harboured ulterior designs in desiring to bestow Urbino itself on his own nephew, does not affect the argument

concerning a sovereign's right to punish or expel a dangerous and disobedient feudatory prince. Likewise, the fact
that the subsequent war proved tedious, expensive and
productive of intense misery, cannot well be imputed as
a crime in the Pontiff, who certainly looked for an easy,
if not a bloodless annexation of the duchy of Urbino.

On Francesco's refusal to betake himself to Rome to
answer the charges formulated, Leo pronounced a Bull
of excommunication against the absent duke ; despatched
an army under Lorenzo de' Medici into his territories ;
and thus speedily drove the almost friendless Della
Rovere tyrant to seek refuge at the hospitable court of
Mantua. Urbino itself being quickly reduced, on 18th
August, 1516, the papal nephew was solemnly proclaimed
Duke of Urbino and Lord of Pesaro, and thus the first
definite step was taken towards creating a Central
Italian state to form the nucleus of that Medicean empire
in Italy, which was equally the fixed desire of the ambitious Pontiff and of his greater compatriot, Machiavelli.

CHAPTER VII

THE COURT OF LEO X

Godiamo ci il Papato, poichè Dio ci l' ha dato. . . . Je crois que là était vraiment sa mission, jouir de la Papauté dans toutes les aises de l'intelligence, et toutes les satisfactions du gout.   Il n'était point politique ; à mon sens il était plutôt encore Athénien que catholique ; Athènes d'abord, Jérusalem ensuite (Armand Braschet, *La Diplomatie Vénitienne*).

IT was the boast of succeeding ages that the first Medicean Pope in his reign revived the sunken glories of classical Rome and made the Eternal City once more the true intellectual and artistic centre of the western world, attracting thither every poet and scholar, every painter and sculptor, every scientist and traveller to receive a warm welcome and a due reward for his talents or his services to mankind at the hands of the Supreme Pontiff.   Certain it is that the court of the Vatican under Leo X. was in reality the most brilliant, the most cultured, and withal the most extravagant that Europe had beheld since the days of Imperial Rome, and that Leo himself moved perpetually in an atmosphere of flattery and splendour such as no Pontiff had hitherto experienced.   The accession indeed of this Medicean prince, in whom past years of indigence and obscurity had only served to inflame a natural taste for art, literature, amusement and magnificence in every form, opened a new era in the annals of Rome ; an era which later writers have not without reason christened

the Leonine Age; whilst the city itself, named by contemporaries "the Light and the Stage of the World,"
became at once the chosen seat of fashion and of learning,
the home of the courtier no less than the haunt of the
poet.   Thus was Rome under Leo X. able to foreshadow
the position held by Paris during the most splendid years
of the Roi Soleil, whose personality has not a few points
in common with that of the first Medicean Pope.   Unfortunately, magnificence can only be obtained by
reckless profusion, and a brilliant court has ever been
shown to be a corrupt one; indeed, the patronage of
Leo X. and the majesty of Louis XIV. proved in each
case a fore-runner of disaster and humiliation at no distant date.

Leo may almost be described as having breathed a
literary and artistic atmosphere from his cradle.   The
erstwhile pupil of the versatile Politian and the erudite
Demetrius of Chalcedon, and the son of a poet, Giovanni
de' Medici had not only been at an early age accounted
a perfect Latin scholar, but also an enthusiastic student
of Greek letters; whilst inherited tastes led him to
appreciate the various writings in the Italian vernacular,
which the classical pedants of that age affected to despise.
He had a passion for all books and manuscripts, both in
the dead and living languages, and these he devoured
with avidity, remembering and quoting their contents
out of an excellent memory.   In Rome he had long
been recognised as a generous patron of literature in
every form, and many a needy scholar had received a
warm welcome at the Florentine cardinal's palace, which
latterly contained the glorious library collected by his
own ancestors, but later confiscated by the Florentine
Republic.   This unique library the Cardinal had by some
means contrived to repurchase in 1508, in which year

its valuable contents, twice paid for by succeeding Medici, were brought to Rome and later were removed to the Vatican. This historic collection, one of the most important and interesting in the world, was again removed by Clement VII. back to Florence and placed in a building near the church of San Lorenzo, specially designed for its reception by Michelangelo and celebrated to-day as the Laurentian Library. But Leo in his youth had aspired to become something more than a mere patron, for he actually attempted to compose music and also to produce Latin verses, which were loudly applauded by the partakers of his bounty, although the only existing specimen of his Muse does not offer much either of originality of thought or charm of diction. Indeed, the poem in question—an ode in the Iambic metre upon an antique statue of Lucretia, excavated in some Roman ruins—has only drawn the faintest of praise from Leo's enthusiastic English biographer, who criticises his hero's attempt "as affording a sufficient proof, that if he had devoted a greater share of his attention to the cultivation of this department of letters, he might not wholly have despaired of success ".[1]   But the worst poet often makes the best of patrons; and the election of Leo X. at once aroused the warmest speculation in the minds of the learned world of Rome, of Italy, and even of Europe. Nor were these eager hopes doomed to disappointment, for that ideal reign of Minerva, for which poets and scholars had long been sighing, became under Leo a reality that surpassed the wildest dreams of the Humanists who applauded the Conclave's choice.   For the pontificate of Leo X. was in very truth the golden age of classical learning; an age wherein scribblers of choice

[1] Roscoe, vol. ii.   See Appendix of this book, where Leo's poem is quoted with a translation into English.

Latin odes or composers of fulsome epigrams gained
such rewards as satisfied the most conceited; an age of
generous, if indiscriminate and undiscriminating patronage;
an elaborate orgy of learning and pseudo-learning; a
millenium of poets and poetasters, of triflers, play-writers,
musicians, singers, pedants and of every sort of personage
who could amuse.   Real native genius alone suffered
the danger of neglect in this ecclesiastical Parnassus, so
that men are nowadays only too apt to remember that
the three chief contemporary writers in Italy—Ludovico
Ariosto the poet, Francesco Guicciardini the historian,
and Niccolò Machiavelli the unrivalled statesman—obtained but a scanty share of that golden stream of patronage which flowed like a veritable Pactolus from its fount
of honour at the Vatican.   Yet Leo's love for learning
was deep and sincere, nor was his liberality, although it
failed to reach Ariosto, wholly confined to those medio-
crities, the Neo-Latinists, whose output of graceful Latin
verse actually exceeded in the few years of his reign the
total surviving mass of genuine classical literature.   For
it was Leo who called the great Greek professor Lascaris
to Rome, and gave every opportunity for the editing and
printing of the masterpieces of ancient Greece.   He protected the Roman Academy and revived its sunken
glories; he reorganised the University of Rome, and
conferred such benefits upon it that his name and memory
were annually kept green by a special service held within
its precincts for nearly four centuries; a pious practice
which only ceased in modern times with the annexation
of Rome to the Kingdom of Italy.[1]

Almost the first act of Leo, dating from the Conclave
which elected him, was the appointment of Pietro Bembo

[1] Lanciani, p. 141.

and Jacopo Sadoleto as papal secretaries-of-state.   These
two writers, both favourable specimens of the scholar-
ecclesiastic, who adorned the court of the cultured Leo,
were selected for this high position on account of their
ripe learning and elegant Latin rather than of their piety
or attention to duty.   But though guilty of moral failings,
which the age laughed at rather than condemned in the
case of a court prelate, the names of Bembo and Sadoleto
undoubtedly shed a lustre on the reign of their master,
whom they served well and faithfully on many diplomatic
missions, and whose letters and despatches they composed in the choicest of Ciceronian Latin.   The high
favour shown to Bembo and Sadoleto not unnaturally
aroused the envy of other aspiring Neo-Latinists, who in
their turn easily obtained offices and preferment by
reason of their learned or witty conversation and their
capacity to produce poems and treatises in the dead
languages.   Thus there rose to fame and affluence a host
of persons whose names alone would fill many pages,
amongst them being the Neapolitan poets, Tebaldeo and
the more famous Sannazzaro, who rated himself a second
and superior Vergil ; Vida, the author of the *Christiad ;*
the elegant Molza of Modena ; Fracastoro, the bard-
physician, who chose a most unpleasant theme for his
principal poem ; that conceited but inferior genius, Bernardo Accolti of Arezzo, " the Only Aretine "—*l' Unico
Aretino,*—as Ariosto styled him at a court which would
have considered crazy anyone daring to prefer his own
impassioned cantos to the vapid productions of Accolti.
This last was perhaps the favourite, the *primus inter pares,*
of that band of fawning Neo-Latinists on whom Leo was
wont to shower bishoprics, canonries, governorships and
public offices of all kinds ; the lucky members of which
sometimes received a purse of five hundred pieces of gold

in return for a flattering epigram, or an abbey for a poem
in the manner of Horace or Vergil to celebrate a day's
hunting in the Campagna.   It was an age that mistook the
glitter of tinsel for pure gold, that deliberately preferred
the frigid and artificial productions of an Accolti or a
Bembo to the immortal stanzas of an Ariosto.   For in
spite of natural talents, which the harshest critic has never
dared to impugn, Leo in his pronounced partiality for the
Latin tongue—that bond of the literary brotherhood of
all Europe—failed to distinguish between the excellent
and the mediocre ; he could pass by Ariosto's appeals
with benevolent but condescending praise, yet in Accolti's
case he must needs fling open the doors of the Vatican to
the crowd and proclaim a general holiday, in order that
the citizens of Rome might not lose an opportunity of
hearing the recitations of one who surpassed all the poets
of antiquity ; he could bestow a friendly kiss on the cheek
of the court-bard of Ferrara,[1] but the gold and the public
appreciation were reserved for a pompous pedant such as
"the Only Aretine ".   And in this case Leo's neglect of
his old friend Ariosto must be adjudged ungrateful as well
as ungenerous ;—"until the time when he went to Rome
to be made a *leo*," writes the poet with suppressed bitterness in his *Fourth Satire*, "I was always agreeable to
him, and he himself apparently loved few better than myself. . . . Whilst the Lion was a whelp, he fondled his
playmate the spaniel, but when he arrived at lion's estate,
he found so many foxes and wolves about his den, that
he cared little for his former playfellow."   Various theories
have been propounded to account for the Pope's cold-
ness towards the first Italian poet of his age, and certain
writers have affected to find its true explanation in

[1] "La mano e poi le gote ambe mi prese.   E' l santo bacio in l' una
e l' altra diede."

Ariosto's political attachment to the House of Este rather than in an obvious lack of understanding of the merits of the *Orlando Furioso*. But whatever the cause, it remains an indisputable fact, that whilst the Vidas, the Beroaldos and the Accoltis found ample encouragement and wealth at Leo's court, the great poet of Ferrara was soon made to realise that his presence in Rome was superfluous, if not irksome to the Papal Mæcenas. With regard to Guicciardini, as a prominent compatriot and a supporter of the Medici, the Florentine Livy obtained high diplomatic posts, although his talents as a historian were ignored. Concerning Leo's recognition of Machiavelli's unique genius, we have only to record that such little attention as he received proceeded from the Cardinal Giulio de' Medici rather than from the Pope. And the same want of sympathy is to be observed in the case of the leading scholar outside Italy, for notwithstanding the court paid him by Erasmus, who dedicated his famous Greek Testament to the Pontiff, Leo ever refrained from inviting the greatest of the Humanists to Rome ; in spite too of the latter's unmistakable hints for such a favour. For in April, 1515, Erasmus had written a long letter to the Pontiff, first excusing himself for his assurance in addressing "one who is as high above Mankind, as is Mankind above the brutes" ; and concluding with the words, " Oh, that it were granted me to throw myself at your most holy feet and imprint a kiss thereon!" But although Erasmus was obviously so anxious to visit Rome and often spoke of his longing to return thither, his *desiderium Romae*, His Holiness did little for him beyond accepting graciously the dedication of Erasmus' Testament and giving him a letter to Henry VIII. of England. Even granting, therefore, that Leo's indifference to the

claims of Erasmus, Machiavelli, Guicciardini and Ariosto
has been unfairly pressed by some modern critics, the
simple fact remains that the four leading men of letters
of that age received scant attention and less recompense in the golden days of Pope Leo X.

Ranking below the classical scholars and literary
prelates of the court, but almost equally favoured by
this Papal Mæcenas, were the musicians, buffoons and
improvvisatori.   "It is difficult to judge," remarks
the satirist, Pietro Aretino, who accepted Leo's bounty
for some years, "whether the merits of the learned or
the tricks of the fools afforded most delight to His
Holiness."   In the science of music Leo, who possessed
a correct ear as well as a pleasing voice, displayed an
intense interest, sometimes even himself condescending
to take part in ditties, on which occasions he used invariably to bestow purses of gold upon his lucky fellow-
performers;—"when he sings with anyone, he presents
him with 200 ducats and even more"; so writes the
Venetian ambassador to his government.   But usually
Leo preferred to listen in a state of dreamy rapture,
softly humming the melody to himself and gently
waving a white be-jewelled hand in response to the
rhythm of the song or to the delicate strains of Brandolini's violin.   For Raffaele Brandolini, the blind musician
and *improvvisatore*, was a particular favourite with Leo
—"he was the apple of the Pope's eye"—and it was
one of the patron's delights to arrange friendly contests
between Brandolini and another violin-player, Marone
of Brescia, whose interesting face is so well known to
us from Raphael's beautiful portrait.[1]   Both these
musicians ranked likewise as the leading *improvvisatori*
of the court, where they were wont to practise that art

[1] Formerly in the gallery of the Sciarra-Colonna Palace, Rome.

of giving expression to poetical feeling in impromptu
verse which is peculiar to Italy, and was at that date
especially appreciated by the Florentines.   Leo, like
his father before him, loved these duels of wit and
poetry, which sometimes took the form of spoken arguments in Latin elegiacs ; indeed, the Pontiff himself on
more than one occasion proved himself as skilful in these
contests as any professional member of his court.   This
curious Italian art probably reached its height of elegance,
and also of abuse, at the gay court of Leo, who not only
applauded the choice extemporary verses and sweet
melodies of Marone and Brandolini, but loved likewise
to extract uproarious fun from the efforts of their feebler
and less refined imitators.   An unfortunate creature,
Camillo Querno by name, but universally termed the
Arch-Poet, who had composed a ridiculous epic of
twenty thousand lines and had been formally crowned
in derision by the wits of the Roman Academy with a
wreath of laurel, cabbage and vine leaves in allusion to
his bad verses and his drunken habits, was occasionally
invited to improvise at the Pope's table.   Plied with
strong wines till he could scarce stand upright and be-
sought to spout his halting hexameters, the poor wretch
was continually insulted and quizzed in the presence of
His Holiness, who even stooped on one occasion to
bandy repartee with Querno.   Turning towards the
Arch-Poet, already hopelessly intoxicated, the Pontiff
in his blandest manner begged him to repeat an impromptu hexameter.

> " Archipoeta facit versus pro mille poetis,"
> (Worthy a thousand poets thine Arch-Bard,)

hiccoughed Querno in reply to the Pope's challenge ;
whereupon Leo at once observed with mock severity—

" Et pro mille aliis Archipoeta bibit."
(Of all the poets none e'er drank so hard.)

With throat parched from his recent recitation, the Arch-
Poet next addressed his host thus :—

" Porrige quod faciat mihi carmina docta Falernum " ;
(Grant me good wine to make my songs more sweet ;)

to which sentiment Leo retorted in tones of solemn
warning :—

" Hoc enim enervat debilitatque pedes."
(Wine enervates the brain and clogs the feet.) [1]

This spectacle of the tipsy Arch-Poet being chaffed
by "the Jupiter of Earth," "the Thunderer of the
Vatican," "the Thirteenth Apostle" (as one clerical
flatterer did not scruple to address the first Medicean
Pope), does not afford us an edifying picture of the
Roman court ; but that love of low buffoonery and insatiable craving for amusement, which seem to have been
innate both in Lorenzo the Magnificent and in his
second son, were destined to lead the Pontiff into yet
more outrageous follies.   A certain Baraballo, a priest
of Gaeta and a man of good family and reputation, was
unhappily for his own peace of mind an indifferent
spinner of rhymes, who fancied his own feeble compositions fully equal to those of Petrarch, and therefore worthy
of special recognition from the Supreme Pontiff.

Arrived in Rome, the foolish Baraballo openly announced the true cause of his visit, whereupon the
courtiers, scenting the possibility of a merry escapade at
the expense of the poet's conceit and incapacity, at once
set to flatter the vain aspirant to the top of their bent.
A public coronation on the Roman Capitol, argued they,

[1] Fabroni, pp. 163, 164.   Roscoe, vol. ii., pp. 224, 225, note
115.

such as Petrarch had once received, could scarcely afford
sufficient recompense to such a Heaven-sent genius, and
the foolish old fellow swallowed all this nonsense without for a moment perceiving how the whole court from
the Pope downward was giggling with suppressed mirth
at the crude and inane verses he was made daily to re-
cite.   Finally, Leo himself with honeyed words of encouragement persuaded the conceited poet to demand a
coronation on the Capitol, such as had been conceded to
his master, or rather fore-runner, the divine Petrarch.
In spite of the entreaties of his horrified family, who saw
with shame and indignation the mean trick that was
being played on their elderly relative, Baraballo's self-
sufficiency was so boundless that he fell easily into the
cruel trap prepared for him.   He even listened to the
Pope's suggestion that the elephant, which King
Manuel I. of Portugal had recently sent as a present
to His Holiness and the like of which had not been seen
in Rome since the days of the Empire, should be gorgeously caparisoned for this very purpose, so that the unique
bard might ride on the unique quadruped from the Vatican
to the Capitol, where the coveted laurel wreath awaited
him.   All Rome hastened to be present at so strange
an exhibition; the windows and terraces of the Vatican
were filled with cardinals, nobles and prelates, all striving
to conceal their pent-up mirth; whilst "the Jupiter of
Earth" himself, seated in a convenient balcony, smilingly
surveyed the animated scene through his spy-glass.
With some difficulty the latter-day Petrarch, clad in a
scarlet toga fringed with gold, was lifted into a richly
decorated saddle on the animal's back, and his sandalled
feet thrust into a pair of gilded stirrups.   The merriment
of court and populace alike was now at its height; the
affair was, in fact, the extreme triumph of Renaissance

practical joking. "I could never have believed," writes
Paolo Giovio, who was an eye-witness both of the
splendours and the follies of the Leonine Age as well as
of the horrors of the sack of Rome which succeeded them,
—"I could never have believed in such an incident, if I
had not seen it myself and actually laughed at it : the
spectacle of an old man of sixty bearing an honoured
name, stately and venerable in appearance, hoary-headed,
riding upon an elephant to the sound of trumpets !" [1]
For to the accompaniment of music and the now unrestrained laughter of the whole assembly, this strange
procession with Baraballo in antique festal robes, perched
proudly aloft on an Indian elephant led by its impassive
oriental keeper, began its progress towards the Capitol,
where the eager poet looked to receive the expected
crown of merit.   But the shouts of the populace, the
braying of the trumpets, and the general absurdity of
the whole proceeding so alarmed the sagacious beast,
which certainly owned more sense than the rider on its
back, that it positively refused to cross the bridge at
Sant' Angelo, whereupon Baraballo was forced to dis-
mount amidst roars of laughter from the Pope to the
meanest street-urchin. [2]   So tickled with this feat was the
merry Pope, that he at once commissioned Gian Barile,
who was then engaged in carving the beautiful doors
and shutters in the Vatican, to introduce the elephant's
picture into the cornice he was at that moment design-

[1] Jovius, lib. iv.
[2] Alexander Pope confuses and combines the two separate incidents connected with Querno and Baraballo :—

> "Not with more glee, by hands pontific crowned,
> With scarlet hats wide waving circled round,
> Rome in her Capitol saw QUERNO sit
> Throned on seven hills, the Antichrist of wit !"
>
> (*The Dunciad*, book ii., 13-16.)

ing, and even the Prince of Painters was requested to
confer immortality by his brush upon Baraballo's steed.
It is not surprising, however, to learn that graver men in
Rome, particularly foreign ambassadors and chance
visitors, were not a little scandalised by this elaborately
planned and unfeeling jest, as well as at the plain circumstance that the most august personage in Christendom could obtain satisfaction out of such frivolity. Yet
Leo was a true Florentine, and this disagreeable type of
practical joking was prevalent in his native city, where
even at the present day a carefully prepared hoax at the
expense of a conceited compatriot is reckoned as the
highest form of human wit; nor are recent instances of
this antiquated form of elaborate and heartless merriment
wanting in the provincial town which was once the
capital of Tuscany.

Another markedly Florentine trait in the Pope's
character was his intense and never-failing delight in
the antics and jests of dwarfs and buffoons, numbers of
whom haunted the Vatican, where every description of
silly prank was played upon human beings who are
nowadays regarded as the objects of pity rather than of
sport. Taste in viands and in amusement has changed
so completely, that it is difficult to realise that in Leo's
days the presence of the half-crazy or the deformed at
the banquet was reckoned fully as essential as the strange
indigestible dishes that no modern palate would tolerate.
Many and many a time was the Pope's table set in a
roar by the sight of these hungry sycophants greedily
devouring carrion that had been disguised in rich sauces
under the impression they were eating choice meats
daintily prepared; or by the dexterity of some brutal
courtier, who had contrived to hit one of these poor
creatures full in the face with a bone or a hot batter

Alinari

CARVED SHUTTER WITH MEDICEAN EMBLEMS
IN THE VATICAN

pudding;[1] even the very lacqueys were permitted to pander to their masters' perverted sense of the ridiculous by teasing and bullying these papal parasites.

On a higher plane than these buffoons was the arch-jester of the court, the redoubtable Fra Mariano Fetti, a personage of some distinction, since he had succeeded the great architect Bramante in the office of *plumbator*, or keeper of the papal seals : an appointment that naturally had raised most unfavourable comment in exalted quarters. This strange friar, who to a certain extent possessed the same contradictory nature as his master, is said to have been originally a barber in the household of Lorenzo the Magnificent, and later to have been converted to a serious view of life by the sermons of Savonarola. Entering the Dominican fraternity as a lay-brother, Fra Mariano became for a time one of the most prominent of the *Piagnoni*, or "Snivellers," as the more ardent of the followers of the prior of San Marco were contemptuously nicknamed ; but it is evident that by the time Leo X. ascended the papal throne, all the good effects of a religious revival had long vanished. His coarse but amusing sayings, his witty insolence towards the grandees of Rome and his insatiable appetite at table all combined to tickle the Pope's thoroughly Tuscan sense of humour, so that "the Cowled Buffoon" —Il Buffone cucullato—soon grew to be a prominent and even an influential member of the Roman court, where his magic gift of arousing Leo's merriment or of removing his wrath at any moment and under any

---

[1] " The Arch-poet was so disfigured by a wound given him in the face by some person who had taken offence at his intemperance and gluttony, that he was deterred from attending the banquets of the Pontiff so frequently as he had before been accustomed to do " (Roscoe, vol. ii., p. 225).

circumstances was of such obvious value that many an intending suppliant found it well worth his while to gain the Frate's good-will. He is said to have eaten forty eggs at a sitting in order to win a smile from His Holiness; and he was the constant butt of the younger cardinals at the hunting-parties at La Magliana or Palo. Yet Fra Mariano was in reality no fool, seeing that he was also the discerning patron of that great master, Fra Bartolommeo, who adored this strange being, as well as of the artist Baldassare Peruzzi, who by his orders decorated a beautiful chapel in the church of San Silvestro, adjoining the Dominican convent wherein the Cowled Buffoon usually resided. It would not prove a difficult task to moralise at length upon the curious character of Fra Mariano and upon this highly unpleasant aspect of Leo's court and daily life, as also upon the sharp contrast afforded by the Pope's praiseworthy patronage of letters and the fine arts thus counterbalanced by the gross pleasure derived from such disgusting exhibitions of human folly and weakness. But the Medici was a true child of his age; a true Florentine in his tastes. Moreover, every prince, and almost every prelate, of the Italian Renaissance possessed in varying degree the same love of letters, art, amusement and ribaldry; it was Leo's peculiar fault that he allowed his natural bent for frivolity and low company to obtain an undue ascendancy in the daily life of his court.[1]

Far less culpable than this passion for silly jesting was Leo's delight in dramatic performances, the proper development of which was not a little enhanced by his patronage. The *Sophonisba* of Gian-Giorgio Trissino

---

[1] Pastor, chap. x., pp. 350-424; Jovius, lib. iv.; Roscoe, vol. ii., chap. xvii., etc., etc.

and the *Rosmunda* of his own cousin, Giovanni Rucellai
—two of the earliest of historical tragedies in blank verse
(*versi scolti*) and therefore the Italian fore-runners of the
Shakespearean plays—had drawn the highest of praise
from the fastidious Leo, whose perpetual craving for
amusement, however, led him to prefer the broad comedies
of Ariosto, Machiavelli and the Cardinal Bibbiena. The
last-named, as the author of the *Calandria*, has sometimes been styled "the Father of Italian comedy,"
although the real merit of invention undoubtedly rests
with Ariosto, who had already written the *Cassaria* and
the *Suppositi* some years before the Cardinal composed
his all-too-famous farce. The author of the *Calandria*,
which is largely adapted from a classical model, the
Menoechmi of Plautus, in the prologue excuses his use
of the Italian language ;—"because the tongue that God
and Nature have given us is worthy of no less esteem
than Latin, Greek and Hebrew"—a patriotic sentiment
which can hardly have been relished by the many
pedantic Neo-Latinists who witnessed it. The plot
of the play, which was arranged to suit existing conditions
of life in Italy, centres round the crass stupidity of a
certain Calandro, desperately in love with a charming
girl, who has a twin-brother so closely resembling herself in voice, figure and general appearance, that the
eager lover is completely mystified, when sister and
brother for a freak exchange their garments. The
delicate situations, most indelicately treated, that are
caused by this premeditated confusion form the chief
incidents of the Cardinal's play, which is full of the
coarsest of Tuscan humour and "little more than a farce
stuffed with gross and obscene jests".[1] Yet with the
best actors procurable to present the piece, with the

---

[1] Villari, vol. ii., p. 341.

illustrious author himself superintending, with the first
artists of the day engaged to arrange and paint the stage-
scenery, and with a brilliant audience composed largely
of Florentines, it is easy to understand how the *Calandria*
was received with rapturous applause when it was acted
at the Vatican for the special entertainment of Isabella
d' Este in the autumn of 1514. For it was not only
the absurdity and nastiness of the comedy that entranced
the Pope, his guest the Marchioness of Mantua, and the
cardinals, courtiers, prelates and maids-of-honour, but
likewise the excellent acting, the interludes of choice
music, and most of all the marvellous and novel effects
of perspective, which Baldassare Peruzzi had introduced
into the scene-painting and which in after-years drew a
well-merited tribute of praise from Giorgio Vasari, the
Plutarch of Italian painters. Since, therefore, the *Calandria* may fairly be ranked as the first comedy, acted in
the vulgar tongue, adapted to the uses and customs of the
day, and fitted with proper stage effects and accessories,
Vasari's brief description of this historic performance at
the Vatican ought not to be omitted here :—

"When the *Calandria*, a drama written by the
Cardinal da Bibbiena, was performed before Pope Leo,
Baldassare prepared all the scenic arrangements for that
spectacle in a manner no less beautiful . . . and his
labours of this kind deserve all the more praise from the
fact that these performances of the theatre had long
been out of use, the festivals and sacred dramas having
taken their place. But either before or after the representation of the *Calandria*, which was one of the first
comedies seen or recited in the vulgar tongue, in the
time of Pope Leo X., that is to say, Baldassare painted
two of these scenic decorations, which were surprisingly
beautiful, and which opened the way to those of a

similar kind, which have been made in our own day.
Now it appears difficult ever to imagine how this artist
has found it possible, within the closely limited space to
which he was restricted, how he has found it possible, I
say, to exhibit such a variety of objects as he has depicted ;
such a number of streets, palaces, temples, *loggie* and
fanciful erections of all kinds, so perfectly represented
that they do not look like things feigned, but are as the
living reality. Neither does the piazza, which is the
site of all these edifices, appear to be, as it is, a narrow
space merely painted, but looks entirely real and of noble
extent. In the arrangement of the lights also, Baldassare
showed equal ability in those of the interior, which are
designed to enhance the effect of the views in perspective
more especially. Every other requisite demanded for
the occasion was added with similar judgment, and this
is the more remarkable, because the habit of preparing
such things, as I have said, had been totally lost."[1]

The marked success of the *Calandria* paved the
way for further representations of sprightly but indecent
farces, which even included a performance in the year
1519 of Machiavelli's *Mandragola* (sometimes called the
Nicias), which is still accounted one of the most witty
comedies ever written in the Italian tongue, although its
main action revolves around a plot that is absolutely
revolting to modern taste.[2] The fun, moreover, that the
great Florentine satirist openly pokes at the hypocrisy
and covetousness of the Italian clergy would seem to

[1] Vasari, *Life of Baldassare Peruzzi of Siena*, Bohn's edition, vol.
iii., pp. 165, 166.
[2] Performances of the *Mandragola* (to which young persons are
never admitted) are still given in Machiavelli's own city of Florence,
where his masterpiece was acted in the autumn of 1906. For an
English appreciation of the *Mandragola*, see Lord Macaulay's *Essay
on Machiavelli*.

mark this drama as more likely to offend than to amuse the chief priest of Christendom ; yet we learn on the authority of Paolo Giovio that the reported success of the *Mandragola* in Florence and its perusal in manuscript induced Leo to command a repetition of the play in Rome, with the same Florentine actors and the same set of stage scenery, "in order that the City might also participate in its delights"; these delights including of course the amusing but shameless sayings of its leading character, Fra Timoteo, the canting parish-priest.[1] Nevertheless, Leo X. was a true son of his House, the very personification of the versatile spirit of his native Florence, so that in his particular case nothing, however incredible, could be deemed impossible, although if any further proof were needed to testify to the appalling and universal corruption of Italian society, priestly and secular, it would be found in the circumstance that this cynical exposure, in the guise of comedy, of rottenness in Church and State was permitted openly with the approval of the Supreme Pontiff. Less objectionable, if less witty than Machiavelli's famous farce, was Ariosto's *Suppositi*, which by papal command was represented on a celebrated occasion in the great hall of the castle of Sant' Angelo on the Sunday preceding the Carnival of 1519, within a few weeks, that is to say, of the young Lorenzo's death and of the consequent extinction of Leo's own family. The immense frescoed saloon was crowded with a jostling audience of bishops and priests, of courtiers and nobles, so that even the ambassadors with their trains came to be hustled somewhat in the assembly, which is said to have numbered nearly two thousand persons. Seated on a daïs above the struggling throng of his guests, the Pope from beginning to end expressed his

liveliest satisfaction in the entertainment.   First extending his hand in benediction above the distinguished
crowd below, His Holiness after making a prolonged ex-
amination of the drop-scene which concealed the stage,
suddenly burst into unrestrained mirth, as his spy-glass
revealed to him a clever representation from the brush
of Raphael of poor Fra Mariano being teased by a
number of tiny devils with horns, hoofs and spiky tails.
To the softest strains of music the painted curtain was
then slowly raised, whereupon the stage appeared to
view, fantastically lighted by means of numerous lamps
placed in clusters so as to form the official papal cipher.
But more effective than this artistic illumination was the
scenery itself, for the divine Raphael had been actively
employed in painting a picture of the town of Ferrara,
which must have eclipsed easily the earlier marvels of
his inferior rival, Peruzzi.   After gazing long and lovingly
at this triumph of scenic art, the Pope's attention was
next attracted by the appearance on the boards of a
herald, who recited a prologue, so comical that it sent
the papal court into hearty fits of laughter, and so highly
indecorous that the foreign envoys, even those of the
Italian states, were quite scandalised ;—"what a pity
such an unseemly prologue should be spoken in the
presence of so august a sovereign!" was the comment
of the none-too-particular Alfonso Paolucci, the representative of Ferrara at the papal court.   In the play
itself, however, which as the work of his own compatriot,
Messer Ludovico Ariosto, this Ferrarese censor of Roman
morals was bound to admire, Paolucci found nothing objectionable, which was fortunate, since Innocenzo Cybò,
Leo's own nephew and youngest cardinal, was actually
taking a prominent part in the dialogue.   Paolucci
likewise admired the dances and the *moresca* with which

the entertainment concluded ; also the incidental music, and particularly the sweet tones of an organ that the Cardinal of Aragon had lately presented to His Holiness, —"although they were not to be compared with the performances at your Majesty's own court of Ferrara". Perhaps the Ferrarese envoy's praise would have been less faint had he not nearly broke his leg, in spite of the Pope's preliminary benediction, in the ugly scramble that ensued at the close of the entertainment, whilst the vast audience was forcing its way into an adjoining room where a splendid collation was laid out for the papal guests ; even a pleasant conversation at the supper-table with the Cardinals of Aragon and Salviati, who of course lauded Messer Ariosto to the skies before his countryman, failed to remove Paolucci's chagrin.[1]

Performances of the newly-invented comedy appear however somewhat rare when compared with the frequent masques, ballets, processions, mummings and *moresche*, which the new dramatic revival was destined later to supplant in popular favour.   These older-fashioned diversions were constantly given on the most lavish scale, especially at Carnival time or during any state visit to the city, which was thus ever kept interested and amused in accordance with the policy formerly pursued by Lorenzo the Magnificent in Florence.   Nevertheless the *moresca* and the ballet were sometimes made the vehicle for expressions of popular opinion, since Leo's notorious levity and intense sense of humour served to embolden the contrivers of these entertainments, who thus wished to notify their views on passing questions of the day.   Instead of a trite classical theme, such as the Labours of Hercules or the story of Ariadne, some burning topic of

---

[1] Reumont, *Geschichte der Stadt Rom*, vol. iii., pp. 133, 134; Pastor, chap. x., etc.

the hour would be treated in an allegorical fashion, and
the easy-going Pope led to draw his own conclusions
from the incidents represented. Perhaps the most remarkable of these mummings with a purpose was a certain
moresca undertaken by Sienese actors in the courtyard
of Sant' Angelo during the spring of the very year that
witnessed Leo's own death. The schism of Luther and
the subsequent religious struggle in Germany were in
everyone's thoughts, and all reflecting Christians had
lately been much excited by the action of the monks of
Wittenberg, who had openly and with intent broken their
monastic vows. That this heinous behaviour was not
altogether reprobated, even in Italy, would appear evident
from the extraordinary spectacle which Leo and his court
witnessed—apparently without protest or annoyance—
and which Castiglione has described in a letter addressed
to the court of Mantua. On an empty stage is placed
a pavilion of sad-coloured drapery, from which emerges
a beautiful young female, who in elegant verses calls
upon the Goddess of Love to procure her a husband. A
blast from an unseen trumpet is supposed to announce
that Venus has granted her fair suppliant's natural request, whereupon eight hermits in flowing robes of dark
grey rush upon the boards. Suddenly perceiving a
statue of Cupid, the grey-clad figures, who presumably
are intended to personate cloistered monks, shoot with
arrows at the son of Venus, who promptly comes to life
on his pedestal and runs for protection to his mother, at
that moment advancing on to the stage. The hermits
next accept an opiate from the hands of the rejected
damsel, and immediately sink to sleep on the floor.
Venus then supplies bow and arrows to her son, who in
his turn transfixes the prostrate bodies of the sleeping
hermits. The slumberers thereupon awaken, and at

once proceed to make frantic demonstrations of love towards the lady that they have hitherto spurned. Circling madly round her, they fling aside their dusky weeds to appear as handsome youths, who dance a graceful measure to soft and seductive music. Having performed their measure, they invite the damsel to select a husband out of their number, bidding her shoot seven and accept the survivor ; a suggestion that the charming creature acts upon without further ado. The naïve moral, that it is better for a young man to be dead than living as a cloistered monk, and better still to be married than dead, must have been thus made obvious to the quick intelligence of the Pontiff, who seems to have been amused and by no means scandalised by this thinly veiled satire upon the evils of clerical celibacy.[1]

.   .   .   .

Whilst a Cardinal residing in Rome, Leo had lived in a chronic state of debt, so that his subsequent extravagance can have caused small surprise amongst the princes of the Church who had elected him. Indeed, one of the earliest acts of his reign had been to squander 100,000 ducats, nearly a quarter of the whole public treasury, upon the empty pageant of the *Sacro Possesso ;* nor had many months elapsed before the papal coffers, filled with the savings of the frugal Julius, were practically emptied ; in the words of a critic of the day, Leo managed to consume within a twelvemonth the whole revenues of his predecessor, of himself and of his successor. He was naturally a bad financier, but he seems in addition to have had a sovereign contempt for all forms of economy, public or private ;—" the Pope could no more save a thousand ducats than a stone could fly

---

[1] *Letter of Count Baldassare Castiglione to the Marchioness of Mantua*, 1521.   Pastor, chap. x.

up into the sky," was the caustic comment of Francesco
Vettori upon his master's reckless expenditure.   It was
lucky for Leo's personal popularity in Rome that the
Romans themselves were inclined to attribute the increased extravagance flaunted openly on all sides to the
malign influence of his many Florentine dependants
rather than to the Pope's own inclination.   For city and
court alike had been overwhelmed in the late irruption
of sharp-witted, commercial-spirited Tuscans, high and
low, rich and poor, who had crowded into Rome on the
election of their Medicean ruler to the pontifical throne.
Previous Popes certainly had favoured their own countrymen, but never within living memory had the Eternal
City beheld such a horde of alien adventurers descending
upon her, all bent on obtaining offices and grants of
monopolies, so that grumblers in Rome loudly declared
their city had sunk to the condition of a Florentine
colony.   On the other hand, it is fairly certain that the
Pope must ere long have been made bankrupt, had it
not been for the assistance of the Florentine bankers—
the Strozzi, Altoviti, Salviati and other families,—who
were shortly in possession of some thirty houses of
business on the left shore of the Tiber and were ever
ready to lighten the Medici's heavy financial burdens
by advancing money at an exorbitant rate of interest,
sometimes rising to forty per cent.   Lack of funds seems
to have been the root of all evil in Leo's case, for almost
every illegal or unscrupulous act that disgraced his reign
can generally be traced to the Pope's thriftless methods
and inordinate love of splendour; for never perhaps has
any prince, outside an Eastern tale, indulged in greater
magnificence or scattered more profuse largesse.   The
gentlemen and clerks of the court amounted to over six
hundred, whilst the full number of attendants, valets,

scullions, grooms, keepers of hawk and hound must have
been truly prodigious, to judge from the contemporary
accounts of the papal mode of life.   But the normal expenses of the court with its daily banquets and its frequent
entertainments were immeasurably swollen by the vast
additional sums spent on objects so varied as the lavish
decoration of the Apostolic palace itself; the re-building
of St. Peter's—that fatal legacy of the grandiose Julius
to his successors ; the buying of ancient manuscripts ;
the endless stream of charities to the old, the poor and
the religious ; the innumerable commissions to artists and
goldsmiths, and the purchase of French hound and Ice-
landic falcon for the Pope's sport.   Nor in this list of
expenses must mention be omitted of the money
squandered at the gaming-table, where Leo was often
wont to play for hours at his favourite *primiero*,[1] punctu-
ally paying his losses, but carelessly flinging his winnings
over his shoulder to the surrounding crowd of parasites.
A medley of intricate politics and of unseemly frivolities,
of indecorous farces and of elaborate Church ceremonies,
of jovial hunting-parties and of intellectual discussions,
of extravagant entertainments and of theological debates,
of grave discourse with foreign ambassadors and of obscene jesting in low company ;—such was that "enjoyment of the Papacy," which Leo had once invited his
brother Giuliano to share with him on his election.   For
nothing which might tend either to his amusement or instruction came amiss to this true child of the Florentine
House of Medici ;—"the masterpieces of antiquity and
the admirable creations of contemporary artists did not
interest him less than the accounts of newly-discovered
lands, the elegant poems and tasteful speeches of the

[1] *Primiero*, a simple game with cards, somewhat resembling the
English game of " Beggar-my-Neighbour ".

CARDINAL BERNARDO DOVIZI DA BIBBIENA

Humanists; the frivolous comedies of a Bibbiena and
an Ariosto; the delightful concerts of choice music; the
clever verses of *improvvisatori* and the coarse jokes of
the only too-welcome buffoons of the courts of that
period. He avoided all unpleasantness as a fundamental
rule, and gave himself up without restraint to amusement :
a trait that was peculiar to his family, and was increased
by his surroundings. He enjoyed all with the delight
of a spoiled child of the world." [1]

Perhaps our clearest conception of these golden days
of the first Medicean Pope can best be obtained from existing accounts of the visit which the celebrated Isabella
d' Este, Marchioness of Mantua, paid to the papal court
during the winter of 1514-5,[2] when the Marchesa, to
whose infant son Ferrante the Pontiff had stood god-
father some eight years before, resided for four months
in Rome. The wit and beauty of this typical great lady
of the Italian Renaissance immediately won the hearts
of all the princes of the Church in Rome, who were only
too pleased to welcome into their midst that female
element, the absence of which the gallant Bibbiena was
wont so often to deplore. Received in full state at the
papal frontier by her old friends Bibbiena and Giuliano
de' Medici, Isabella made her way to the Vatican, where
Leo received the fair diplomatist (for the Marchesa was
combining political business with enjoyment on this occasion) in his suavest and most paternal manner, albeit the
princes of the Houses of Este and Gonzaga, old Medicean
friends in days of poverty and exile, were no longer held
in good odour by the ambitious Pontiff. He even refused to permit his graceful suppliant to remain on her

[1] Pastor, chap. x.
[2] For this incident see Signor Alessandro Luzio's study, *Isabella d'
Este ne' primordi del Papato di Leone X.*, etc. (Milano, 1907).

knees at his throne, but bade her sit beside him like a
queen, and was lavish of gifts, promises and expressions
of good-will towards herself, her husband and her charming children. The Pope's cordial reception was the signal for an endless stream of invitations to the Marchesa
and her sprightly maids-of-honour, who during their sojourn in Rome found themselves plunged into a positive
whirlpool of banquets, balls, processions, hunting-parties,
popular festivals and dramatic performances (amongst
the last-named being the historic production of Bibbiena's
Calandria, already mentioned). In the rare intervals
permitted by this sequence of gaieties, the Marchesa,
escorted by Raphael, was wont to visit the antiquities of
the city or to inspect the many treasures of ancient and
contemporary art in its principal palaces. Of a truth,
however, there was very little leisure to spare for such
matters, seeing that the entertainments organised in her
honour scarcely allowed her sufficient time for sleep, still
less for intellectual study. "Yesterday," writes Isabella's
secretary to his master in Mantua, "the very reverend
Cardinal Riario gave us a supper so extraordinarily
sumptuous that it might suffice for all the queens in the
world. We sate for four full hours at table, laughing
and chatting with those most reverend Cardinals."[1]
Contemporary accounts of these banquets leave modern
readers astounded at the variety, quantity, and incon-
gruity of the viands offered on state occasions. Sweet
and savoury, pastry and game, were all served at one
and the same time, whilst the spirit of vulgar ostentation
was satisfied by endless courses of rich dishes, so that
only the trained gluttons of the period, such as Fra
Mariano, were able to do them justice. Merriment
amongst the guests was commonly aroused by some

[1] A. Luzio, *Isabella d' Este*, etc.

such device as a huge pie filled with blackbirds or nightingales, which, in the manner of the old nursery ditty, flew twittering up to the ceiling when the host cautiously cut the enclosing crust. At other times applause was easily evoked by such puerile absurdities as a dish of peacocks' tongues or by a monster pasty, whence a child would emerge to lisp some complimentary or indelicate verses to the assembled guests. Loud and often uncouth music was kept up incessantly throughout these long-drawn-out feasts, a tolerable idea of which can be gleaned from the Venetian envoy's description of one of Cardinal Cornaro's dinners. "The meal was exquisite," writes the astonished ambassador; "there was an endless succession of dishes, for we had sixty-five courses, each course consisting of three different dishes, all of which were placed on the board with marvellous speed. Scarcely had we finished one dainty, than a fresh plate was set before us, and yet everything was served on the finest of silver, of which his Eminence has an abundant supply. At the end of the meal we rose from table gorged with the multiplicity of the viands and deafened by the continual concert, carried on both within and without the hall and proceeding from every instrument that Rome could produce—fifes, harpsichords and four-stringed lutes in addition to the voices of hired singers."[1] Nevertheless, Cornaro's festal dinner must have been far inferior to the banquet provided for the Marchioness of Mantua by Raffaele Riario, who had the finest palace and the largest revenue of all the cardinals in Rome, and whose wealth was only surpassed by the income of the Sienese banker, Agostino Chigi. This famous merchant-prince and patron of the fine arts had himself on one occasion given a memorable

[1] *Relazioni degli Oratori Veneti.*

entertainment to the Supreme Pontiff, whereat the feast was prepared in a new building fitted out for a stable. The walls of this beautifully proportioned hall had however been hung with the finest of tapestry so that the general effect was pleasing in the extreme. The Pope and the distinguished guests present were astonished not only at the luxury of the meal and the splendid hangings of Chigi's supposed new dining hall, but were also amazed to find every piece of plate in use already engraved with the armorial bearings of the persons invited. At the conclusion of so sumptuous a feast, the Pontiff himself began to congratulate his host on his magnificent chamber, regretting that even the Vatican could show no room equally spacious or richly furnished; whereupon Chigi, who was evidently expecting the expression of some such sentiment, gave the signal to his servants to unfasten the cords supporting the arras, which immediately fell in a mass to the floor, exhibiting to the astounded Pope the empty racks and mangers of the steeds that were shortly to be installed in the vast apartment which had so excited the envious admiration of the splendour-loving Medici—"Your Holiness, this is not my banqueting hall; it is merely my stable!"

As Carnival approached, the fun waxed faster and more furious, since each cardinal in Rome strove to invent some fresh pastime for the fair stranger, who could bandy repartee with the witty Bibbiena or discourse well of Greek letters with the cultured Leo. "Yesterday," so writes Isabella on the 29th January, 1515, to her lord, "to make a beginning of the festivals and merry-making of Carnival, His Magnificence Lorenzo de' Medici invited us to dine at his house . . . where we saw a splendid bull-fight in which four bulls were killed. The performance lasted about three hours. When dusk set in, we fell to dancing for about three hours' space. At the festival appeared the most reverend the Cardinals of Aragon, Este, Petrucci and Cybò, all masked; but the Cardinals Bibbiena and Cornaro, who were likewise supping there, went unmasked. The sisters and nephew of the Pope were present. The banquet was very fine and choice, and lasted about two hours, after which we again set to dancing, and enjoyed ourselves thus until eight of the clock." [1]

The Papal court moreover was not too proud to attend at such a season the humbler diversions of the people, which included processions of triumphal cars, a regatta on the muddy Tiber and the time-honoured ceremony at the Monte Testaccio—that grass-grown mound near the Porta San Sebastiano, which was once the public dumping-ground of Imperial Rome. This sport consisted in the rolling of barrels containing fat pigs down the steep slopes of the hillock, whilst on the flat sward at its base, peasants fought like wild beasts for the heavy casks which were hurled with appalling velocity into their midst from above. Members of the Roman court found pleasure in this squalid spectacle, and from their safe post on the crest of the Testaccio were greatly diverted by the quarrelling and knife-thrusting of the *contadini* in their efforts to obtain these prizes. To "a battle of oranges," which it seems Leo himself with his keen Tuscan sense of humour had suggested as a suitable novelty for Carnival-tide, the Marchesa received a special invitation from the Pope. "I was requested by His Holiness," she writes, "to go to the Castle of Sant' Angelo to see a regatta on the Tiber . . . after which there was a battle of oranges, that would have been a delightful spectacle but for the

[1] A. Luzio, pp. 110-112.

rain and storm stopping all the fun.   At the end of the
entertainment I was received most affectionately by
His Holiness, who provided us with a most sumptuous
collation."[1]   The battle of oranges, which the inclement
skies of February so cruelly spoiled for the Marchesa,
seems to have raged round a fortress, and barricades
constructed of wood, which was defended by one party
of the papal lacqueys against the attacks of their fellow-
servants, both sides pelting each other vigorously with
the yellow fruit, of which an unlimited supply had been
provided to serve as missiles.   Isabella and her august
host were also much pleased with the time-honoured
feste di Piazza Navona, which were on this occasion
marked by special expenditure.   Cars representing Italy,
the Tiber, the She-wolf of Rome, Alexander the Great
on horseback, and several of the pagan divinities slowly
filed past the admiring eyes of the court amidst wild
cheering from the populace, which was particularly
attached to this local festival.   Two hundred youths,
selected for their graceful bearing and good looks, took
part in the affair habited as Roman soldiers, whilst two
camels and other strange animals from the gardens of
the Vatican were also made to figure in this incongruous
and tasteless procession, at the rear of which followed a
huge globe surmounted by an angel to symbolise the
triumph of Christianity.

    These costly pageants in the city were varied by
occasional hunting-parties in the Campagna, of which
that arranged by the Pope on his preserves at La
Magliana was the most remarkable, seeing that 3000
horsemen took part in this gigantic beat (*caccia*), and
the game killed included fifty stags and twenty wild boar.
But so important a feature was the chase in Leo's daily

[1] A. Luzio, p. 113.

ARMORIAL TROPHY OF LEO X

IN THE VATICAN

existence, that an account of the papal hunting and its incidents has been reserved for the following chapter.

On 27th February, Isabella d' Este regretfully left Rome to return to her impatient husband at Mantua. Her departure, as may well be imagined, was the cause of genuine grief to her special friend, Bibbiena, as also to Petrucci d' Aragona, Cybò and the younger and less reputable members of the Sacred College, who had thoroughly appreciated the prolonged visit of the Marchesa and her maids-of-honour. The gaiety, the vice, the paganism, the cynical indifference to religion and morality, the extravagance in every form of the Leonine Age, all were thus seen at their worst and at their brightest by the pleasure-loving but shrewd Isabella d' Este, who is herself the female incarnation of that fascinating but corrupt period. Little could she have foreseen, when she quitted the Eternal City that February morning to the deep concern of Leo's frivolous cardinals, that twelve years later she was destined to behold with her own eyes the carnage and desolation which were the inevitable consequence of all those meretricious and illicit splendours. For the Marchesa was actually residing in Rome during that terrible summer of 1527, when her own residence, the Colonna Palace, was almost the only house in the whole city that escaped the frenzied onslaught of bloodthirsty Spaniards and heretical Germans.[1] It was indeed a strange irony of fate that allowed the Marchioness of Mantua to participate in the glories of Leo's semi-pagan rule, and later to become an eye-witness of the fearful and total collapse of all that glittering but insecure fabric of magnificence which the Medici had contrived to erect upon the ruins of Imperial Rome.

[1] See chapter xiii.

CHAPTER VIII[1]

LEO'S HUNTING

Taxing the folly and madnesse of such vaine men that spend themselves in those idle sports, neglecting their business and necessary affairs, Leo Decimus, that hunting Pope, is much discommended by Jovius in his life, for his immoderate desire of hawking and hunting, insomuch that (as he saith) he would sometimes live about Ostia weeks and months together, leave suters unrespected, Bulls and Pardons unsigned, to his own prejudice, and many private mens loss. —"And if he had been by chance crossed in his sport, or his game not so good, he was so impatient, that he would revile and miscall many times men of great worth with most bitter taunts, look so sowre, be so angrie and waspish, so grieved and molested, that it is incredible to relate it." But if he had good sport, and bin well pleased on the other side, *incredibili munificentià*, with unspeakable bounty and munificence he would reward all his fellow-hunters and deny nothing to any suter, when he was in that mood (Burton's *Anatomy of Melancholy*, Part I., sect. 2, subsec. 13).

IT is rarely that we find in the same individual a pronounced taste for letters combined with an insatiable passion for the chase;—indeed, in our own times the breach between the spheres of sport and of learning has been yet further enlarged, so that now an almost bridgeless chasm seems to yawn between the scholar and the sportsman. Nevertheless, Leo contrived to become known to posterity not only as the Papal Mæcenas, but also as the Papal Nimrod. As a cardinal Giovanni de' Medici had been much addicted to hunt-

---

[1] Throughout this chapter considerable use has been made of Count Domenico Gnoli's charming and valuable study—*Le Caccie di Leone X.*, in *La Nuova Antologia*, vol. cxxvii.

ing in the Roman Campagna, often forming one of the
large parties arranged by his wealthy colleagues, Ascanio
Sforza and Alessandro Farnese.   Indulgence in the
chase had never been considered improper in the case
of a cardinal, but as yet no Pontiff had ever condescended,
either by reason of choice or sense of official dignity,
to take more than a passing interest in this form of
amusement.   Leo must be adjudged therefore the first
Pope regularly to abandon himself to sport, to organise
hunting-parties on a scale hitherto unsurpassed and to
preserve whole districts in the Campagna to supply
himself and his guests with the necessary game.   But
even in this case precedent was strong, and there can be
little doubt that at first Leo X. hesitated to persist in a
practice that had not been seriously condemned in the
Cardinal de' Medici.   For in July, 1513, only a few
weeks after his accession, we find him sending a regret-
ful refusal to a tempting invitation from that inveterate
sportsman, Cardinal Farnese: "Oh, that I could but
enjoy your own freedom, so as to accept your offer!"
But if his refusal was really due to ecclesiastical scruples
(as seems highly probable) these had certainly been overcome by the close of the year, since in January, 1514,
that is within a twelvemonth of his election, we find Leo
openly engrossed in his favourite occupation.   The
Pope's nominal excuse for this changed attitude was the
advice of the court physicians, who insisted on a life in
the open air as beneficial and even essential to his health.
Yet, assuming that the doctors of their own free will
were urging this point without merely recommending
what was agreeable to Leo's obvious wishes, it is impossible to imagine the Pope ignorant of the strict pro-
hibition of such a form of recreation by the canon law,
and indeed we find the Papal Nimrod in the course of

his reign forbidding the Portuguese clergy to indulge in those very pursuits to which he himself was so notoriously addicted.

The chief scene of Leo's hunting expeditions was his favourite residence, the Villa Magliana,[1] situated on the road to Porto, at about five miles' distance from the city. Erected by Innocent VIII. and embellished by Julius II., the Magliana had for some time served as an occasional country retreat for the Popes, who seemed quite careless or ignorant of the unhealthy nature of its site; a flat meadow reeking of fever at no great distance from the Tiber. To-day the old papal hunting-lodge, which is utilised as a farm building, though standing un-inhabited, presumably on account of the local malaria, consists of a range of low stone buildings in a fair state of preservation, enclosing a courtyard with a broken fountain, at present used as a watering trough. A graceful little balcony of marble looking eastward across the grassy plains of the Tiber towards the purple-hued range of the Alban Hills, as well as a loggia and a broad staircase on its northern side remain intact. Everywhere are to be seen escutcheons of the Cybo and Della Rovere Popes, but by a strange coincidence not a single Medicean emblem has survived the ravages of time. From the damp dilapidated chapel and the dis-mantled halls the fading frescoes of Raphael and Lo Spagna have long since been abstracted, but it is still easy to trace the *tinello* or dining-hall, the great kitchen and other domestic arrangements of this tiny palace, "this Vatican in miniature," as contemporaries named the Magliana. Mulberry and acacia trees occupy the space once covered by the admired pleasaunce of the

---

[1] La Magliana stands within a stone's throw of the main line running north to Genoa.

first Medicean Pontiff with its aviaries and fountains;
otherwise a flat thistle-grown expanse follows the curves
of the river towards distant Ostia.   Close to the deserted
villa the muddy, turbulent stream of the Magliana
rushes past through thickets of willow and aspen to join
the yellow Tiber, whilst northward extends for miles and
miles a scrub-covered undulating country, which even
to-day affords ample shelter both for winged and ground
game.   The Magliana was of course papal property,
and as all the neighbouring territory belonged to the
Orsini family, his own relatives, it was no difficult matter
for Leo to obtain an immense tract of land suitable for
purposes of sport; indeed this papal hunting estate
stretched from the Tiber on the south into the Campagna
as far north as the Isola Farnese, its boundary to westward being the sea-coast and to eastward the ancient
Via Cassia.   At the villa itself the Pope, whose love of
venary was by no means confined to the chase, had
erected an enormous *gazzara*, or netted enclosure, wherein hundreds of jays (*gazze*), doves and herons were kept
ready for the sport of hawking, of which Leo was pas-
sionately fond.   By thus reserving birds in confinement,
the trouble and delay of finding the necessary quarry in
the open were saved, so that the Pontiff could at any
moment, when the desire seized him, follow with his
spy-glass from the balcony of the villa or from a shady
seat in the garden the spectacle of a favourite falcon
and its destined prey mounting upward in graceful
spirals into the clear blue of the Roman sky.[1]   At the
papal mews hard by were housed numerous hawks from
the tiny merlin to the powerful goshawk; whilst a neighbouring structure was reserved for the ferrets.   The
Pontiff seems to have been devoted to ferreting, since

[1] Jovius, lib. iv.

he had at great expense caused a large area of sandy
waste near Palo to be surrounded by a palisade and then
well-stocked with rabbits.   The interior of this *conigliare*
(which must have closely resembled the modern rabbit-
warren constructed on so many English estates) was
thickly planted with myrtle and juniper scrub, and large
quantities of meal and fodder were also supplied to the
captive coneys, as sundry entries in the papal accounts
of the period testify.   As both the rabbits in the *conigliare*, the birds in the *gazzara* and even the valuable
French hounds suffered much from the attacks of
scorpions and snakes, high rewards were always paid to
the peasants for any noxious reptiles killed near La
Magliana or the warren at Palo.

The hunting season for ground game usually opened
in the middle of September, and continued throughout
the whole of the autumn and winter, during which period
the Pope was often absent from Rome for so long a
space as six weeks at a stretch.   Popular as Leo undoubtedly was and lax as was the age, yet this craving
for sport and open indulgence in hunting at first aroused
a certain degree of opposition at the Roman court.
Paris de Grassis, whose varied experiences under the
two last Pontiffs could not have rendered him particularly
strait-laced, was horrified, at least in the opening year of
his reign, by Leo's total disregard for papal etiquette and
by his hunting costume which, though no doubt convenient for the purpose, appeared highly indecent to his
master of the ceremonies.   " He left Rome without his
stole, and what is worse without his rochet, and what is
worst of all, he wore long riding boots (*stivali*), which is
most improper, seeing that then the people cannot kiss
the Pope's feet!"   But in reply to the anxious de
Grassis' expostulations, the Medici only assumed his

blandest smile without taking further trouble to excuse
or justify his queer apparel.   And if the garb of their
master appeared uncanonical and unsuited to his lofty
position, that of his accompanying cardinals showed even
less regard for what was seemly in princes of the Church,
so that we read of the observant Venetian, Matteo
Dandolo, commenting severely upon Cornaro's unclerical
appearance in a close-fitting jacket of brown Flemish
cloth and with a broad ungainly Spanish hat.

The name of Domenico Boccamazzo, the Pope's
trusted head-keeper, who was responsible for the preservation of game in the papal hunting zones at La
Magliana, Palo, Cervetri, Toscanella and elsewhere,
frequently occurs in the chronicle of the private expenses
of the papal household, and Boccamazzo has a still
further claim on our remembrance, if not on our gratitude, as the author of a treatise composed quarter of a
century after Leo's death, wherein he laments the passing
of the golden days of the Papal Nimrod and relates
some of his own experiences as papal huntsman.[1]   This
keeper of the Italian Renaissance, who as an author
must certainly be reckoned unique in his profession, describes with commendable exactness the terms and
methods of the hunting of his own day, and thereby
quite unconsciously draws for us a most valuable picture of
that brilliant society of the Leonine Age amusing itself
in the free air of the Campagna after a long spell of
indulgence in the political, learned and artistic atmosphere of the city.—"Finding myself in a declining old
age," writes Boccamazzo in the opening sentences of his
modest work, " after having spent all my life and all my
substance in the chace, . . . I thought it suitable to in-

---

[1] The title of this curious little work seems to have been *Il
Cacciatore Signorile di Domenico Boccamazzo.*

scribe in this my book the ways of hunting and of hunting parties in my prime;" and it is from the pages of Leo's
literary keeper that we are enabled to learn many interesting details of the Papal Nimrod and his court.

On the day previous to the hunt an under-keeper,
skilled in the lore of wild animals and assisted by a well-
trained dog, would select a convenient spot, teeming with
game of every description, from hares and porcupines to
stags and wild boar.   Under the eye of the *capo-caccia*,
that is of Boccamazzo himself, the chosen area, which
was probably a small woody valley debouching on the
plain, would be wholly enclosed by immense strips of
stout sail-cloth (*tele*), each piece some twenty feet long
by six feet high and fastened together with hooks, for
in the days of Leo the old Italian use of nets (*reti*) for
this purpose had been superseded by the new French
hunting fashions.   These *tele* were firmly secured by
stout poles driven into the earth and were watched
during the progress of the day's sport by soldiers of the
Swiss Guard aided by peasants, whose duty it was to
prevent the terrified boars from breaking through the
enclosing material, or the stags from leaping bodily over
it in their frantic endeavours to escape.   Next day at
the appointed hour for the hunt, the *armata*, or armed
sporting party, was carefully marshalled on the plain
outside the enclosed space, the principal post of vantage
being reserved for the *Principe Cacciatore*, or Master of
the Hunt, that is for the Supreme Pontiff himself.   The
cardinals and nobles of the papal court were next led to
suitable positions so as to obtain the cream of the sport;
riders on horseback were disposed in such a manner as
to prevent the on-rushing game from escaping into
neighbouring marshes or thickets; whilst the grooms
holding the greyhounds and mastiffs in leash were like-

wise appointed to their proper places. When all was ready, the *Principe Cacciatore* gave the signal to begin by waving aloft a white kerchief, whereupon a long blast on the horn was sounded, and the under-keepers with peasants to act as beaters entered the enclosure with fearful yells, shouts, blowing of horns and even explosions of gunpowder in order to drive the imprisoned game out of cover towards the open, where the company was awaiting its appearance. Amidst the wildest excitement and a deafening chorus of shouting, barking and cheering the frightened beasts rushed pell-mell hither and thither, being skilfully guided towards the fatal opening ready prepared for them. With a roar of delight cardinals, nobles, knights and prelates with their attendants flung themselves upon the half-stupefied prey, attacking with energy, but apparently without much science, boar, wolf, goat, deer or hare with every kind of weapon save the musket, which for obvious reasons was forbidden on these occasions.

Whilst some of the sportsmen tried to spear the flying hart or, sword in hand, to face the enraged boar, others would follow the greyhounds on horseback across the open plain in pursuit of hare or bustard. Meanwhile His Holiness, the Master of the Hunt, a conspicuous figure on the white horse that had borne him at Ravenna, was smilingly surveying from his secure and lofty position the general tumult through the inevitable glass : now applauding the Herculean Cardinal Sanseverino (who in imitation of his favourite antique god constantly bore a lion's skin on his broad shoulders) for his pluck in meeting the on-rush of a wounded boar, now warning some favourite page to keep clear of the fray, and anon laughing consumedly at the absurd antics of Fra Mariano struggling with a refractory mule, or at Paolo Giovio, his own historian, who in the excitement of the chase had come to grief in some muddy ditch and was floundering in the oozy slime.

Yet even more important than Boccamazzo in the management of the papal hunts was Leo's private chamberlain, Giovanni Lazzaro de' Magistris, universally known by his nick-name of Serapica, "the Mosquito," which he presumably owed to his small shrill voice. A hard-bitten wiry little fellow, originally a parish priest at Aquila in the kingdom of Naples, Serapica had gained the confidence of Leo equally by his tact at court and by his indomitable pluck in the field, where he would face a charging boar, and even on one occasion was badly tossed by a stray bull before his master's eyes. Both as a courtier in the palace and as custodian of the papal kennels, this Neapolitan sporting priest served his magnificent patron faithfully during his life and mourned him with sincerity after death. It is not difficult, however, to understand why Serapica's undeniable influence with the Pontiff became the cause of much jealousy amongst the more prominent members of the Roman court, whose outraged feelings were expressed in the foul-mouthed Aretino's sarcastic epigram upon Serapica's strange advancement from the papal kennels to the papal presence.[1] Whilst Boccamazzo was held answerable for the constant supply of game, Serapica was responsible for all the arrangements of the hunt, a matter of no small concern when Leo penetrated into the more remote districts of the Campagna, where only a few fever-stricken hamlets existed to afford shelter for the Pontiff and his luxurious suite, which often contained a hundred or more guests, to say nothing of the ruck of humbler followers, such as beaters, grooms, and dog-keepers. In fact, the expected

---

[1] Serapica stregghiò i cani; e poi fu papa.

ALESSANDRO FARNESE (PAUL III)

arrival of the Papal Nimrod brought no little anxiety to
the local governors of the small towns of the Roman
State, so that we can easily imagine the mixed feelings
wherewith the Castellan of Civittà Vecchia must have
received the ensuing communication from His Holiness
on the 18th October, 1518 :—

"MY BELOVED CASTELLAN,

"I shall be at Cività Vecchia on the 24th day
of this month with a large suite. You must arrange for
a good dinner with plenty of fish for me, as I am most
anxious to make a display of state before the men of
letters and others who will be my companions. I shall
reimburse all your expenses on our behalf. I command
you to let nothing be wanting at this banquet, since I
wish to entertain thereat persons of the highest consideration, who are very dear to my heart. We shall be 140
in number, and that will serve to guide you, so that there
may be no mistakes nor deficiencies through ignorance.
I bestow my blessing upon you.

"Your most loving
"SOVEREIGN"[1]

But this number, large as it appears, was moderate
in comparison with the immense crowds which attended
the hunts of Cardinal Farnese, when he entertained the
Pontiff on his estates at Viterbo or Cannino. These
visits to the feudal domains of the Farnesi, made usually
in the summer months, gave occasion to immense holo-
causts of feathered game, chiefly pheasants, partridges and
quails, which were captured by most elaborate and ingenious devices, whilst smaller birds, such as thrushes,
ortolans and larks, even robins and goldfinches, were
snared in thousands by means of the *uccellare*, the

[1] Quoted by Count Gnoli (*Le Caccie di Leone X.*).

historic bird-snare of Italy. The warm weather likewise
drew Leo to the beautiful wooded shores of the Lake of
Bolsena, which had long been familiar to him, since as
legate of the patrimony of St. Peter he had occasionally
resided at the town of Bolsena, where a stately palace and
a fountain enriched with Florentine coloured terra-cotta
still proclaim to-day the taste and bounty of the
Medici. The Pontiff bore such an affection for this smiling district, partly from old associations but chiefly on account of the splendid fishing afforded by these prolific
waters, that a summer rarely passed unmarked by his
presence on these shores. "Every year," sings the house-
poet of the Farnesi, "doth Leo condescend to visit our
domain and to bathe his holy countenance in our waves."
Taking up his residence in a villa belonging to his host on
the islet of Bisentina, Leo was frequently rowed over the
shining expanse of Bolsena in a specially constructed
barge manned by sixteen oarsmen; sometimes to indulge in a long day's fishing or sometimes to visit his
own preserve of pheasants on the island of Martana.
Owing to the sparse population on the shores of Bolsena,
boatmen and fishermen had to be brought from Lake
Trasimeno to minister to the pontifical pleasure and to
assist in the immense hauls of fish, and particularly of
the famous eels of Bolsena, which, according to Dante,
had caused the death of Leo's predecessor Pope Martin
IV., whose gluttony for eels and white wine was punished
by a course of starvation in Purgatory :—

> "E purga per digiuno
> L' anguille di Bolsena e la vernaccia." [1]

Nevertheless, in addition to his fishing preserves at sylvan
Bolsena, Leo had constructed near Ostia a huge *bacino*,

[1] *Purgatorio*, canto xxiv.

or artificial pond of salt water, teeming with all kinds of
Mediterranean fishes, wherein the Pope and his guests
frequently diverted themselves.[1]

These expeditions at Bolsena and Ostia, however,
were reckoned as simple amusements, which could not
be compared with the sterner pleasures of the chase,
which afforded Leo far keener enjoyment.   But although
the author of these hunting-parties and their most devoted
observer, we must ever bear in mind that Leo was seldom
anything but a spectator or an umpire of the exciting
scenes and personal encounters around him.   His chronic
malady forbade him to indulge in vigorous exercise either
on horseback or afoot, assuming moral or official scruples
were insufficient of themselves to restrain him ;—in boggy
or dangerous places even His Holiness had to be carried
in a litter in order to reach the proposed scene of operations.   More than one contemporary poet has fortunately
left us accounts of these papal hunts, and though their
Latin verses are full of pedantic allusions and of fulsome
praise of the Pontiff, his cardinals, his courtiers, his dogs,
his very buffoons, we have been presented with striking
glimpses of a day's hunting in the golden age of the first
Medicean Pope.   Through the *Palietum*,[2] for example,
of Baldassare Molosso, commonly called Tranquillo and
known to history as the tutor of that human fiend, Pier-
Luigi Farnese, first Duke of Parma (then a stripling
described by Leo himself as "possessing high courage,
praiseworthy manners and a good disposition"), we are

---

[1] Jovius, lib. iv.   Paolo Giovio was himself the author of one of the
earliest Italian treatises on the natural history of fish ; his *De Piscibus
Romanis* being published shortly after Leo's death.   It is probable
that the historian obtained his information on this subject during
these fishing expeditions at Bolsena and Ostia.

[2] *Tranquilli Molossi Palietum*, Bossi-Roscoe, vol. xii., pp. 129-
134.

able to obtain a valuable picture of an event of this nature which took place on 17th January, 1514, when Leo was the guest of the poet's patron, Cardinal Alessandro Farnese, afterwards Pope Paul III. In graceful flowing hexameters Tranquillo salutes the Pontiff as "the Jupiter of Earth," and then alludes to the young Cardinal Petrucci of Siena as "that most beautiful of youths, to whom Cupid has yielded his bow, his arrows, and his very quiver, whereby to make havoc in the hearts of the nymphs and tender maidens". Innocenzo Cybò, the Pope's own nephew, the poet flatters by professing to foresee in him a future Pontiff, a curious and rather dangerous compliment, seeing that Leo himself had barely reached his thirty-ninth year. All names, however, are presented to us in classical guise, with the result that not a few of them can no longer be identified; yet it is easy to recognise the intrepid little Serapica in the line—

Fortis equo sumptisque minax Serapitius armis.

In the midst of this brilliant array of nobles and prelates, all bent on amusement, appears Leo with the genial smile, prominent like Jove himself surrounded by the minor deities of Olympus. Beside him rides Farnese, unarmed and only intent on his august master's wishes; but the other cardinals all bear lances, swords or darts, which they employ with varying degrees of skill upon the big game that is driven for them out of the enclosed thickets. The gigantic Sanseverino, who once bore Alexander VI. in his arms like a baby and who can still despite his years vie in bodily strength with the younger cardinals, deftly transfixes with his short sword a charging boar of prodigious size : a daring feat which wins for him the warm approbation of His Holiness, who at the same time implores his host not to allow his precious heir, the little Pier-Luigi, to mingle in the sport for fear of some injury. Meanwhile Fra Mariano—purposely, perhaps, who can tell?—manages to fall off his mule within sight of the Pontiff's glass and thus arouses his patron's mirth by his comical struggles and shrill appeals for assistance. And thus for hours the merry-making proceeds apace to the united sounds of beaters calling, dogs giving tongue and wild beasts screaming with fear or agony. The sun declines towards the western horizon; all are grown weary of the sport; the enclosed space is well-nigh denuded of its game; so that the papal command to cease is received with general satisfaction. In the picked phrases of the poet thus does the great Leo now address his brother prelates and sportsmen. "The Gods have granted our prayer, for this day's hunting has been most prosperous, although at the first uprising of the sun the morn was dim with clouds and showers. But later Phœbus Apollo changed his aspect and shone out radiantly with face serene as on a day in springtime. Thus do the Gods show favour to such as never despair.[1] Enough of dart and hound! Our slaughter for to-day is sufficient. Lay aside your weapons, and tie again the swift hounds to the leash. Whatever game remains in cover will afford us sport another season."

With the setting sun the long train slowly proceeds homewards to Farnese's castle at Cannino, where at the gates of the little town groups of peasants applaud the returning Pontiff, who smiles genially in response and flings handfuls of coins from the purse of crimson velvet at his girdle, which it is Serapica's duty constantly to replenish. For Leo is very popular with the people of the Campagna, whom he loves to converse with and also

[1] Compare with this, chapter iii., p. 55.

pays handsomely in return for any forced labour he may exact. Moreover, he constantly bestows largesse upon whole families, and gives dowries to enable pretty sunburnt girls to marry their sweethearts;—his very coming enriches the fields and brings a golden harvest, so aver the grateful *contadini* not without reason.[1] Leaving the cheering crowd and the improvised festal arches of the town, Farnese's guests enter the castle hall, where an elaborate supper is being prepared. The interval of waiting is passed in animated conversation concerning the incidents of the past day's sport, or else in admiring the fine tapestries and pictures of the chamber. At the conclusion of the meal, Grapaldo of Parma sings to his lute Latin hexameters, of which the theme is Diana surprised in her naked loveliness by the rash hunter Actæon, whom the indignant goddess forthwith changes into a stag that is straightway torn to pieces by his own hounds. By midnight all have grown weary from their past fatigues or sleepy from the effects of the Cardinal's choice wines, and on Leo giving the signal to retire all gladly seek their couches. For ten days this life is pursued at Cannino without a break, and then with hundreds of happy and enriched peasants wishing him God-speed, the Jupiter of Earth returns once more to Rome, where the citizens hasten to the gates to meet the papal cavalcade and to admire the trophies of the late hunt proudly displayed; particularly the huge tusker slain by the hand of the Cardinal Sanseverino. Before the portals of the Vatican His Holiness turns to address his erstwhile companions of the chase: "Fellow-hunters, it is not meet that I alone should obtain the whole of the booty, which has been secured by your own exertions. Take it therefore away

[1] Jovius, lib. iv.

with you, and suspend the horns of the stags as votive offerings above the temple doors. All the spoil belongs to you; the sight of it affords sufficient pleasure to Leo." And with these words each sportsman selects his share out of the mass, and triumphantly bears it through the streets of Rome to his own palace.

But a yet more lively and realistic account of one of these expeditions, which took place at Palo in the autumn of 1520, a year before the Pope's death, has been handed down to us from the pen of Guido Silvester, commonly called Postumo, a poet in the train of Cardinal Rangone of Modena, highly praised for his talents by the generous Ariosto, who speaks of this Postumo as doubly crowned by Minerva and Phœbus Apollo.[1] The writer first indites of the gay procession issuing from the town for the day's sport. There is the Earthly Jove, "the Thunderer of the Vatican," with his portly form enveloped in a robe of rich white brocade—*albo insignis amictu*—and surrounded by the Cardinals Giulio de' Medici, Cybò, Ridolfi and Salviati, all his near relations, and also by Bibbiena and Rangone, his tried and devoted friends. There is Bernardo Accolti, "the Only Aretine," swaggering and brandishing a spear, which to do full justice to that mediocre genius he was wont to employ more skilfully than his quill. That perfect courtier with grave face, dark hair and cold blue eyes, Baldassare Castiglione; the poets Molza, Vida and Tebaldeo, with a host of learned members of the Roman Parnassus are present; but the renowned Bembo and his colleague Sadoleto, being absent on their master's political missions, are sadly missed by the remainder of the company. Again the poet describes for us the driving of the game from the enclosed area; the tense expectation of the

[1] *Ad Petrum Pactium*, Bossi-Roscoe, vol. viii., Appendix CLXIX.

Pope and his guests at the entrance of the plain; and the ensuing scenes of confusion and slaughter. But Postumo mentions also certain incidents of the day's sport;—how he himself is knocked down and nearly killed by a savage boar to the momentary alarm of the Pontiff, who has perceived the poet's danger; and how one of the knights, Licaba by name, actually spears a valuable shaggy hound in mistake for a wolf, which causes much mirth to His Holiness, when shown the carcase of the stupid blunderer's "wolf". Postumo too is greatly diverted at witnessing a fierce duel between a certain Falloppio of Modena (an exile from his native city on account of a murder committed there) and a soldier called Lica, who quarrel and finally come to blows over the disputed possession of a slain wild boar. In the ensuing fight Lica loses an eye and is rescued with no little difficulty from the clutches of the brutal Falloppio, to be led away to his patron's tent blinded, limping and howling with the pain. But even more amusing in Postumo's opinion than poor Lica's fate appears the merry accident (*jocus*) which terminated the career of Lancetto, Cardinal Cornaro's favourite kennel-man, celebrated equally for his skill in training dogs and for his drunken habits (*quo non vinosior*). Lancetto, evidently in his cups at the time, contrives to transfix with the spear one of his best hounds, Argo by name, whilst close upon the heels of a wounded boar. Horrified at his own clumsiness and maddened by the fumes of the wine he has lately swallowed, Lancetto with a mighty effort must needs leap right upon the back of the flying boar, and try to strangle it by squeezing its gullet with both his sinewy hands. But the tortured quarry soon succeeds in flinging its human rider to earth, whereupon it gores the prostrate body from head to foot, till

life is extinct.   Lancetto's companions at length slay the
infuriated animal and carry the mangled corpse of
Cornaro's kennel-man to his master's pavilion, where
the Venetian cardinal orders his dead servant's visage
to be washed with the best of old wine, whilst he pauses
for a moment to compose a suitable epitaph to place on
Lancetto's tomb :—"Here lies Lancetto, whose death-
wound was the work of a wild boar, or rather of the
wine-cup".[1]   Such a jovial adventure as this quite throws
into the shade the drolleries of Fra Mariano (Charmides),
who is engaged in quizzing that handsome but petulant
youth, Valerio Orsini, for being unable to restrain his
tears at losing the stag he has been pursuing.   But the
bag is enormous, and as the party returns to Palo, His
Holiness can be overheard muttering to himself from
time to time, "What a glorious day!"

Now is the right moment for a prelate desiring
another *commendam*, or the courtier with a hankering
after some coveted lordship, to approach and present the
ready-drawn parchment, which requires the pontifical
signature alone to make its terms binding.   Leo is in
high good humour, and therefore signs anything and
everything that is placed before him, nor is he sparing
of genial smiles to his cunning suppliants.   How different
is the behaviour of His Holiness on an evening when
the day's sport has been poor!   Scowls and bitter
sarcasm followed by a sharp refusal are pretty sure to
fall upon any indiscreet applicant on such an occasion,
no matter how simple or necessary the request.   "It is
quite incredible," observes the learned Paolo Giovio,
who elsewhere comments on his master's invariable
courtesy, "that after an ill day's hunting he should

[1] . . . Hic Lancettus ab apro
Sed magis a vino saucius ora jacet.

exhibit so much disappointment and annoyance both in his face and in his temper." But sport and weather have alike proved propitious this fine November day, so that Leo will grant all demands with his accustomed grace and generosity.

Nevertheless, the day's adventures are not quite exhausted, although the shades of evening are beginning to fall, for suddenly a buzzard is spied aloft hovering against the gold and crimson of the western sky. Promptly the falconer of Cardinal Orsini releases his master's best peregrine, which darts upward in pursuit of the bigger hawk and sets to attack its less active opponent with beak, wings and talons. But whilst the whole party is gazing rapturously at this aerial combat, suddenly there sails into ken an immense eagle, which in its turn assails the Cardinal's falcon. In vain does the anxious *strozziere* sound the accustomed call of return; the plucky falcon engages in battle with the king of birds, and is incontinently slain. Headlong falls the lifeless mass of blood-stained feathers with a thud to the ground at the feet of its weeping trainer, whilst Orsini himself proceeds to moralise on the high spirit of his unfortunate pet. The gallant falcon shall be buried, he declares, with full honours of war upon the battlement of some lofty tower. Her chains and jesses shall lie beside her in the tomb, and an achievement bearing the proud arms of Orsini shall mark the spot, above which skulls of doves and herons shall yearly be suspended for a votive remembrance of the bird's past victories.

As in Molosso's poem, the banquet, the jest, the music and the recitation, which crown the labours of the day, are duly recorded; but in this case it is Messer Tiresia, a canon of Bologna and a papal secretary, who

delights the august company with choice verses composed
by the absent Bembo, whose genial presence and witty
conversation are so sorely missed.

.   .   .   .

However interesting they may be deemed from an
historical or social point of view, these contemporary
accounts of Leo's hunting-parties must inspire disgust
in modern minds and serve to prejudice us against a
Pope, who not only delighted in these crude exhibitions
of wholesale slaughter, but also squandered vast sums
of the public revenue upon their arrangements. We
are shocked, and rightly so, by the callous descriptions
of Postumo and Molosso, and still more so by the
account of a certain driving of big game at Santa
Marinella on the coast, whereat numbers of stags, goats
and boar were hurried down a steep bosky ravine headlong into the sea. Close to the shore the papal court,
stationed in boats, was awaiting the appearance of the
game, which was slaughtered amidst the wildest scenes
of noise and confusion, whilst His Holiness, seated
comfortably in a luxurious barge amidst the blood-
stained surf, eagerly followed every detail of a revolting
spectacle, worthy the eyes of a Nero or a Commodus.
Nevertheless, we must digress for a moment to remark
that the cruelty and barbarism we so condemn were
necessarily inseparable from the hunts of the Renaissance ; nor must we forget that the dexterous use of
modern fire-arms has deprived sport on a large scale
of some of its objectionable features, seeing that the
breech-loading, self-ejecting guns of to-day kill with
merciful precision, whereas four centuries ago the victims
of large hunting-parties, such as Leo attended, were torn
or hacked for hours with clumsy sword or spear. As
a son of Lorenzo the Magnificent, the Pope had in-

herited a natural taste for sport in the brutal forms then
of necessity prevalent; and as a Cardinal there were
none to forbid, and very few to censure the Medici's
open indulgence in this form of amusement, however
unseemly in a Churchman.   And again, most of the
younger cardinals of princely rank, his own friends and
companions, were inordinately devoted to sport in every
form, so that Medici was only too ready from natural
inclination to follow their bad example.   But as Supreme
Pontiff he might and should have set his face firmly
against such waste of time and treasure, to say nothing
of loss of reputation, by refraining from pastimes which
were expressly forbidden by the canon law and were
highly indecorous in one holding the most exalted office
in Christendom.   But instead of setting a good example,
Leo, after one feeble effort at self-control, yielded
completely to a temptation which his wealth and position
now offered.   Nor was there a shadow of excuse for
his doing so, since on account of his physical infirmity
he was unable to engage actively in the sport which he
patronised, or to share in its real dangers or fatigues,
which form the usual excuses urged for an excessive
devotion to the chase.   On the contrary, seated in
comfortable security he used invariably to obtain his
satisfaction from watching thus the scenes of torture and
massacre enacted below, whilst his active participation
was confined to giving the required *coup de grâce* to
some stag or boar that had become entangled in the
enclosing bonds.[1]   On such occasions, Leo would descend from his palfrey and be led in state to the spot
where the wounded beast was struggling hopelessly
in the toils.   With spear poised in his right hand, and
with the left hand employed in holding the spy-glass to

[1] A. Luzio, p. 64, note 3.

guide the coming thrust, His Holiness amid applause of sycophants and servants would advance to deliver the final death-blow to the exhausted animal.   It is therefore obvious that it was the actual bloodshed and brutality of the chase rather than its attendant risks and hardships, which urged Leo to these hunts; it was the constant spectacle of indiscriminate slaughter and not any genuine desire for the pure air and free life of the open country (as his eulogistic biographer Giovio asserts), which induced the Pontiff to waste so much time due to public business and his holy office.   And yet Count Bossi, the able Italian commentator of Roscoe's biography of Leo X., expressly defends the Pope's conduct for this very reason; declaring him blameless, since he only honoured the sport by his august presence, "with all the dignity appertaining to his exalted office".[1]   Such is a modern Italian view of the ethics of papal hunting.

But if it was unseemly, as we have already shown, for the Supreme Pontiff to be hunting at all, how much the more severely is Leo to be judged for allowing this forbidden pastime to become a positive craving, an obsession, pervading his very existence, diminishing the papal revenues, of which he was but the temporary guardian, and setting a terrible example of selfish frivolity to the whole Christian world, of which he was the acknowledged Head, and thereby helping not a little to foment that growing spirit of disaffection and schism which was so soon to rend in twain Western Christendom? As Leo's brilliant, merry, cultured life draws towards its close, it becomes instructive and also sad to observe this desire for sport assuming proportions that would have been reprehensible in a secular prince, and therefore tenfold more culpable in the case of a Supreme

[1] Bossi-Roscoe, vol. xii., p. 130.

Pontiff. Like the bad King Rufus of England who loved the brave red deer like his own children (and certainly far better than his own subjects), did Leo grow more and more enamoured of venary in its most brutalising forms. There appears something ominous in the simple circumstance that during the very last days of Leo's reign, at a moment when all Europe was seething with ecclesiastical revolt and secular aggression, the Supreme Pontiff can yet find leisure and means to squander large sums on hawks for the papal mews. On 20th November, 1521, the faithful Serapica makes his last entry in the *private spese* of his magnificent patron:—"To John Brand of Malines, 30 ducats apiece for six jer-falcons; 10 ducats each for two goshawks; 15 ducats for a tiercel jer-falcon, and 10 for a young goshawk; that is in all 225 ducats".[1] Eleven days later, and the Papal Nimrod is lying dead in a chamber of the Apostolic Palace.

[1] Gnoli, *Le Caccie d' Leone X.*

CHAPTER IX

LEO X. AND RAPHAEL

During my residence in Rome, I often saw the great Raphael on public occasions walk from his house, near the rising edifice of St. Peter's, to the court of Leo X., followed by forty or fifty artists, so generally was his superiority acknowledged. I also frequently met him at the Vatican. His celebrity made every stranger seek his acquaintance. His elegant figure and interesting physiognomy attracted attention, while the fulness of his conversation and the amenity of his manners fascinated the spectators of the divine creations of his pencil. I observed with pleasure his manner of communicating information to his pupils. It was neither the condescension of the pride of knowledge, nor the forced and brief precepts of the hired lecturer, but the ample and generous communication of a mind as liberal as it was enlightened. He not only quitted his own performances to instruct theirs, but he freely gave his pupils designs of his own composition, and hence it was that in my travels through Europe I found so many of his sketches in the cabinets of the curious. The kindness of Raphael's disposition diffused itself among his scholars. They copied his manners as well as his mind, and this honourable emulation therefore never degenerated into illiberality or envy (*The Travels of Theodore Ducas*).

LEO X. was undoubtedly "the incarnation of the Renaissance, not in its purest but in its most brilliant form," and the world in consequence still owes a deep debt of gratitude to the liberality and fine taste of the first Medicean Pontiff, whose name will ever remain associated with that of the divine Raphael of Urbino. Yet the same carping criticism that has been passed upon his choice in literature has been even applied to the Pope's patronage in the domain of art. The ostensible reason for this dissatisfaction is to be found in the continued absence from the Roman court during his reign of two out of the three leading Italian artists of the day, namely, Lionardo da Vinci and Michelangelo Buonarotti. Neglect of the latter, the Pope's own fellow-citizen, has been constantly urged by modern writers as an instance of Leo's conspicuous lack of real artistic insight or knowledge. Nevertheless, it is not hard to comprehend the Medici's failure to appreciate the stupendous genius of Michelangelo, whose gigantic conceptions in stone or marble possessed small attraction for this papal patron, who seems to have been less partial to sculpture than to the sister arts of painting, engraving and architecture. Like most short-sighted persons, Leo found a surer delight in the minute and delicate productions of jewellers and goldsmiths such as Tagliacarne and Caradosso, which he loved to examine closely with spy-glass or spectacles, than in the vast naked groups of statuary which the Florentine master was then devising for the monument of the late Pope Julius. Nor was Leo's antipathy due merely to artistic reasons, for the two qualities which he specially demanded in the recipients of his bounty, alacrity and an unquestioning obedience, were utterly absent in the egotistic temperament of the fierce Michelangelo. The genial but erratic Pope had therefore small sympathy with the conscientious but morose Florentine, ever nursing some grievance, real or imaginary, against his employer for the time being, and resenting the scant deference that was usually displayed towards the leading artists of the period, who were then held on a lower level than the scholars and poets of the court and were treated as skilled decorators rather than as distinguished men of genius. With the fiery Julius II., himself of plebeian origin, Michelangelo had been more content, for in that case both patron and sculptor were moved by the same combative and impatient spirit; both shared some measure of that *terribilità*, which was so common a characteristic of their turbulent epoch. How different in the eyes of the fastidious and cultured Medici was the behaviour of the discreet young painter from Urbino! If the great Florentine was always alert to find some cause of discontent, the new master from Urbino ever showed himself anxious to please and ready to undertake any task from the most profound to the most trivial, from decorating the halls of the Apostolic palace to designing the drop-scene for a licentious farce, from painting the Supreme Pontiff himself to drawing the likeness of poor Baraballo's elephant;—anything, in short, that the capricious mind of the mighty Leo might care to suggest on the spur of the moment. No wonder then that the Medici openly preferred the divine Raphael to the unique Florentine, seeing that Leo's own easy-going nature was not a little reflected in that of the handsome and charming young painter from Urbino. Silent and self-centred, the great sculptor was wont to regard with bitterness of envy the rapid progress of his fascinating rival, now basking in the full sunshine of the papal favour, whose steps were everywhere dogged by a crowd of admiring pupils hanging intent on every sentence that fell from the lips of Raphael. "You go about your business," said the jealous Michelangelo with a sneer, "like a general with his staff!"—"And you," was the prompt retort of the artist thus needlessly provoked, "all solitary like the hangman!"

Leo, however, did give employment to his great fellow-citizen, who at the Pope's suggestion reluctantly abandoned his cherished design of completing the colossal monument for the late Julius, in order to under-

take the building of a façade for the basilica of San
Lorenzo in Florence, and on this task Michelangelo was
nominally at least engaged from the year 1515 until the
close of the Medici's reign.   Certain biographers of
Michelangelo have hinted that Leo was not in earnest
when he gave this commission,[1] yet it is hard to admit
the possibility of such a theory, seeing the peculiar connection of this famous church with the Medici and the
boundless pride of the Medici themselves in their House.
But it would be futile to dwell here on the miserable
story concerning the precious years of the sculptor's life
that were irretrievably wasted amongst the marble
quarries of Carrara, whilst obtaining material for this
façade ordered by the Pope.   It is sufficient to state the
dismal fact that throughout the nine years' pontificate
of the Papal Mæcenas the marble statue of the Risen
Christ in the Roman church of Santa Maria sopra
Minerva was almost the sole work of note produced
by the chisel of Michelangelo.   By a strange coincidence
this figure, which is commonly accounted one of the
master's least happy efforts, stands close to the tomb of
the Medicean Pope, who, whatever excuse may be advanced on his behalf, certainly failed to avail himself
of the most profound genius in all Italy.   And even
making full allowance for the incompatibility of temper
in artist and patron, this treatment appears all the more
remarkable, since the Pope had known Michelangelo
from boyhood (the two men being almost of an age);
indeed, their acquaintance dated from the early days
when the sculptor, then a promising lad, was studying his
art in the gardens of the Magnificent Lorenzo, before
ever Leo had been raised to the dignity of the purple.

[1] For the cause of this theory, see J. A. Symonds, *Life of
Michelangelo*, vol. i., p. 350.

In spite of all this regrettable waste of time and this misunderstanding, let us hope however that the Venetian painter, Sebastiano del Piombo, was sincere when he wrote to the offended master, on 27th October, 1520, a little more than a twelvemonth before the Pope's death ;— " I know in what esteem the Pope holds you, and when he talks of you, it would seem that he were speaking about a brother, almost with tears in his eyes ; for he has told me that you were brought up together as boys, and shows that he knows and loves you. But you frighten everybody, even Popes ! "[1]   Yet in any case it was a heavy loss to posterity that Leo omitted to turn to account the talents of Michelangelo as he did those of Raphael, for the melancholy fact remains prominent that the reign of the splendid Leo constitutes a barren spot in the fertile garden of Michelangelo's career.

It is a pleasant relief to turn from this sorry tale of neglect and misunderstanding to the account of Leo's patronage of Raphael.   Here at all events the artistic temperament of the second son of Lorenzo the Magnificent found full scope in turning the powers of the wonderful painter of Urbino to the glorification of himself and his House in the exquisite productions, which all admire to-day in those halls of the Apostolic palace, that are themselves called the Stanze di Raffaelo, in honour of him whose genius is therein shown at its best - and brightest.   Only seven years younger than the Pontiff he was permitted to serve so faithfully, Raffaelo Santi, or Sanzio, was born in the old hill-set city of Urbino on the sixth day of April, 1483.   The little capital was then in the heyday of its independence, whilst the court of its dukes of the ancient and honoured House of Montefeltre was the centre of an artistic and intellectual

[1] J. A. Symonds, *Life of Michelangelo*, vol. i., p. 347.

life, whereof Raphael's bosom friend, Baldassare Castiglione, has left us such charming recollections in the pages of his *Cortigiano*. Sprung of a respectable but by no means noble stock, the youthful Raffaelo Santi, better known in latter days as the divine Raphael of Urbino, undoubtedly learned the elegant arts of the polite world of his time in the atmosphere of the ducal court of the Montefeltre, who in the painter's childhood frequently entertained in their beautiful palace the exiled members of the House of Medici, so that Raphael must have been slightly acquainted with the Cardinal and his brother Giuliano at a very early age. The Medici were undoubtedly glad to welcome the promising young painter, when in the year 1508 he made his appearance in Rome as a rising artist, whose increasing fame was likely soon to eclipse the renown of his late master, Pietro Perugino. In the Eternal City the ever-growing reputation of this youthful genius from Urbino scarcely seemed to need the assistance of his influential supporter, the great architect Bramante, for Raphael quickly obtained numerous commissions in high quarters, amongst his many patrons being the Cardinal Giovanni de' Medici, who speedily formed the loftiest opinion of his capabilities. In all probability it was Raphael who now designed for the Cardinal's titular church of Santa Maria in Domenica on the deserted Coelian Hill its charming little portico with the five arches, above which appears the inscription that tells the stranger of the Medici's bounty in restoring this ancient fabric.[1] And it was probably also by Raphael's advice that the marble copy of an antique ship was erected in front of its façade, a circumstance which has gained for this church the local

---

[1] *Divae Virgini Templum in Domenica dirutum Jo. Medices Diac. Card. instauravit.*

name of " La Navicella ". This tasteful restoration of
an ancient Roman basilica was of course but a trifling
event in the midst of innumerable commissions of far
greater importance ; for in addition to other duties
Raphael had already been entrusted by Julius II., on the
warm recommendation of Bramante, with the re-de-
coration of the official apartments of the Vatican, although
these rooms were largely covered with the frescoes of
Peruzzi, of Sodoma and of Perugino, the new master's
own teacher, whose influence can so easily be traced in
the earlier productions of his brilliant pupil. With that
naïve modesty which was characteristic of his sweet
nature, Raphael pleaded earnestly for the retention of
these beautiful but now despised frescoes, and it is solely
due to the unselfish entreaties of the Prince of Painters
that any portion of these already existing works was
spared in the Halls of the Incendio, the Eliodoro and
the Segnatura.

Without digressing further concerning his achievements under Julius II., it will be sufficient for us to state
that at the Pope's death in the early spring of 1513,
Raphael, who had not then passed his thirtieth birthday,
had already completed the decoration of the whole of
the Sala della Segnatura[1] with those splendid semi-
classical, semi-theological compositions, which are perhaps
the most truly spiritual in feeling of all his frescoes in
the Vatican, and are generally held in the highest esteem
by modern critics. In the adjoining Sala di Eliodoro
he had likewise finished his glorious *Expulsion of Helio-
dorus from the Temple of Jerusalem*, together with the
still more lovely *Miracle of Bolsena*, two faultless
masterpieces which represent the highest level reached

[1] So called from the signing (*Segnatura*) of the various papal
briefs and documents in this chamber.

in fresco and which incidentally confer an unmerited immortality upon the bloodthirsty old Pontiff, who was paying the master the not over-generous sum of 1200 ducats for each room thus adorned with the most beautiful conceptions that could possibly emanate from any human brain. For the tall venerable figure of the warrior Pope is made to appear prominent in both these magnificent compositions; borne aloft in full panoply of pontifical state, Julius surveys with kindling eye the discomfiture of the sacrilegious invader of the Jewish sanctuary, much as he would have regarded the butchery of every barbarian Frank or Spaniard still remaining on the sacred soil of his own Italy. The painter was still engaged upon this chamber when the Pope's decease forced him to suspend the work, until such time as the result of the sitting conclave of March, 1513, was made known—a most critical and anxious period in the career of Raphael, who was so deeply engrossed in the task which was intended to rival, if not to surpass, the mighty achievements of Michelangelo in the Sistine Chapel hard by.

The subsequent election of Giovanni de' Medici to the vacant throne at once put an end to the artist's suspense, for in Leo X. he felt certain of gaining a sympathetic and generous patron. Even were he not already possessed of so many powerful and devoted friends, Raphael would soon have won the favour of the new Pope, "for not only had he become the most celebrated painter of his day, but also the most finished courtier. Left to himself whilst still a boy, the young Urbinese had felt the necessity of developing those diplomatic qualities wherewith Nature had so richly endowed him."[1] Indeed, Leo, as we shall presently show, proved all too

[1] Muntz.

STANZA DI ELIODORO
IN THE VATICAN

Alinari

appreciative a patron of the master, who was evidently
a man after his own heart, combining, as Raphael did,
supreme genius with the graceful manners of the accomplished courtier and possessed of the utmost willingness
to work in addition to his marvellous capacity for every
variety of task.   He was courtesy itself—*la gentilezza
stessa*—as Vasari, no blind admirer, was fain to admit ;
"no less excellent than graceful, he was endowed by
Nature with all that modesty and goodness, which may
be occasionally perceived in those favoured persons,
who enhance the gracious sweetness of a disposition
more than usually gentle by the fair ornament of a winning charm, always ready to conciliate and constantly
giving proof of the most refined consideration for all
persons and under every circumstance ".[1]

With zest the happy artist resumed his interrupted
labours upon his uncompleted fresco in the Stanza di
Eliodoro, the *March of Attila upon Rome*, which is
merely an allegorical painting of the recent defeat of
the French at Novara.   Before the gates of Rome,
whose ancient walls and aqueducts are clearly delineated
in the background, the Pope St. Leo advances to
forbid the impious king of the invading Huns to enter
the Holy City, whilst the Pontiff's action is supported
by the appearance of the avenging Apostles Peter and
Paul, who hover overhead in a blaze of golden light.
But the artist has made no secret of his open intention
to magnify the deeds of the Medici under this transparent
guise.   St. Leo is in fact an excellent portrait of Leo X.
in shining robes and mounted on the milk-white palfrey
that had borne him on the field of Ravenna, whilst the
discomfited barbarian monarch, shrinking in terror before the heavenly effulgence shed by the angry Apostles,

[1] *Vita di Raffaello Sanzio.*

is none other than the Most Christian King, Louis XII. of France. The papal cross-bearer, who gazes with rapturous awe at the splendid figure of the Pontiff, is represented by Raphael himself, and close to him appears a somewhat stolid cardinal seated on a mule, whose features again recall those of the Medicean Pope. This remarkable double representation of Leo both as Pontiff and as Cardinal in a single group has given rise to the theory that Raphael, who had already completed a portion of this fresco at the date of the death of Julius II., added the portrait of the newly elected Pope, whom the painter had lately witnessed proceeding in full state from the Vatican to the Lateran in the famous pageant of the *Sacro Possesso*.[1] Certainly we have in this picture a clear portrait of the Medici as he rode across Rome on that memorable occasion, clad in the white and gold pontifical vestments and with the jewelled tiara on his head. In the same hall, at right angles to this fresco, Raphael added the striking *Deliverance of St. Peter*, one of his best known and most popular works, wherein under the incident of the Angel leading the Apostle out of prison, he recalls the escape, deemed almost miraculous at the time, of Leo X. himself a few months before his elevation to the papal throne.[1] The contemporary armour worn by the Roman soldiers in this impressive composition—an anachronism of which the learned Raphael could only wittingly be guilty—seems intended expressly to connect this story from the Acts of the Apostles with the fortunate liberation of the captive Medici during the retreat of the French army from Milan in the summer of 1512.

In spite of endless interruptions caused by divergent

[1] See chapter v.

duties, the Stanza di Eliodoro was finished by the
middle of the year 1514, whereupon Raphael set to
adorn the third hall, usually styled that of the Incendio,
because one of its chief compositions commemorates a
miraculous event, which is said to have occurred under
Leo IV. in the ninth century, when a conflagration that
had broken out in the Borgo, or suburb lying round the
Vatican, was quenched by means of the earnest prayers
of that Pope.   Even so unpromising a subject for artistic
treatment has been rendered attractive through the
unique talent of the painter, who in this case presents us
with a delightful composition conceived in the true spirit
of antiquity.   For Raphael has shown us here the
destruction of ancient Troy by fire, with naked figures
forced into graceful attitudes at the sudden impulse of
alarm;—there is pious Aeneas escaping with the aged
Anchises on his back; there is the little Iulus following
in his sire's footsteps and clasping the precious Lares
and Penates in his tiny arms; there is the unhappy
Cassandra mourning over her own fulfilled prophecy of
impending disaster, whilst in the distant background
of this scene of confusion can be observed the form of
a mediæval Pontiff, who tries to extinguish the raging
flames with outstretched palms, as he stands above the
portico of old St. Peter's, which was itself a ruin at the
time this fresco was designed.   More closely connected
with the policy of Leo X. is the fine group of the *Coronation of Charlemagne*, a glorious tribute to the not
very creditable treaty lately concluded between Pope
and French King at Bologna.   In the centre of this
great painting kneels the Emperor with the visage of
Francis of France before the Medici depicted as his
predecessor Leo III., whilst the merry little page who
upholds the imperial mantle is Giuliano's bastard son,

the future Cardinal Ippolito de' Medici.[1] Facing this fresco of the Emperor's Coronation is the *Victory of Leo IV.* over the Saracens at Ostia, wherein the Medici's form is prominently displayed, as he sits in a somewhat theatrical pose attended by his favourite counsellors, Bibbiena and Giulio de' Medici. This hall, in spite of its acknowledged beauty, exhibits only too plainly the effects of the high pressure of work at which the artist was constantly kept, for the signs of the inferior handiwork of pupils are everywhere apparent, causing us to lament uselessly that the divine Raphael was not permitted to secure the leisure requisite for the completion of these magnificent creations. Still deeper is our regret in the Sala di Costantino, the last and most spacious of this suite of official rooms, for in this case the hand of death had already beckoned to the painter before ever his magic pencil had touched the walls of this apartment. Of its decorations, the splendid *Triumph of Constantine*, the most spirited and most harmonious battle-piece that ever was conceived in imagination, was alone copied exclusively from the master's original cartoon by his trusted pupil, Giulio Romano, whilst the remaining compositions, interesting as they are, owe nothing either to the hand of Raphael or to the bounty of Leo X.

Apart from the inestimable artistic value of these frescoes, the halls of the Segnatura, the Eliodoro and the Incendio incidentally present us with a well-filled portrait gallery of those cardinals and bishops, scholars and diplomatists, painters and poets, who thronged the court of the Vatican during the pontificates of Julius II. and Leo X., thereby affording us an additional source of interest and instruction. "The rooms painted by

[1] See chapter vi.

Raphael," so writes the learned Bembo in one of his letters to the Cardinal Bibbiena, "are quite beautiful, not only on account of the skill shown in the execution, but also on account of the great number of clergy whose portraits he has introduced."[1]   We ourselves to-day, who can but behold all this splendour after it has been dulled by centuries of neglect or injured by sacrilegious restoration, and who must perforce survey this shrine of art in the company of an unromantic train of fellow-tourists, of necessity find it difficult to realise the original appearance of this series of paintings in their pristine freshness of colour.   How entrancing must have been the aspect of these apartments when peopled with a constant come-and-go of gorgeously clad prelates and courtiers, who as they swept proudly through the Stanze paused from time to time to admire, to criticise, to compare, or to examine with pleasure or envy the speaking likenesses of their friends or rivals, portrayed on these glowing walls by the brush of the Prince of Painters! On reflection, as we traverse these rooms we come to perceive only too clearly the havoc wrought here during the passage of four centuries, and to understand the lack of a fit environment.   With such thoughts in our minds, we can then enter into the feelings of that fastidious scholar Bembo, who considered these frescoes merely as an adequate setting to the official court life of the Vatican in the golden days of the Leonine Age. "The halls," he writes, "which Raphael has painted, are already beautiful beyond compare, but their charm is enhanced not a little by the crowds of passing cardinals and prelates."

From the gloomy grandeur of the Sistine Chapel, peopled with Michelangelo's stately but sinister Prophets

[1] Letter dated 19th July, 1517.   Muntz, p. 154.

and Sibyls, we turn to enter a new world of allegory, a
world of light and gladness, when we ascend to the
Rooms of Raphael.   Although the beautiful frescoes of
these halls are not without their admitted defects, yet
the general impression produced on the beholder at
entering the Stanze is so bright and joyous, so bewilder-
ingly full of charm, that hostile criticism is at once dis-
armed.   The mind may become more elevated amongst
the Titanic masterpieces of the Capella Sistina, but the
human spirits are cheered and warmed in regarding this
succession of pictures which present to us in alluring
form only the pleasant side of the life of the Italian
Renaissance.   The Sistine Chapel indeed reflects the
fierce mind and unbending nature of the rugged Julius,
but the Stanze di Raffaello are all eloquent of the liberal,
ostentatious, easy-going, extravagant Medici, who made
it a fundamental rule during his short but fortunate reign
to avoid all unpleasantness and to obtain the full enjoyment of the Papacy, which, so he verily believed, Heaven
itself had bestowed upon him.   In these splendid halls the
divinities of Paradise and of Olympus, the philosophers
of the antique world and the confessors and martyrs of
Christendom, the sages of Greece and Rome and the
poets of mediæval Italy meet, converse and argue together in sweet reasonableness, so that we are shown
thereby the very essence of the Humanism of the Renaissance, which did not hesitate to put the virtuous
counsels of Socrates and Plato on an equal footing with
the dour theology of the Middle Ages.   No note of
gloom or sorrow or pain is allowed to intrude within
these realms of bliss and brightness.   Everywhere the
Church is made to appear triumphant, but never does
that triumph suggest war or rapine in its train.   Calmly
do the great Pontiffs Julius and Leo watch the celestial

emissaries scatter the evil forces of idolatry and dark-
ness; even the great battle-piece in the Hall of Constantine exhibits no gruesome scenes of slaughter, for
the only harrowing incident portrayed therein is the
pathetic sight of an old warrior bending in silent grief
over the lifeless form of a 'standard-bearer slain in the
flower of his youthful beauty.   The Stanze of Raphael
constitute in short an epic poem in painting of the preservation of the arts, the learning, the religion, and last
but not least of the secular papacy of Italy from the
impious hands of ignorant and brutish barbarians.   And
this work is accomplished by celestial agency, whilst her
venerable Pontiffs, the guardians of threatened Italy, the
seat of culture and true religion, merely stand aside, to
permit Peter and Paul with all the heavenly host to carry
out the pious task of deliverance.[1]   Cheerfulness and
confidence are the predominant notes in the various
scenes depicted by the Prince of Painters; an all-pervading pessimism is the main characteristic of the Sistine
Chapel;[2]—it is our peculiar good fortune that in these
latter days we can derive an equal but diverse pleasure
of the intellect from the contemplation of each of these
shrines of Italian art.

Of the countless thousands who annually traverse this
world-famous suite of apartments, few persons have paused
to admire the exquisite wood-carving that completes the
general scheme of their ornamentation.   Yet the doors
and shutters of these rooms, which were carved by
Giovanni Barile of Siena under the personal supervision
of Raphael, constitute of themselves a study in Medicean

---

[1] " In the Stanze of Raphael the triumphs of the Popedom over
all its foes are set forth with matchless art and with matchless unvera-
city " (J. Bryce, *The Holy Roman Empire*, p. 289).

[2] J. Michelet, *La Renaissance.*

heraldry, that serves to link the series of historical
frescoes on their glowing walls with the pontificate of
the Medici.   For every panel is carved in high relief
with designs that embody the Diamond with the triple
Plumes,[1] the *Broncone*, or branch, of the young Lorenzo,
the Medicean lions with globes at their feet, and of
course the inevitable ox-yoke of Leo himself with his
favourite legend of *Suave;* whilst in the central panel
of each shutter a frieze of interlaced diamond rings surrounds the papal tiara and the familiar shield with its six
pellets.   The somewhat gloomy ante-chamber of the
papal pages and equerries, that lies between the Sala di
Costantino and the diminutive chapel of San Lorenzo
wherein Leo used daily to hear Mass, is likewise heavily
enriched with the various emblems of the Medici.   In
its splendid cassetted ceiling, gorgeously gilded and
painted, the form of the Medicean diamond is throughout utilised as a pendentive, and in the flat compart-
ments of the roof are everywhere conspicuous the well-
known devices of Lorenzo the Magnificent and of his
second son, the Supreme Pontiff.   The heraldic and
emblematic wood-carving in the Stanze di Raffaelo may
be reckoned of trifling consequence to the passing visitor,
yet in so famous a place it is interesting to note these
memorials of the pomp and pride of the first Medicean
Pope, to whose love and patronage of art is largely due
the very existence of those masterpieces of the Urbinese
artist, which engross our full attention to the exclusion
of their historical interest.

Whilst he was yet striving vainly to obtain the
necessary time to complete the paintings of the Stanze,
the over-worked artist was commissioned by his ap-

[1] The motto of this emblem consists of the erudite rebus, *Super
adamas in pennis.*

preciative but inexorable patron to adorn the newly erected *Loggie,* or open arcades that mask the façade of the palace overlooking the great courtyard of San Damaso, which their architect Bramante had left un- finished at his death in 1514. This fresh task, in which Raphael was largely aided by his talented pupil, Giovanni da Udine—the first decorator of his day, though not numbered in the front rank of its artists—must have proceeded concurrently with the work carried on in the adjoining suite of the Stanze, for the so-called Loggia of Raphael can be entered from the portals of the Sala di Costantino. This spacious and lofty gallery, which was originally intended to lie open to the strong light and pure air of Heaven and was only enclosed with glass in the course of the past century, consists of thirteen broad bays, each of which contains a domed ceiling enriched with four subjects selected from the Old and New Testaments, all treated with a peculiar charm and sim- plicity that have earned for this series of fifty-two sacred pictures the well-chosen title of " the Bible of Raphael ". More conspicuous, however, than these frescoes placed high in the domed ceiling amidst the usual adjuncts of Medicean emblems, are the countless wall-paintings, now terribly defaced and faded by centuries of ill-treat- ment and neglect, which are well known to artists from the engravings of Volpato and Ottaviani. This mass of mural paintings represents every possible variety of subject, antique or contemporary—gods and goddesses, nymphs and dryads, peasants and monsters, birds, beasts, and fishes, garlands of fruit and flowers, fantastic archi- tecture, domestic implements of elegant form, and in short any and every object or creature that invited artistic treatment. This positive riot of the exuberant fancy of a master-mind was certainly the direct result of

Raphael's deep interest in the vanished life of the ancient world, for he had long been an enthusiastic student of the *grottesche*,[1] the classical wall-paintings and stucco designs found in the recently excavated halls of the Palatine and the Coelian. To transplant in an amended and yet more beautiful guise this long-lost art from the decaying chambers of pagan emperors to the palace of the Roman Pontiff became a cherished ambition of the painter, who was not only the chief artist, but also the first antiquary of his day. So changed, however, is the aspect of this Loggia since the glazing of its arches and so hopelessly ruined the Renaissance *grottesche* of Raphael and Giovanni da Udine, that we find it very difficult under present conditions to conjure up the appearance of this broad corridor in its original state as Raphael designed and adorned it for the Pope. We miss the effect of the open air ; we note the pitiable condition of the once gay and glowing mural decorations ; and we look in vain for the splendid pavement of glazed and coloured tiles, an admirable example of Luca Della Robbia's art, which has long since perished. The far-famed Loggia of Raphael, thanks to the ill-usage of man and the vagaries of the Roman climate, exhibits to us in these days but the shadow of its pristine glory.

So damaged in short is this fine specimen of the arts and architecture of the Renaissance, that we can but echo the lament of the critic Lanzi, who declares "that the exposure of this gallery to the inclemency of the weather has almost reduced it to the squalid appearance of the ancient grotesques ; but they who saw it after it was finished, when the lustre of the gilding, the snowy whiteness of the stuccoes, the brilliance of the colours,

---

[1] Hence the word "grotesques," the decorations found in the *grotte*, as applied directly to this style of ornament.

THE LOGGIA OF RAPHAEL

IN THE VATICAN

and the freshness of the marbles made it resplendent
with beauty on every side, must have been struck with
amazement as at a vision of Paradise".[1]   Says Vasari,
" it is impossible either to execute or imagine a more
beautiful work," and with such reflections we must try
to picture for ourselves the general aspect of this gorgeous
corridor, as it was originally conceived by the genius of
Raphael and embellished by the skill of Giovanni da
Udine.   In any case, though it seems but a wreck of
its former magnificence, the Loggia has fared better than
another celebrated work of the master in the Vatican,
the so-called Bath-chamber of the Cardinal Bibbiena.
This apartment in the papal palace was undertaken at
the request of Raphael's especial friend in the Sacred
College, Bernardo Dovizi ˙of Bibbiena, who himself
proposed to Raphael the decoration of a room in the
Vatican in imitation of one of the frescoed chambers recently unearthed in the ruins of the Palatine.   "Thus
far had I proceeded," writes Bembo to his friend Bibbiena in a letter dated 19th April, 1516, "when Raphael
himself entered.   He seems to have guessed that I was
speaking of him to you, so that he begged me to add
that he wished you to tell him any other subjects you
might desire to have painted in your bath-room.   Send
him full details of them as soon as you can, because
those designs already chosen will be started upon the
walls this week."   The theme chosen by the witty and
learned cardinal was taken from the venue of classical
mythology, for he had selected the story of Venus
and Cupid, which, it must be frankly admitted, was
hardly suited to the environment of the palace of the
chief celibate in Christendom.   But the commission was
highly congenial to the taste of the artist, whose de-

[1] *History of Painting*, vol. i., Roman Epoch.

corations of Bibbiena's bath-room, marvellously imbued
with the true spirit of the antique, were greatly admired
in Rome, and probably caused the envious Chigi's demand for the painting of the allegory of Venus, Cupid
and Psyche, which the master designed for the frieze of
a hall in the Sienese banker's splendid villa on the Tiber.[1]
This room at the Vatican with its exquisite frescoes has
long been closed to the public, ostensibly on account of
its almost ruined condition, but also perhaps because a
prudish reticence refuses to allow even artists admission
to a chamber that proclaims only too clearly the "pagan"
proclivities of the Medicean Pontiff and his cardinals.
Fortunately, copies have been made from time to time
of these justly admired frescoes, so that a tolerable idea
can still be gleaned therefrom of the original charm and
harmony of what must have been one of the painter's
finest works.

Such, told briefly and baldly, is the story of Raphael's
main achievements in the Vatican during the seven
years from 1513 to 1520 under the direct patronage of
Leo X., who has certainly left the mark of his taste and
influence upon the palace of the Popes. And whilst we
have good reason to deplore the Pontiff's attitude towards Raphael in hastening unduly the artist's labours
and in heaping fresh tasks upon his already over-
burdened shoulders, we ought in fairness to recognise
our enormous debt of gratitude to the bounty and
insight of the Medici.

From the decoration of the actual fabric of the
Vatican, we now pass to another celebrated work of the
master, the set of tapestries ordered by Leo for the
embellishment of the blank wall-spaces in the Sistine

[1] Now known as the Villa Farnesina. It is to-day in a pitiable
condition of neglect and dilapidation.

Chapel, already a treasure-house of art with its painted roof from the brush of Michelangelo and its many frescoes dating from the distant reign of Sixtus IV. It was Leo's fixed intention to obtain two sets of tapestries, one to illustrate the Acts of the Apostles and thereby to symbolise the historical institution of the Papacy; whilst the other was to represent the Life and Death of Christ. Upon the necessary cartoons for the former set, the artist hastened to employ his characteristic skill and energy, with the happy result that all the Christian world is still marvelling at the combination of simplicity and grandeur displayed in his conception of the leading events in the lives of St. Peter and St. Paul. The subjects chosen by Raphael are too well known to need any hint of description here,[1] for they have been made familiar to us all from our childhood, and it is truly no slight proof of Raphael's matchless genius that his pictures of the Bible appeal with equal force and charm both to the infant and to the scholar. Few persons however, even of those who visit Rome, where these splendid relics of the master-mind of Raphael and of the liberality of Leo are preserved in the Galleria degli Arazzi in the Vatican, have made observation of the smaller subjects below the large Biblical groups of figures. Yet these little-noticed designs serve to connect this famous set of tapestries with the great Pontiff who was primarily responsible for their production. For besides the customary display of Medicean shields and devices in the rich and variegated borders of each piece of tapestry, we are presented with a number of quaint but vigorous scenes from the early career of Giovanni de' Medici before he was elected Pope. Amongst the

[1] Or to remind the reader of the existence of seven of the original cartoons in the South Kensington Museum.

many incidents of his busy life, already described in
these pages, we can recognise the Cardinal's flight in
disguise across the wild Apennine passes; the looting of
his palace in Florence; his dramatic capture by the
victorious French at Ravenna (perhaps the best of this
series); the triumphal entry of the Cardinal into Florence
after the sack of Prato, and his reception at the conclave
of March, 1513, whence he emerged as Leo X. No
doubt the second set of tapestries, illustrating the Life
of Our Lord, was meant to contain subsidiary scenes of
a like nature depicting Leo's pontificate.

The cartoons, when completed, were dispatched to
Brussels and there retained after the copies in tapestry
had been duly sent to Rome. On the arrival of these
precious hangings (for their cost amounted to 150,000
ducats, all told), by order of Leo X. they were publicly
exhibited in the Sistine Chapel on St. Stephen's Day,
1519, and loud were the praises from all quarters
showered upon the popular and successful artist. "All
in the chapel," so writes Paris de Grassis, "were struck
dumb by the sight of these hangings, for by universal
consent there is nothing more beautiful in the world."
Nor can we wonder at this outburst of delight and con-
gratulation, when we recall Vasari's description of the
splendid guise in which Raphael's majestic designs were
thus exhibited to the admiring crowds of high and low
in Rome on St. Stephen's Day. "The work was so
admirably executed that it awakened astonishment in
all who beheld it, as it still does to-day; for the spectator
finds it difficult to conceive how it has been found possible to have produced such hair and beards by weaving,
or to have given so much softness to the flesh by means
of thread; a work which certainly seems to have been
performed by miracle rather than by the art of man,

seeing that we have here animals, buildings, water, and innumerable objects of all kinds, so well executed that they do not look like a mere texture woven in the loom, but like paintings executed with the pencil." It is true that Vasari's unstinted praise is directed to the execution rather than to the design of these tapestries ; yet we can well imagine the breathless admiration of the connoisseurs of Leo's court before this blaze of colour and their warm adulation of the modest artist, whose end followed so quickly upon the heels of this moment of proud satisfaction.

Nevertheless, all this mass of artistic employment, finished or unfinished, amounted to but a fraction of the manifold duties which the hard-pressed Raphael was expected to perform. Ever since the death of Bramante in the spring of 1514, the youthful painter had been entrusted by Leo with the superintendence of the rising edifice of the new St. Peter's ;—in the actual words of the papal brief of appointment to this honourable but arduous task, the flattering reason is advanced, "because thou not only excellest in the art of painting, as all men agree, but hast also been nominated by Bramante on his death-bed as being skilful in the science of architecture, and fit to continue the erection of that temple to the Prince of the Apostles, which he began". And again, shortly before the over-taxed artist's death, Leo X. (who to his eternal credit appears as the sole Pontiff of the Renaissance who made some slight effort to save the existing relics of classical Rome from the impious hands of the architects and builders) charged the all-too-willing Raphael with the drawing-up of a full list of the many surviving ruins of Rome and with the compilation of a plan of the ancient city. And with commendable courage the great painter, architect, scholar and antiquary in the opening lines of his report pleads to the sympathetic Leo for increased care in the preservation of the precious objects still remaining; nor does he scruple to remind the Medici of the evil example set by his own predecessors in so important a matter. "The very persons," so he declares, "who should have been the special champions of the desolate remains of ancient Rome, have shown themselves the most forward in robbing and injuring her. How many Pontiffs, O Holy Father, endowed with your present dignity, but possessing neither your knowledge, your merit, nor your breadth of sympathy, have allowed the destruction of antique temples, of statues, of triumphal arches, and other glorious monuments of the founders of our country! How many among them have permitted the foundations of ancient buildings to be laid bare for the sake of the cement, and have thus reduced them to ruin! How many antique figures and other carvings have been turned into lime! I am saying only what is true, when I declare that this modern Rome, with all its grandeur and beauty, with its churches, palaces, and other monuments, is built with the lime made from our ancient marbles." It is almost too tantalising to speculate on what might have been accomplished in these comparatively early days of Roman vandalism, had but the enthusiastic Raphael and the enlightened Leo been spared to contrive between them an adequate scheme for the better preservation of the priceless antiquities of the city.

It was whilst thus engrossed, amongst a multitude of other duties and commissions, on the preparation of his report on the Roman ruins that the divine artist was suddenly struck down with his mortal illness in the spring of 1520. Hastily summoned from his work at Chigi's

villa by a message from Leo, who wished to confer with
Raphael concerning one of his innumerable schemes,
the master hurried on foot along the Lungara to arrive
heated and weary at the Vatican, where he caught a
severe chill whilst conversing with the Pontiff beneath a
draughty arcade.   A constitution naturally delicate,
added to the ceaseless strain upon mental and physical
powers during the last seven years, assisted the progress
of the malady, which was further increased by the absurd treatment of the ignorant physicians, who merci-
lessly bled and physicked their exhausted patient.   The
picturesque but melancholy story of Raphael's last days
—of his death-bed scene in the chamber containing his
great unfinished masterpiece of the Transfiguration,
that he was executing for the Cardinal Giulio de' Medici ;
of the wild grief of the Roman Pontiff, court and people ;
of his stately interment in the Pantheon of Rome ; of
his lofty epitaph from the pen of Bembo—lies outside
the scope of a work dealing with his papal patron.   On
6th April, "on Good-Friday night, or rather at three
o'clock on Saturday morning, expired the noble and
excellent painter, Raffaelo da Urbino.   His death
caused universal sorrow, particularly amongst learned
men, for whom more especially, although also for
painters and architects, he had drawn in a book (as
Ptolemy drew the configuration of the world) the ancient
buildings of Rome, with their proportions, forms and
decoration, and so faithfully, that he who has beheld these
drawings might almost assert that he had seen antique
Rome itself. . . . But Death interrupted this useful and
glorious enterprise, for he carried off the young man at
the age of thirty-four (*sic*).[1]   The Pope himself felt
intense grief, and he had sent at least six times during

[1] In reality thirty-seven.

the fifteen days that his illness lasted, to enquire for fresh news. You may judge then of what others did. And as on precisely the same day the Pope's palace was menaced with destruction, so much so, that His Holiness was forced to seek refuge in the apartments of Monsignore Cybò, there are many people who say that it was not the weight of the topmost Loggia which caused this accident, but that it was a portent to announce the passing of him who had toiled so long at the adornment of the palace.

"And in truth an incomparable master no longer exists. Lamentations for his death should not merely be expressed in light and fugitive words, but by serious and immortal poetry. And poets, if I am not mistaken, are preparing in great numbers for the task.

"It is said that he leaves a fortune of 16,000 ducats, 5,000 being in silver specie, the greater part of which is to be divided amongst his friends and servants. To the Cardinal of Santa Maria in Portico[1] he has bequeathed his house, which formerly belonged to Bramante and which he bought for 3,000 ducats.

"He has been interred in the Pantheon, whither he was borne with great honour. His soul has doubtless gone to contemplate the edifices in Heaven, which are not subject to destruction. His name and memory will live long in his works and in the remembrance of all honest men.

"Far less important, in my opinion, although it may appear otherwise to the multitude, is the loss the world has just sustained in the death of Signor Agostino Chigi, which happened last night. I shall not speak much of

[1] The official title of Bernardo Dovizi da Bibbiena, commonly called the Cardinal Bibbiena (*vide passim*), who only survived Raphael seven months, dying on 9th November, 1520.

him here, as it is not known yet to whom he has devised his property. I merely gather he has left to the world 80,000 ducats in ready money, letters of exchange, loans, estates, sums placed at interest in banking houses, plate and jewels.

"It is rumoured that Michelangelo is ailing at Florence. Tell our Gatena of this, that he may be upon his guard, since great painters are threatened. God be with Youth!

"ROME, 11*th April*, 1520 "[1]

And following on the Venetian Michiel's letter, that perfect courtier Castiglione writes to his mother : "I am in good health, but it seems that I were not in Rome, since my poor Raffaelo is here no longer. May his blessed soul be with God!" Perhaps of all who mourned for the departed artist, none was more sincere or steadfast in his sorrow than Castiglione, who had lately assisted Raphael in his exploration of the Roman ruins and whose portrait from his departed friend's hand constitutes to-day one of the chief treasures of the Louvre. "My love for my Raphael," he writes at a later period, "is just as strong and enduring in death as ever it was in life."

Thus expired on his thirty-seventh birthday, Raffaelle Sanzio da Urbino, the chief glory and ornament of the splendid pontificate of Leo X.

As has been already remarked, we have not enumerated a tithe of the multitude of commissions begun, if not completed, by Raphael during the reign of his principal patron, Leo X. Cardinals, foreign potentates, courtiers, prelates, merchants, struggling artists, all alike

---

[1] Extract from a Letter of Marcantonio Michiel of Venice, staying in Rome, to Antonio di Marsilio in Venice. Quoted by Passavant, Muntz, etc.

besieged the great master with requests for Madonnas, family portraits, designs for palace or villa, drawings of ornate chalices and ewers, whilst the good-natured painter, who seemed unable to say no to any suppliant, however importunate or however humble, sapped his strength in trying to satisfy their endless demands. But of the numerous works we are compelled to pass over, we must make at least one exception out of the many portraits executed by the master. This is of course the world-famous likeness of Leo X., familiar to all from photographs and engravings, if not from the actual painting which hangs in the Pitti Palace of Leo's own city of Florence. This work has been described again and again, yet it would be impossible to omit a brief notice of it in these pages. For here Raphael exhibits to us the utmost height of his genius as a portrait-painter, since not only does he present us with an excellent likeness of the first Medicean Pontiff, but he verily seems to usher us into the presence of Leo himself, so natural is the pose and so lifelike the countenance. Seated at a table, covered with a cloth, whereon lies an elaborately chiselled bell, the great Pontiff appears to gaze straight into the eyes of the advancing spectator, whilst his expressive and enquiring face seems but to lack that quality which alone marred the reputed perfection of Donatello's statue of St. George,—human speech. Without stooping to flatter his magnificent patron, the artist has with his inimitable skill contrived to invest the sensual unattractive countenance and the ungainly form with an air of real majesty. The finely moulded white hands are prominently displayed, as with the right the Pope carelessly fingers a leaf of the illuminated manuscript before him, and with the other grasps the inevitable spy-glass. The crimson cap and *mozzetta* trimmed with fur and the rich

white brocade of the rochet provide warmth of colouring
in this splendid composition, which for historical interest
combined with artistic treatment must stand unrivalled
amongst the masterpieces of the world.   Depicted with
equal force of character but with less minute detail appear the figures of the two cardinals, Leo's relatives,
who stand beside the papal chair.   These are Giulio
de' Medici, afterwards Clement VII., whose sharp
features and handsome but saturnine face, afford a
marked contrast with the full fleshy countenance of his
cousin, the Supreme Pontiff.   With hands clasping the
ornate woodwork of the Pope's chair, stands Cardinal
Luigi de' Rossi, presenting a common-place type of
ecclesiastic but serving admirably as a foil to the prominent central figure of the group.[1]   As Rossi was one
of that batch of thirty-one cardinals created by Leo in
1517, and died in the year but one following, we can
fix with tolerable accuracy both the date of the work and
the age of the Pope, who must have been about forty-two
or forty-three at the time of this portrait, though the
heavy flabby countenance betokens a more advanced
age.   Nothing can give the student of the Italian
Renaissance a closer insight into the inmost aims and
real character of the Medicean Pope than this masterpiece of Raphael, which clearly displays the outward
geniality of Leo, yet hints also at the underlying ambition
and lurking cruelty of his varied nature, so that this
portrait seems truly a clue to all the events and actions,
private and public, which adorned or disgraced the reign
of the Papal Mæcenas.

[1] In a fine copy of this celebrated work by Giuliano Bugiardini
of Florence, which hangs in the Corsini Gallery at Rome, the figure
of Luigi Rossi has been replaced by that of the Pope's nephew,
Cardinal Innocenzo Cybò, who ordered Bugiardini to make this change
in the copy ordered (see Vasari, *Life of G. Bugiardini*).

CHAPTER X

CONSPIRACY OF THE CARDINALS

Il n'eut jamais plus plaisant pape. Sur ce nom grave et *léonin* Jean de Médicis était un rieur, un farceur, et il est mort d'avoir trop ri d'une défaite des Francais. . . . Il croyait avoir peu a vivre, et vivait double, menant la vie comme une farce, aimant les savants, les artistes comme acteurs de sa comédie. . . . Ce n'est pas que cette cour si gaie n'ait eu aussi ses tragédies. Les cardinaux, qui avaient cru nommer un rieur pacifique, furent un peu étonnés lorsque, tout en riant, il entrangla un, le Cardinale Petrucci. Profitant de cet étonnement et de cette terreur, il fit (ce que n'avait osé Alexandre VI.) trente-et-un cardinaux en un jour, faisant d'une pierre deux coups, assurant à sa famille la prochaine élection, et remplissant ses coffres par cette vente de trente chapeaux (J. Michelet, *La Reforme*).

BUT Leo's gay and brilliant court, wherein the headlong pursuit of learning and of pleasure ran its course unchecked, was not fated to continue without its due share of gloomy and repulsive tragedies, nor can the Pope himself be deemed blameless for their occurrence. It was not long after his accession that a sense of disappointment began to affect the minds of the score or so of Italian cardinals who had elected Giovanni de' Medici, and though Leo both from natural inclination as well as from set policy showed himself invariably courteous and conciliatory towards the members of the Sacred College, yet by degrees this simmering discontent tended ultimately to develop into a real revolt against his person and authority. The causes contributing to this new-sprung spirit of disaffection at the Roman court were many and various, but the papal favour openly shown in Rome to the Florentine adherents of the Medici and the determined prosecution of the war of Urbino were of themselves capable of arousing the hostile jealousy of many members of the College. Amongst others, Raffaele Riario, the wealthiest Churchman in Rome and the senior cardinal, had been greatly exasperated by Leo's forcible expulsion from his realm of Francesco Della Rovere, the late Pope's nephew and Riario's own kinsman, and this personal displeasure was felt, though in a less degree, by the other cardinals who for divers reasons were attached to the interests of the Della Rovere family.   Francesco Soderini shared this dislike, though for a totally different cause, for he had been greatly incensed by Leo's open determination to wed his nephew Lorenzo, now styled the Duke of Urbino, with a French princess of royal birth instead of with a daughter of the burgher House of Soderini, according to the scheme originally arranged by Bernardo da Bibbiena at the late conclave ; and this impending breach of faith on Leo's part revived more fiercely than ever the slumbering enmity of the Florentine Cardinal. The whole College moreover had been deeply angered by the Pope's recent bestowal of scarlet hats, contrary to the pledge exacted from him prior to his election, although the number of cardinals so created before the spring of 1517 had not exceeded eight in number.[1]   For in the first year of his pontificate Leo had conferred the supreme honour upon his secretary Bernardo Dovizi and upon Lorenzo Pucci, both of them Tuscans, and

[1] Amongst them stands prominent the name of Thomas Wolsey, who had succeeded the late Cardinal Christopher Bainbridge in the see of York.

also upon Lorenzo Cybò, a youth of twenty, his own nephew and the grandson of Pope Innocent VIII., who had been the original promoter of the Medici's career in the Church;—"that which Innocent gave to me, to Innocent I restore," was the smiling Leo's sole retort to the many sharp criticisms passed upon him for this action. This moderate use of his legitimate prerogative proved however highly distasteful to the older members of the Sacred College, but that which especially served to rouse their jealousy and ire was the Pope's questionable conduct in regard to his cousin Giulio de' Medici, the most devoted but by no means the ablest counsellor Leo had at his command. Giulio, who had long wavered between the choice of a secular or an ecclesiastical career, had ridden at his kinsman's coronation procession in the capacity of a knight of Rhodes, but a few days later he made a final decision, accepting the archbishopric of Florence from Leo, who met the inevitable objection to Giulio's base birth by granting the new-made prelate a special dispensation enabling him to fill so exalted an office. This unusual form of favouritism gave no little offence, which was immeasurably increased, when shortly afterwards the Pope appointed a commission to inquire into all the circumstances of his cousin's alleged parentage with the obvious intention of declaring him the legitimate son and heir of that Giuliano de' Medici, who had been murdered by the Pazzi conspirators in the Duomo of Florence in 1478. This inquiry was so patent a sham and a subterfuge, that boundless indignation but little or no surprise was manifested, when this packed body of commissioners reported the new archbishop of Florence to be verily the actual child and heir of the murdered Giuliano by his true wife, a certain Florentine lady by name Simonetta Gorini, with whom he had contracted a secret marriage.[1]   On 20th September, 1513, accordingly, a papal proclamation, professing to be based on the finding of this commission, affirmed Giulio de' Medici to be legitimate, whereupon the scarlet hat was formally presented to the late Medicean bastard, the future Pope Clement VII.   Without doubt it was a natural impulse in Leo to raise to the purple, even by an artifice, one who was both closely related to him and deeply attached to his private interests, yet a proceeding so irregular and so unpleasantly reminiscent of bygone Borgian methods, caused the most unpleasant impression throughout all Italy.   Upon the newly created *Porporato*, bastard and upstart as he was generally regarded, fell the jealous dislike of his unwilling colleagues, whose hatred waxed hotter when they began to perceive the immense and increasing influence wielded by the Cardinal Giulio.   For it soon became evident that the more subtle and selfish counsel of this interloper was gradually supplanting the influence of the easy-going and less ambitious Bibbiena, the waning of whose intimacy with Leo can be traced in the growing power of the Cardinal de' Medici, albeit the latter was in taste, character and appearance the complete antithesis of his master.   "He was rather morose and disagreeable," writes Guicciardini, "than of a pleasant and affable temper; reputed avaricious; by no means trustworthy and naturally disinclined to do a kindness; very grave and cautious in all his actions; perfectly self-controlled and of great capacity, if timidity did not sometimes warp his better judgment."[2]

In spite however of the general dissatisfaction felt at

[1] Perhaps "la Bella Simonetta," whose portrait, ascribed to Botticelli, hangs in the Pitti Palace in Florence (Creighton, vol. v.).

[2] *Storia d' Italia*, lib. xi.

the sudden rise to power of this unpopular Medicean
bastard and at the long disastrous war of Urbino, it is
doubtful whether this state of discontent would ever have
broken out in open insurrection, but for the unbridled
passions of the boy-cardinal of Siena, the dissolute
Alfonso Petrucci, who had previously shown himself so
warm an advocate of Leo's claims during the late conclave. At the time of his visit to Florence in the past
winter, Leo had presumed to meddle in Sienese politics
by abetting the removal of Alfonso's brother Borghese
from the governorship of that city, and by helping to sub-
stitute for that young tyrant the more respectable
Raffaele Petrucci, a member of the same family, who
was Castellan of Sant' Angelo. Alfonso, not without
reason, now began to complain bitterly of the Pope's
ingratitude in return for his past services, and his indignant threats of vengeance found a ready echo in the
minds of several of his colleagues. The old Raffaele
Riario, willing to wound in secret and yet afraid to strike
openly, appears to have encouraged the silly youth,
whose fury was likewise inflamed purposely by Soderini,
Sauli and other malcontents in the Sacred College, including the Cardinal Adrian of Corneto, who is said to
have desired his master's speedy death for no other
reason than that a soothsayer had once declared to him
that the next Pontiff was destined to be one Adrian, a
person of mean birth but of great culture.[1] Assuming
this description of Leo's successor to apply to none other
than himself, the Cardinal Adrian with incredible folly
did not shrink from approving of Petrucci's violent
suggestions, which included a plan for stabbing the
Pontiff on some convenient occasion whilst out hunting.

[1] A curious prophecy which was actually verified in the election
of Adrian VI. in the Conclave of 1522. Jovius, lib. iii.

Willing instruments of assassination at that time were never lacking for the accomplishment of any plot, no matter how diabolical or dangerous of execution, so that a certain medical charlatan from Vercelli, one Gian-Battista by name, on overhearing Petrucci's unguarded threats and complaints, at once made known his readiness to compass the Pope's death on consideration of a suitable recompense. The plan proposed by Gian-Battista and adopted apparently by Petrucci and his friends, was that the doctor should be introduced at the Vatican as a skilful physician, who was well qualified to alleviate the Pope's painful ailment, and that, having once gained Leo's confidence, he should then secretly murder his unsuspecting patient by means of poisoned bandages. A secretary of the Cardinal Petrucci and also a Sienese captain, bearing the suggestive nick-name of Poco-in-testa, offered to participate in this horrible scheme, which might easily have been crowned with success, but for Leo's unexpected reluctance to admit another surgeon into the palace. Efforts were still being made to induce the Pope to accept the new physician's services, when the existence of the plot was suddenly revealed through the carelessness of a page, although Petrucci's own behaviour in withdrawing from Rome and opening negotiations with the Pope's enemy, the dispossessed Duke of Urbino, formed of itself a sufficient cause to excite the alarm of Leo, who, it must in fairness be admitted, had already warned the young cardinal of the peril of his treasonable conduct. Furious at his discovery of Petrucci's abominable plot, yet with true Medicean craft keeping his information a profound secret, Leo now invited Petrucci with affectionate words to return to Rome and even allowed the Spanish ambassador to send the young cardinal a safe-conduct couched in the most explicit terms. And the Cardinal of Siena, who seems to have been as gullible by nature as he was violent, was apparently satisfied with the papal promises, for he now proceeded towards Rome, although the court was marvelling at his extreme rashness in venturing thither under such circumstances. On reaching the gates, Petrucci was joined by Sauli, and the two princes of the Church with a large train of servants made their way without a thought of treachery to the Vatican, where on their arrival a most dramatic and disgraceful scene took place. For scarcely had the two cardinals entered the courtyard of the palace than by order of the Pope they were arrested and seized in spite of their indignant protests, Sauli tearing his rochet to shreds in his impotent rage, whilst Petrucci set to cursing Leo at the top of his voice. From the Vatican the two unfortunate men were forcibly removed to the castle of Sant' Angelo, to be thrust " into the most horrible of its underground dungeons, full of a cruel stench ".[1] Nor would the hard-hearted Medici allow even a single servant to attend to their wants, until the Sacred College in a body came humbly to entreat this favour on behalf of its imprisoned members. In vain did the Spanish envoy plead and reproach, quoting to the Pope the terms of the safe-conduct lately issued; Leo remained fixed in his resolve to make an example of these two conspirators against his authority. Meanwhile the Pontiff, who without any reasonable shadow of doubt had really been terrified by his late discovery, ordered the gates of the Vatican to be kept closed and securely guarded against an attempt upon his person which he averred was imminent. Having called public attention to his alarm by such measures of precaution, Leo's next step

---

[1] Jovius, lib. iii.

was to order the seizure of the venerable Cardinal Riario,
an incident which caused a profound impression in the
city, where people were heard openly to exclaim that
the House of Medici was at last about to wreak its long-
delayed vengeance upon the old envoy of Sixtus IV.,
who nearly forty years before had been present at the
conspiracy of the Pazzi in the Florentine Cathedral.   So
overcome with fear did this aged and luxurious prince of
the Church show himself at the moment of his arrest,
that being unable to move from sheer terror he had to be
borne in a litter from the papal ante-chamber to a distant
room in the Vatican, where although kept a close
prisoner he was treated with more consideration than his
luckless colleagues in the neighbouring fortress of Sant'
Angelo.

The consistory was now convoked in the utmost
haste, and here Leo, trembling with an angry excitement,
which some considered to be assumed rather than real,
fiercely demanded of the cardinals present the names of
all who were implicated in the recently unmasked plot.
After a lengthy and most undignified altercation, which
could be clearly overheard outside the apartment and became indeed in two hours' time the common talk of all
Rome, the dozen members present, dreading the Pope's
fury and quaking at the evil fate of Petrucci and Sauli, at
last compelled Francesco Soderini and Adrian of Corneto
to come forward and entreat for mercy upon their knees,
albeit in all probability their crime consisted in little else
than the uttering of coarse jests and the open expression
of their private ill-will against Leo.   The cardinals, now
thoroughly cowed and crestfallen, gladly submitted to
the immense fines, which were inflicted upon their companions kneeling in an agony of terror at the feet of the
enraged Pontiff, who scarcely deigned to notice their

presence or attitude. So high were the penalties fixed, that Soderini was shortly forced to retire from Rome, nor did he return thither during Leo's lifetime, whilst the Cardinal of Corneto at the first opportunity fled by stealth from the city, and having been hunted hither and thither by the papal minions was finally lost sight of and died in obscurity : truly a tragical ending to the prosperous career of that able but lowly born ecclesiastic, who for many years held the English see of Bath and Wells.[1] With regard to Riario, the Pope, somewhat to the surprise of those around him, showed a measure of his traditional clemency towards the old antagonist of his family, who had thus fallen helplessly into the toils. Riario was certainly mulcted in a huge ransom, but after an humiliating expression of repentance in public was eventually re-instated in his former dignities, although he prudently decided to spend the few remaining years of his long life at Naples.

As for the miserable Sauli and Petrucci, the former of whom is said to have shrieked at the very sight of the rack, both cardinals were before long induced to make a full confession of their aims, and indeed it was the admissions they had disclosed under stress of the most exquisite torture that had formed the gist of the charges subsequently brought against Riario, Adrian and Soderini. Sauli, as a Genoese citizen and therefore claimed as a subject by the French King, was able to secure the good offices of Francis I., as well as of the Pope's own brother-in-law Francesco Cybò, with the result that he was finally pardoned and released from his pestilential dungeon in Rome to be kept under strict

---

[1] For an account of Adrian, or Adriano da Castello as he is sometimes styled, the reader is referred to the article on this Cardinal in the *Dictionary of National Biography*, vol. i.

surveillance at Mont Rotondo, where he expired after much suffering during the ensuing year, not without some suspicion of foul play.   But Petrucci, that "Cupid of the Cardinals," the Medici's late playmate and favourite companion, seems to have possessed no friend powerful enough to intercede successfully on his behalf, and after some hesitation on Leo's part he was accordingly executed in his foul and gloomy cell by one Orlando, a Mohammedan hangman of the Roman court.   Common report averred that Petrucci was strangled on the night of 6th July, but others declared that he was beheaded with a kerchief tied over his eyes, cursing his perfidious master to the last and angrily refusing to make his confession or to receive the sacraments, telling the scandalised priest in attendance that "if he were doomed to lose his life, he cared nothing what became of his soul".[1]   The corpse of the late Cardinal of San Teodoro, only twenty-two years of age, was secretly interred after nightfall outside the walls of the city, and though the cruel fate of this comely youth, "who was surely born beneath some star of malign influence," may excite our compassion, it must be borne in mind that his cold-blooded execution, however harsh and ungenerous in Leo, succeeded in ridding the Sacred College of one of its most turbulent and disreputable members.   But the horrible story of Petrucci's career and ending serves well also to illustrate for us the swift variations of Fortune in the days of the Italian Renaissance, when in the briefest space of time a powerful nobleman or Churchman could be suddenly and without warning dashed down from a pinnacle of wealth and power into an abyss of infamy, such as can scarcely be conceived in our own days.   But if the punishment meted out to a cardinal of loose morals be accounted

[1] Fabroni, Appendix L.

bloodthirsty, what can be said concerning the awful
barbarities perpetrated upon the more humble accessories
to the crime—Gian-Battista of Vercelli, Poco-in-testa
and Petrucci's secretary—who after endless stretchings
upon the rack were dragged on hurdles through the
filthy streets of Rome, torn to pieces with red-hot pincers
and finally gibbeted whilst still breathing on the parapet
of the bridge of Sant' Angelo?

Some modern writers have essayed to prove that no
definite conspiracy ever existed on this occasion, and
that the actions of Petrucci and his associates were confined solely to vague threats against the life or authority
of Leo.   Nevertheless, all contemporary historians seem
to have believed in the actual existence of a deep-laid
plot of a terrible and even of an unparalleled nature
against the person of the Pontiff, whom the conspirators
were anxious to replace by a master more congenial to
their tastes and private ambitions.   How many of the
cardinals were privy to Petrucci's "accursed madness"
(*scelerato furore*), as Guicciardini styles it, it is impossible to conjecture, and of the five arrested it would be
no easy task to apportion the exact amount of guilt appertaining to each, though it would seem as if Riario and
Adrian sympathised with rather than abetted the scheme
of assassination.   That Leo was truly alarmed and
horrified there is no reason to deny, and even if his conduct throughout be adjudged both harsh and treacherous,
it is not unlikely that under the more severe Julius II.,
Sauli, Soderini, and perhaps Adrian would have shared
the evil fate of the wretched ringleader, Petrucci.   On
the other hand, it is evident that the versatile Medici,
perhaps at the advice of his cousin Giulio, contrived to
turn to good account his late alarm at the discovery of
the plot, which afforded him an excellent excuse for

levying heavy fines wherewith to replenish the empty
treasury out of the ill-gotten wealth of his greedy cardinals, with whose pecuniary losses nobody was likely to
sympathise ; and doubtless it was this reflection that induced Leo to extend an unexpected degree of mercy
to the unhappy Riario.   Nevertheless, regarded from
any and every point of view, the Conspiracy of the Cardinals forms one of the ugliest incidents in the whole
course of the Italian Renaissance, leaving the most unpleasant impression of the appalling corruption of the
Roman court and also of Leo's signal lack of that spirit
of clemency and forgiveness which had once been
reckoned his predominant virtue.

Having crushed the revolt in the Sacred College by
these prompt and drastic measures, Leo proceeded to
make a merciless use of his late victory in deciding to
create forthwith a batch of thirty-one cardinals : an unprecedented stroke of policy against which the surviving
members of the College were now powerless to protest.
Not only was such a step an event of the highest political
importance at the moment, but it may also be said to
have destroyed for ever that supremacy which a handful
of Italian cardinals, often consisting of the worst-
principled members of the College, had usurped since
the middle of the preceding century.   For during the
last four or five conclaves the election of a new Pope
had rested practically in the hands of a small and by
no means representative clique of Italian ecclesiastics,
who had at least on one occasion openly offered the
gravest dignity in all Christendom to the highest bidder ;
and it is therefore to Leo X. that the definite and final
overthrow of this corrupt and unedifying system is due,
although he deserves perhaps little credit for his action,
seeing that his immediate object in view was to subdue

the Sacred College for his own ends rather than to
purify it.   Nor were mercenary motives for Leo's policy
lacking, since it was no secret that the Pope was hard
pressed to find not only the funds necessary to the up-
keep of his luxurious court but likewise the money
needed to prosecute the dragging campaign in Urbino.
Very welcome in these financial straits were the fines
lately levied from Riario and Sauli, yet the total amount
thus raised did not prove adequate for the requirements
of the moment, and in consequence several of these
new-made *Porporati* were forced to contribute heavily
to the papal treasury as the price of their recent honours.
Yet it cannot be denied that Leo's choice of new
members showed in many instances his sharp discern-
ment of merit and his appreciation of learning and piety,
since the lengthy list includes such names as those of
the excellent Egidius of Viterbo, the historian and
principal of the Augustinians; of Tommaso de Vio of
Gaeta, head of the Dominican Order, commonly termed
the Cardinal Cajetan and celebrated as the theological
opponent of Martin Luther ; and the pious Adrian of
Utrecht, the simple and austere preceptor of the Archduke Charles, who was to become Leo's own successor.
Old kindness from the Lady Bianca Rangone of Modena
was repaid by a hat bestowed on her son Ercole, whilst
princes of the Royal Houses of France and Portugal
received the highest dignity of the Church in the persons
of Louis de Bourbon and of Alfonso, the infant son of
King Manuel I.   The ill-fated name of Petrucci was
still commemorated in the College by the elevation of
Raffaele Petrucci, the espousal of whose claims by Leo
had been the original cause of the late conspiracy with
its subsequent failure that had broken for ever the
usurped power of the Cardinals, and at the same time

LEO X CREATES THIRTY CARDINALS

had strengthened enormously the position of Leo and all his successors.   Three Florentine relations—Niccolò Ridolfi, Giovanni Salviati and Luigi Rossi—were likewise invested with the purple, and contrary to the best advice Leo advanced several Roman prelates, amongst them being that violent would-be patriot, Pompeo Colonna, whose bitter enmity towards the second Medicean Pontiff was destined ere long to prove so disastrous.   Royal birth, learning, piety, wealth, claims of family, claims of gratitude—all are represented in this list of cardinals, the largest creation in the annals of the Papacy.   But although many types of men were selected, it is clear that the prevailing intention of the Pontiff and his cousin Giulio was to obtain a subservient College, upon whose attitude full reliance could be placed for furthering the cherished but secret policy of extending the dominion of the Medici throughout Italy.   Of this historic nomination of cardinals in the autumn of 1517 an interesting memorial is still to be found in the great fresco executed by Vasari and his pupils in after years at the command of Cosimo I., the first Medicean Grand-Duke of Tuscany, Leo's distant kinsman in the male line, but his great-nephew on the distaff side, since Cosimo's mother had been a daughter of that Jacopo Salviati who had espoused Contessina de' Medici, the Pope's sister.   This large painting, which appears above the mantel-piece of the ante-chamber of the *Quartiere di Papa Leone X.* in the civic palace of Florence, affords us portraits of almost all the personages who took part in this ceremony.   Beneath an elaborate canopy upheld by twisted columns Leo X. is shown seated upon his throne in the act of investing the crowd of new-made cardinals, who pass before the papal chair in rapid succession.   The older members of the College appear sitting on benches with Giulio de' Medici and Bibbiena prominent in the fore-ground, whilst at the back of the scene the painter has introduced the figures of Michelangelo, Castiglione and other celebrated laymen, who regard the solemn rite with a languid interest. This fine fresco exactly faces the large representation of Leo's state entry into Florence, to which we have already made allusion, and forms an admirable pendant to it; indeed, the whole of this spacious but rather gloomy apartment is decorated with scenes, real or allegorical, to illustrate the leading events in the career of Giovanni de' Medici, Pope Leo X.

With this decisive victory over the Sacred College, Leo may be said to have attained the zenith of his fame and power, so that the road seemed clear of all obstacles in the way of that supreme mastery of Italy which constituted his hidden but undoubted aim, now that both Florence and Rome were safe in the hands of the Medici. The Council of the Lateran, so unwillingly convoked by the late Pope, had been already decently dismissed in the spring of 1517, so that there was little fear of inconvenient criticism in that quarter; the subdued College of Cardinals was believed to be ready to abet his future policy; his nephew, officially styled Duke of Urbino and created Captain-General of the Church, was shortly to be allied with a princess of the royal blood of France. In the early spring of the following year, 1518, the haughty young Lorenzo set out with a train surpassing in luxury and splendour that of any reigning monarch, and made his way towards Paris in order to represent his uncle at the approaching baptism of the Dauphin, as well as to celebrate his own nuptials with Madeleine de la Tour d'Auvergne, cousin of the French King. " Now that the Duke of Urbino has been expelled from his dominions, a similar fate awaits His Majesty of Ferrara," writes a bitter German critic of Leo's ambitious schemes, perhaps the great Ulrich von Hutten himself. " When both these dukes are dispossessed of their realms, then we shall have to salute that Florentine merchant, Lorenzo Medici, as King of Tuscany! . . . And since Fortune is variable and Leo may himself expire before his desires are fulfilled, and his successor may chase the papal nephew from his ill-gotten duchies, therefore Lorenzo must needs espouse some princess of France and purchase a principality in that land, in the event of his own expulsion from Italy in the future. Already the bargain has been struck, the documents have been attested, and the pledges on either side have been exchanged. ' Long, aye, too long, have we remained mere apothecaries' (*medici*), cry these upstarts, 'now is our opportunity to make ourselves kings and princes'!"[1] Such was the expression of opinion indulged in by German malcontents and reformers concerning the splendid embassy dispatched from Rome to the court of Francis, with the evident object of making the coming alliance of the heir of the Medici with the Princess Madeleine an imposing affair in the eyes of the rulers of Europe, for it was intended to be a glorification, conceived in an ostentatious and somewhat vulgar spirit, of the new-sprung sovereignty of the Florentine mercantile family which was now claiming to rank amongst royal Houses.

Even the prodigal Francis of France was amazed and visibly impressed by the young Lorenzo's show of state and by the costly nature of the Pope's gifts, which included thirty-six horses with attendants and fine harness, and also a gorgeous matrimonial bed for the

---

[1] *Exhortatio viri cujusdem*, etc., Roscoe, Appendix LXXIX., also vol. ii., p. 244, note 12.

betrothed pair constructed of tortoiseshell inlaid with mother-of-pearl and encrusted with numerous precious stones.[1] The Seigneur de Fleurange declared the jousts and banquets in Lorenzo's honour at the royal castle of Amboise to have been the most sumptuous ever held in France or even in all Christendom ; but he proceeds to pass some significant comments upon the bridegroom's state of health, which marked him out as wholly unfit for marriage, in consequence of which the French historian extends his pity to the innocent young bride, who in his sight was "trop plus belle que le marié ". But moral considerations weighed little or nothing in the selfish minds either of the King or Pope, each of whom had his private reasons for desiring the projected union, and thus this loveless political match was duly concluded amidst a succession of the usual bridal festivities. After a lengthy sojourn at the gay court of Francis, Lorenzo and his bride at last set their faces southward for Florence, where the duke, already in an advanced stage of his malady, took up his residence in the old palace in Via Larga. Haughty and self-centred, Lorenzo had ever been regarded with dislike or indifference by the Florentines, with the exception of the extreme partisans of his House, so that scant sympathy was shown for the dying prince or even for his youthful wife, who had also fallen into a pitiable state of ill-health. Restricting himself to the society of his secretary, Goro Gheri of Pistoja, and his boon companion and pander, Moro de' Nobili, the unpopular duke spent miserably the last months of a brief but wasted existence in the palace of his ancestors, which had once been tenanted by the wise Cosimo and the Magnificent Lorenzo. His increasing sickness made the duke either unable or unwilling to proceed to Rome,

[1] Fabroni, Appendix LXIX.

where the greatest anxiety was felt with regard to the expected heir of the House of Medici, and bitter was the chagrin of the disappointed Pontiff, when on 13th April, 1519, the news was brought him that the Duchess of Urbino had been delivered of a daughter.   Any further hope of a male heir to all the newly acquired glories of the Medici was shattered a fortnight later, when information was sent of the death of the unhappy Madeleine, who was herself followed to the grave on 6th May by her wretched husband, a perfect wreck of manhood, although only in his twenty-seventh year.

This stream of catastrophes spread perfect consternation within the Vatican, and moreover certainly caused the death of that intriguing woman, Alfonsina de' Medici, Lorenzo's mother, whose restless ambition had so often goaded on her husband, her son, and even her brother-in-law to acts of folly or aggression in the past.   With the tidings of the fatal illness of the last legitimate male of the Medicean House (save the Pontiff himself), the Cardinal Giulio, now become more than ever a personage of importance in his family, had been hastily despatched to Florence, but though he arrived there before the duke's actual decease, he does not seem to have visited the dying prince, who had invariably treated the base-born Churchman with disdain.   But on news of Lorenzo's death Giulio took prompt measures to ensure order throughout the city, and so judicious and conciliatory did he show himself, that public confidence was quickly restored.   The Cardinal took a prominent part likewise in the obsequies of his late cousin, who was interred within the basilica of San Lorenzo, with all the dismal pomp but without any of the genuine regret that three years before had accompanied his uncle Giuliano the Good to the tomb.   Arrogant and rough-mannered,

ambitious and dissipated, Lorenzo II. was truly exhibited
as the heir of his father Piero il Pazzo, and if we may
draw a fair inference from the character of himself and
of his only daughter, it appears no small fortune for
Florence and Italy that Lorenzo's legitimate offspring
was limited to the baby-girl, who was one day to become
famous or infamous as Caterina de' Medici, Queen of
France.

Not only did the Cardinal Giulio attend his relative
to the grave, but it was he who in after years caused
Michelangelo to erect that pair of splendid monuments,[1]
the wonder and delight of succeeding ages, which mark
the last resting places of Giuliano the Good and his unworthy nephew amidst the chill magnificence of that
echoing mausoleum, the New Sacristy of San Lorenzo.
With his form clad in a warrior's tunic and with head
covered by the plumed helmet sits eternally gazing into
space the worthless Medici, who was chosen to be the
ideal prince of Machiavelli's day-dreams. The statue's
air of perfect repose and of calm meditation has won the
epithet of *Il Pensieroso* for the artist's work, which offers
the strongest contrast with his feeble representation of
the charming and more virtuous Giuliano, whose pose
appears as stilted and affected as any despised production of the school of Bernini. But it is impossible for
the beholder to resist the dread fascination of that
mysterious half-hidden countenance of the Duke
Lorenzo, whose earthly existence has been thus im-
mortalised by the chisel of Michelangelo, by the brush
of the divine Raphael, and by the pen of Machiavelli,
albeit the sole grandson of the Magnificent Lorenzo was
undoubtedly the least worthy of remembrance of all
the Medici. Yet it is obvious that Michelangelo's famous

[1] See chapter xii.

STATUE OF LORENZO DE' MEDICI, DUKE OF URBINO

statue does not present us with the human portraiture
of the dissolute Lorenzo, the Medicean Duke of Urbino ;
on the contrary, with its noble air of meditation and its
majestic mien, it perpetuates the master's conception of
that ideal prince, whom Italy in her hour of sore need
and peril so urgently demanded, that perfect tyrant
whom the House of Medici, despite all its reputation for
genius and patriotism, signally failed to produce.   Not
only is that severe and cheerless Sacristy of San Lorenzo
a mortuary-chapel of departed Medici, it is also the
charnel-house of those high hopes of a free and united
Italy, which once centred round the living members of
the great Florentine House.

> There from age to age,
> Two ghosts are sitting on their sepulchres.
> That is the Duke Lorenzo.   Mark him well.
> He meditates, his head upon his hand.
> What from beneath his helm-like bonnet scowls ?
> Is it a face, or but an eyeless skull ?
> 'Tis not in shade, yet like the basilisk
> It fascinates and is intolerable.
> His mien is noble, most majestical.[1]

Cardinal Giulio de' Medici passed the whole of the
summer of 1519 in Florence, busily engaged in making
arrangements for the better government of the city, and
even inviting its leading citizens, and amongst them
Niccolò Machiavelli, who was ever striving to win the
favour of "these Medicean lords," to draw up suggestions for his own guidance.   Such marked ability did
Giulio display with regard to Florentine affairs, and so
tactful was his exercise of power during this and the
following three years, that Roscoe has not hesitated to
call them "the most brilliant period of his life".   Meanwhile the future fate of Florence was left hanging in the

[1] S. Rogers, *Italy*.

balance, for the Pontiff's intentions towards his native
city were quite unknown to his intimate counsellors,
and were probably as yet unfixed in his own mind.
For at one moment he would hint in all sincerity at a
coming restoration of political freedom, seeing that the
legitimate descendants of Cosimo, "the Father of his
Country," were all extinguished save himself, whilst at
other times it appeared evident that Leo was inclined
to keep a firm hand upon the city which he had recovered with such pains a few years before.   But whilst
Florence was thus enjoying a spell of rest and prosperity
under the supervision of the Cardinal Giulio, it was
finally decided that the Duchy of Urbino, which it had
cost so much treasure to seize and still more to retain,
should be forcibly annexed to the States of the Church,
although Lorenzo's infant girl was officially styled
Duchess of Urbino.   The cost of this disastrous enterprise, amounting to the enormous sum of 800,000 ducats,
Leo decided to debit in part to the reluctant Florentines,
who in return for their enforced payment were compensated with the conquered district of Montefeltre and the
great rock-fortress of San Leo.[1]   In October of this
same year Giulio, leaving Florentine administration in
the hands of Cardinal Passerini of Cortona, returned to
Rome, taking in his train the little " Duchessina," Caterina
de' Medici.   On her first appearance at the Vatican the
poor orphan girl was received in full state by the Pontiff,
who must have regarded this frail atom of humanity,
the offspring of diseased parents, with any but pleasur-
able feelings.   Yet such was the versatility of Leo's
mind that he could contrive to turn even so tragical and

---

[1] A vigorous fresco by Vasari, commemorating the capture of
San Leo, is included in the series of pictures in the Ante-chamber of
the *Quartiere di Papa Leone X.*

piteous an incident into an erudite jest; *Secum fert aerumnas Danaûm!*—she brings all the catastrophes of Hellas with her presence!—observed the Pope with an apt quotation out of his beloved classics, and the words thus idly spoken proved certainly prophetic with regard to the country over which the little Catherine was eventually fated to rule. Perhaps the Pontiff's deeply-lying chagrin might have been somewhat assuaged could he but have foreseen that the despised baby-girl before him, his great-niece, only five months of age, was to become a future Queen of France and the mother of three sovereigns and a Queen of Spain. But at this moment there was little indeed to cheer the mind of the Pope, who now found himself forced by a perverse fate to abandon all his cherished schemes of family aggrandisement, when his own burgher line was thus reduced to himself and the frail Duchessina. *Questa è troppo gran casa per si poca famiglia!*—so vast a mansion for so small a number!—had once sighed long ago the Pontiff's great-grandfather, the wise Cosimo of pious memory, as he wandered disconsolate after the loss of a favourite son through the halls of the palace in Via Larga; here was a repetition of Cosimo's sentiment in far more serious circumstances, when all the acquired power and splendour of the aspiring Medici were found concentrated in a priest and a sickly baby-girl. There was the Cardinal Giulio, it is true, the natural cousin whom he had legitimised, his most attentive counsellor and adherent; and there can be little doubt that from Lorenzo's death onward, the influence of the Cardinal gained a complete ascendancy over the forlorn Pontiff, whose foreign policy began to reflect more and more the private aims of that subtle and secretive Churchman. In addition to Giulio, there were the two younger

bastards, Giuliano's handsome and engaging little son
Ippolito, who was a favourite with the Pope, and that
swarthy and singularly unattractive child, Alessandro de'
Medici, whose real parentage remains a subject of
speculation, though in all likelihood he was the natural
son of the Cardinal Giulio himself rather than of his
reputed sire, the late Duke Lorenzo. Without a legitimate male heir save his distant kinsmen of the junior
branch of the family, of whom he took little notice and
was in fact believed to be jealous, Leo's original and
absorbing desire of founding a Medicean empire in Italy
was necessarily brought to an end, so that he began to
tire of the tedious routine of public business and henceforth to pursue his various amusements, particularly that
of the chase, with an ever-increasing ardour during the
few remaining years of his life. The conduct of foreign
policy therefore devolved largely upon the energetic
Cardinal, who, if he lacked Leo's natural talents, owned
far greater powers of application to business, so that he
now became the true exponent of Medicean statecraft
amidst the far-reaching changes impending in Europe.
For in the opening days of the year 1519 there had expired the old Emperor Maximilian, for whose end all
Europe had long been waiting with mingled feelings of
alarm and hope, whilst on 28th June of the same year,
in spite of strong opposition from the courts of Rome
and Paris, the youthful Charles, King of Spain and
Naples, was duly elected emperor with the title of Charles
V., and thus from the very extent and resources of his
vast realms was able to supplant the indignant Francis
of France as the leader of Europe and the natural
arbiter of her fortunes. For nearly two years Leo and
the Cardinal de' Medici continued to play at their
favourite game of political vacillation between the two

rival powers, but on 29th May, 1521, a definite treaty of alliance between Pope and Emperor was signed to the infinite alarm of the French King. Besides the fear of the Imperial displeasure, Charles' promise to restore to the Holy See the towns of Parma and Piacenza, the deprivation of which by Francis had never ceased to rankle in the Pontiff's mind, undoubtedly operated to impel Leo to this compact. For although the hope of founding a Medicean kingdom in Italy had perished eternally for lack of heirs, yet Leo was easily able to fall back on the former ecclesiastical policy of Julius II., which aimed at extending the papal boundaries and at driving the intruding foreigner out of Italy. To keep Urbino and Modena for the Holy See and to regain the lost cities of Parma and Piacenza for the Papacy became now the main object of the Medici's policy, which belongs rather to European than to Italian history.

Early in the summer of the same year the long-threatened war between King and Emperor broke out in Lombardy, that favourite theatre of all military operations. Owing to the poor tactics of the French commander, the Seigneur de Lautrec, the Imperial army, supported by the papal forces, was able to form a junction with the Swiss mercenaries, and to proceed without further difficulty towards Milan. That city quickly surrendered to the vast army led by the Marquis of Pescara, the husband of the celebrated Vittoria Colonna, and ere long Parma and Piacenza were also in the hands of the conquerors of Milan.

CHAPTER XI

DEATH AND CHARACTER OF LEO X

What grieves me most is to hear that your bed is constantly surrounded by physicians, who never agree in any opinion, because it would be accounted derogatory to the dignity of the second to think like the first and repeat his views of the case. It is certain, as Pliny observes, that wishing to make a name by their discoveries they try all manner of experiments upon us and sport with our lives. Physicians acquire their art at our expense, by killing us they learn means of cure, and they are the only persons permitted to slay with impunity. Holy Father! regard as a troop of foes all that crowd of doctors which surrounds thee. Think of the Emperor Hadrian's epitaph—*Turbâ medicorum perii!* (I died of a multitude of doctors!) (*Letter of Petrarch to Pope Clement IV.*).

THE news of the fall of Milan and the subsequent recovery of Parma and Piacenza by the Church was sent to Rome with all possible speed by the Cardinal Giulio de' Medici, who was with the Imperial forces in person, the glad tidings reaching the Pope about sunset of Friday, 22nd November, 1521, at his villa of the Magliana. Leo had just returned from the chase, somewhat tired and heated, but on reading the Cardinal's welcome despatch, he hastily summoned the papal master of ceremonies to his presence in order to confer with him as to the propriety of having public rejoicings in the city. To the Pontiff's eager inquiry, that wary personage made reply that it was not customary for the Holy See thus to celebrate the result of any battle waged between two Christian monarchs, unless the Church had some special interest at stake, but of such a case the Pontiff himself, as head of the Church, would naturally be the best judge.   Leo, amused by this ingenious piece of sophistry, at once answered that he had every reason to rejoice, whereupon Paris de Grassis declared it his manifest duty to return openly thanks to the Almighty for the late benefits obtained.   The Pope accordingly commanded his master of the ceremonies to summon a full consistory of the cardinals for the ensuing Wednesday, and "having said this he retired to his chamber, where he remained resting for some hours, after which he was reported later to complain of feeling unwell.   And indeed on the following Wednesday no consistory could be held."[1]   Such is the bald statement that Paris de Grassis has presented to us concerning Leo's brief but fatal illness, the first symptoms of which undoubtedly appeared on the very evening that brought him the good news of the victory of the Imperial army and of the desired restoration of Parma and Piacenza to the Church, an event on which he had set his heart to an exorbitant degree.

According to common belief the mental excitement induced by this welcome but sudden intelligence, acting upon an unwieldy frame already weakened by chronic disease, was the direct cause of Leo's premature death, a few days before attaining his forty-sixth birthday. Over-heated, fatigued and agitated by the recent news, the Pope was seized with a violent chill, when after a close damp day a bitter north wind arose at sunset, sweeping over the Roman Campagna and blowing with icy breath into the courtyard of the villa, where the papal servants were already lighting a huge bonfire in honour of the victory.   Leaning from his casement in the teeth of the blast to applaud the efforts of his men-

[1] Roscoe, Appendix CII.

at-arms in the courtyard, Leo certainly contracted the
feverish catarrh, which compelled him two days afterwards to return to the Vatican, but which the doctors of
the court declared to be of no great consequence, although
he was far too unwell to attend the consistory fixed for the
following Wednesday.   As we have had many occasions
to remark, it was a superstitious age, that drew strong
inferences from trivial chances or portents, so that, when
Leo on returning to the Vatican found in his own apartment
a large model of the beautiful tomb which Torrigiano,
the Tuscan sculptor, had been commissioned to erect in
Westminster Abbey for the late King Henry VII. of
England, he became not a little distressed in mind at so
ominous a coincidence.[1]   Indeed, the sight of Torrigiano's
model seems to have inflicted a nervous shock upon the
ailing Pontiff, who gradually grew worse until "on
Sunday, the first day of the month of December, at
about the seventh hour, Pope Leo X. expired of a
violent chill without anyone warning him that his sickness was mortal, since the physicians all protested he was
but slightly indisposed owing to the cold he had taken
at the Magliana".

Various highly contradictory accounts have been
transmitted to us of the Medici's last moments.   One
of these relates how Leo expired in an agony of remorse
for his unhappy countrymen butchered nine years before
by the cruel Spanish soldiery at Prato, and how his
dying ears were filled with their piteous groans, whilst
the Pope in his terror shrieked aloud "*Pratum me
terret!*"   Another description is from the pen of Fra
Piacentino, a canon of the Lateran, who moralises at
some length upon Leo's miserable and lonely end, with
nobody beside him save Fra Mariano Fetti, the arch-

[1] Jovius, lib. iv.

jester, who remained with his dying master to the last, "as a straw clings to an empty sack". "Think upon God, Holy Father!" the Cowled Buffoon is stated to have cried on this sad occasion, to which exhortation the poor Pope could only make reply by calling aloud thrice on the Almighty: "Dio buono! Dio buono! Dio buono!"[1] Jovius, on the other hand, who is a far better authority, attributes a more dignified as well as more probable termination to the career of the great Pontiff. "Scarcely," relates the learned Bishop of Nocera, "had Leo recognised the fatal character of his malady and the rapid approach of his last moment upon earth, than he lost all consciousness and was hurriedly taken from this world. Nevertheless, some few hours before his decease, he clasped his hands and raised them to Heaven in all humility, whilst with upturned eyes he gave thanks to God, openly professing that he could meet the stroke of death with calmness, now that he had seen Parma and Piacenza restored to the Church without any spilling of blood, and also the defeat of the Church's haughty foe, the King of France."[2]

It is difficult to extract the true story of Leo's last hours from statements so varied, but all accounts agree in the circumstance that the final stage of the Pope's illness was terribly swift and that a fatal ending was quite unexpected both at the Roman court and in the city. That Leo really died unattended save by Fra Mariano appears most improbable; seeing that the foreign ambassadors were constantly making inquiry and that the Pope's own sister, Lucrezia Salviati (whom the Venetian envoy accuses of laying hands on every object in the Vatican at her brother's death—*sgombrò il palazzo di tutto*) was actually residing in Rome at the

[1] Roscoe, vol. ii., p. 467, note 32.   [2] Jovius, lib. iv.

time. Nor has the well-known story, that Leo expired without receiving the last sacraments, ever been proved, though it is not impossible that his fearfully sudden end may have allowed no time for the due performance of the last rites of the Church. Nevertheless, a rumour to this effect afforded an opportunity to some malicious wit, said on doubtful authority to be no less a person than the poet Sannazzaro, to insult the memory of the dead Pontiff by the composition of a scandalous distich :—

> Sacra sub extremâ si forte requiritis horâ
> Cur Leo non potuit sumere ; Vendiderat ![1]

"Thou didst creep into our midst like a fox ; thou didst live amongst us like a lion ; and thou hast died like a dog "[2]—a repetition of the cruel epigram composed two centuries before on the death of Boniface VIII.— was another of the satirical lampoons published in Rome concerning the deceased Pontiff, who only a few hours previously had been the object of universal flattery. Yet the sound of these chance notes of discord was lost in the general chorus of praise and wailing which supervened on the news of Leo's demise in so sudden a manner and at so early an age, for the poets and scholars of Rome and Florence, whom the Pope had entertained so lavishly during his reign, were vying with each other in the preparation of elegies and laments for the passing of an ideal patron, whose equal both in learning and in liberality they were never likely to look upon again. Extravagant as it may appear, the epitaph placed on the Medici's temporary tomb in St. Peter's echoed

---

[1] Without the Church's sacraments Pope Leo died, I'm told ;
How could he e'er receive again what he himself had sold?
— Fabroni, p. 238.

[2] Apud nos intravit ut vulpis ; vixit ut leo ; exiit ut canis.

faithfully the heartfelt grief of the members of that papal
Parnassus, which Leo had called into existence :—

Deliciae humani generis, Leo Maxime, tecum
Ut simul illuxere, interiere simul.[1]

Scarcely had Leo breathed his last and the court and
city of Rome were filled with utter consternation, than
the physicians, with the Paduan, Bernardino Speroni,
at their head, began to dilate upon the suspicious nature
of the late Pope's illness and death.   The cardinals at
the earnest request of the doctors accordingly ordered
an autopsy of the body to be made, with the inevitable
result that these ignorant physicians at once began to
prate of symptoms of poisoning, that universal bugbear
of an age wherein the science of medicine had sunk to
its lowest depth.   Many persons, from the King of France
and the Duke of Urbino to the meanest scullions of the
palace, were suggested as likely individuals to have com-
passed or carried out a fell deed, for which in reality
there was not a tittle of evidence forthcoming.   Indeed,
Leo's death constituted a typical case in which the utter
failure of the medical men to cure a malarial fever complicated by long-standing disease, and the spirit of the
age which promptly sought for a criminal motive in the
sudden demise of any personage of note, combined together in attributing so unexpected an event to the
agency of poison.   Bernarbò Malespina, the papal cup-
bearer, was now apprehended at the request of these incompetent doctors, and cast into Sant' Angelo, whence
the unfortunate and innocent man was only liberated by
the order of Cardinal de' Medici, who with more common-
sense than the physicians, promptly released Malespina

[1] Great Leo, all the joys of life that be
Go mourning to thy tomb and die with Thee!
                              —Fabroni, p. 239.

on hearing the absurd details of the charge. Even the faithful Serapica, who had everything to lose and nothing to gain by being deprived of a generous master, was regarded with some degree of suspicion, and the poor little man's decent melancholy after Leo's death was with true Italian reasoning set down to the deepest cunning to conceal his supposed crime. Possibly but for the mistaken handling of the medicos, Leo, though in delicate health, might have recovered by means of ordinary measures and by a strict avoidance of the absurd and dangerous drugs supplied to him by Speroni and his colleagues. But, like all the males of his family, Leo did not possess the robust constitution that the time required ; "his head," remarks Vettori, "was always choked with catarrh and his appetite was so capricious that he would hardly touch food one day and on the next would eat to repletion ".[1] A quiet and regular mode of living might certainly have saved the Pope on this occasion, and have preserved his life for many years to come. For in spite of the opinions of several contemporaries, who honestly believed in the fantastic theories of the doctors, it seems fairly obvious that Leo X. expired as the victim of medical incompetence rather than of a crime for political ends, as the Venetian envoy, the personal friend of Speroni, at once hinted to his government.

The Pope's corpse, after having been cut up and dissected to satisfy the curiosity of the physicians, was buried in St. Peter's with great haste and with small pomp, for the papal treasury was well-nigh empty, and the Florentine bankers in Rome, who saw ruin staring them in the face owing to Leo's untimely death, were naturally in no humour to advance large sums of money

[1] Villari, vol. ii., p. 254.

upon a costly funeral worthy of the Papal Mæcenas. Many years, in fact, elapsed before a monument was reared to recall the memory of Leo X., and his existing tomb in the choir of the great Dominican church of Santa Maria sopra Minerva—no inappropriate temple to enshrine the recollection of the brief reign of the Goddess of Learning in Rome—is due to the generosity of the Pope's nephew, Cardinal Ippolito de' Medici, who cherished many instances of Leo's kindness to him in childhood. Antonio da Sangallo is credited with the design, and Baccio Bandinelli with the execution of this mediocre specimen of Renaissance art, which is wholly unfit to serve as the depository of the ashes of Giovanni de' Medici, Pope Leo X., or to rank as "a monument of the Golden Age of Italy, which is for ever associated with the names of Leo and the Medici, just as the age of Horace was linked with those of Mæcenas and Augustus ".[1] In short, this erection of a later period obviously belongs to that type of mausoleum which strives to be imposing through mere size and pathetic by means of expense. The large white marble statue of the Pontiff, with the left hand grasping the keys of St. Peter and with the right elevated in an eternal but languid benediction, stands out clear against the background of dark basalt, but has a singularly heavy and lifeless aspect. Nor can the allegorical figures and bas-reliefs upon the monument itself claim to be considered works of art. Opposite to Leo's tomb, and identical with it in treatment and design, stands that of the second Medicean Pope, Clement VII., whose handsome bearded face and more graceful figure appear to better advantage than the clumsy and undignified form of his happier predecessor. Thus in the choir of the famous church "are

[1] F. Gregorovius, *Tombs of the Popes*, p. 98.

Fortune and Misfortune represented in the tombs of two
kinsmen of a celebrated family ; the two reverses of the
coin of life ".[1]   Both monuments in their heavy classical
setting combine ill with the Gothic architecture and the
gaudy painted windows of the Dominican church, and
comparatively few persons take the trouble to penetrate
behind the choir screen to inspect these rather feeble
productions of Florentine sculptors.   At the foot of
Leo's tomb a marble slab in the pavement proclaims to
the passing stranger that the cultured and erudite Pietro
Bembo, friend and secretary of the Papal Mæcenas,
reposes at the feet of the master whom he survived for
nearly a quarter of a century.   By a curious chance, at
the rear of Leo's ponderous monument, in the northern
ambulatory of the choir, is to be seen a simple effigy,
which is far better known and revered than the monstre
tombs of the Medicean Pontiffs, for it is nothing less than
the carved slab which denotes the last resting-place of
the gentle monk Giovanni of Fiesole, known to all the
world as the saintly painter, Fra Angelico.   It would be
impossible to find a sharper contrast than that afforded by
the two figures of that jovial child of Fortune, the first
Medicean Pope, and his humble countryman, the simple
monk from aery Fiesole, whose emaciated form, worn
with prayer and fasting, meets our eyes with arms
meekly folded across the breast and with the beautiful
head reposing on its stony tasselled pillow.   Yet that
Italy could produce two such diverse types of Churchmen in the years of the Renaissance is not the least of
the many marvels of that incongruous age.   Thus Leo
X. stands for the power, the splendour, the paganism,
the patronage, the learning and the intense worldliness
of that period ; the gifted Dominican monk for the ex-

[1] F. Gregorovius, *Tombs of the Popes.*

treme simplicity and piety that found their vent in the
painting of sacred masterpieces, such as all succeeding
ages have failed lamentably to rival in their naïve but
exquisite loveliness.

> Non mihi sit laudi quod eram velut alter Apelles,
> Sed quod lucra tuis omnia, Christe, dabam—[1]

such are the opening lines of the Latin epitaph of the
holy Tuscan painter, who rejected the gauds and lucre
of this life, and worked solely for the glory of God,
Whose reward, he well knew, far surpassed all that the
rulers of earth could bestow.   On the other hand, we
behold one in whom all the pleasures and duties of life
alike were centred ; one who allowed the spiritual ideals
of the monk of Fiesole to be utterly eclipsed by the con-
tending forces of flattery and worldly power.   Verily,
Leo X. and Fra Angelico have obtained a portion of
their due reward in the verdict of succeeding generations.

.   .   .   .

It ought to be unnecessary to remind the reader that
the character and career of Giovanni de' Medici, Pope
Leo X., ought in all fairness to be judged by a contemporary and not by a modern standard of ethics and ideas.
Like his father before him, Leo was essentially a
Florentine of the Renaissance, endowed with all the
tastes, virtues and failings of the great citizens of Florence during that epoch.

"In everything," remarks Herr Ludwig Pastor,
Leo's latest German biographer, "he was truly a son of
his time, wherein the good and the bad were so closely
intermingled.   His whole nature reveals an extra-

---

[1] Apelles, fame was mine ; 'twas nought to me
Save that, O Christ, I gave all gain to Thee !

ordinary mixture of praiseworthy and un-praiseworthy
qualities ;—that nature, light, gay and many-sided, which
only too willingly cast aside all that was serious, deep
and original.   Shining in all branches of the intellectual
movement of the Renaissance, he is particularly eminent
in this, namely, that he draws to himself men of the
most opposite character and of diverse nationality."[1]

His many political shifts, which were the despair of
contemporary sovereigns and excite the indignant surprise
of modern critics, were, however, by no means censured
severely in his own age ; indeed, men found more to
admire than to reprobate in Leo's selfish and tortuous
policy.   In any case, some excuse for this is to be
sought in the difficult position in which he was placed on
the papal throne, midway between the rival powers of
the Spanish-Austrian Empire on one side and of France
on the other.   As the weakest member of the triumvirate
of Spain, France and the Papacy, Leo always tried
to make up in cunning what he lacked in real support.
And, moreover, taught from his infancy at his father's
court to be both secretive and self-seeking, he had not
been improved by the long years of poverty and enforced exile, during which he had been compelled to
hide even his natural ambition of a Medicean restoration
in Florence.   From an excess of caution in these days
of penury and insignificance, he had grown gradually so
steeped in the arts of dissimulation, that on attaining to
real and settled power, he found himself quite unable
to follow any straight path or to commit himself to any
fixed and open aim, like the more candid Julius II.
In short, duplicity became a second nature to him.
"Never," remarked the legate Aleander in after years,
" have I met with a man so secretive and averse to

[1] *Leo X.*, chap. x.

pursuing a definite policy." Nevertheless, we must give Leo credit for a genuine if vague desire to obtain the expulsion of the French and Spanish invaders out of Italian territory. Such a noble and patriotic aspiration may have been subsidiary to ignoble and private aims, yet it undoubtedly occupied the Pope's mind, even if, in the unkind phrases of an English critic, "it divided his attention with manuscripts and sauces, painters and falcons".[1] But the grand conception, though hidden to many observers, was certainly existent, and was perceptible to the sharp eyes of Machiavelli. "It was this great though mutable ambition of Leo's that continually deceived Machiavelli," writes Professor Villari. "It was thus that the Florentine secretary had been inspired to compose his *Prince*, and had despatched so many letters to Vettori and others in order to feed the flame. But whenever seeming to burn most brightly, the fire always expired on a sudden without leaving a spark behind."[2]

Of Leo's personal character, we trust a correct idea has been formed from the preceding pages of this work. That he ascended the papal throne with the highest reputation for culture, virtue and peaceful inclinations, we have already shown; and we have also endeavoured to explain how this early esteem was lost, both in the eyes of his own generation as well as of posterity, through the Pope's constant frivolity and selfish ambition. It is possible that to a certain extent the Medici's nature was transformed for the worse by the new-found power, the wealth and the adulation, which came to him as Pope after many years spent in adversity; but it seems hard to imagine, if he were in reality so good as he was reputed, that his elevation to the pontificate proved the utter ruin

[1] Macaulay, *Essay on Machiavelli*.
[2] Villari, vol. ii., pp. 253, 254.

of his morals, and that he grew vicious instead of more virtuous. Without speculating further as to this point, it will be sufficient to quote Guicciardini's moderate appreciation of Leo X. as "a prince, who greatly deceived the high expectations entertained of him, when he was raised to the Papacy, since he therein displayed more cunning and less goodness than the world had imagined of him. . . . Yet he passed for a good prince, though I dare not say of an Apostolic goodness, seeing that in our corrupt times the virtue of a Pontiff is commended, when he does not surpass the wickedness of other men."[1]

Grave charges of immorality have been levelled at Leo certainly, but only by those who lived in later ages and were highly prejudiced, and such persons seem to have based their attacks mostly on a somewhat obscure passage in the Fourth Book of Jovius' *Life of Leo X.* These scandalous whispers may promptly be rejected, since there is to be found no definite charge in any contemporary writer of personal impropriety on the Pope's part, in whatever degree he may be held answerable for the evil morals prevailing at his court, or for the vicious tone in the society of Rome during his pontificate.

Even more serious, but likewise more improbable, than this vague accusation of gross conduct is that of blasphemous infidelity, still occasionally to be encountered in old-fashioned works of a markedly Protestant tendency, for it is true that "the most fruitful cause of animosity against Leo X. is to be found in the violence of religious zeal and sectarian hatred".[2] It is easy to comprehend how such a charge came at a later date to be levelled at the Papal Mæcenas, the "pagan" Pope, who delighted

[1] *Storie d' Italia*, lib. xi.
[2] Roscoe, vol. ii., p. 475.

in the art and language of antiquity, but it ought to be superfluous to describe this insinuation as a base calumny. For it is founded mainly on a famous and oft-quoted, but impudently mendacious statement contained in a scurrilous treatise called the *Pageant of Popes* by John Bale,[1] who therein openly professed it his intention "to give the Roman Church double according to her works". This tract, which bristles throughout with historical inaccuracies, contains the following outrageous anecdote concerning Leo X. : "On a time when cardinal Bembus did move a question out of the gospell, the pope gave him a very contemptuous answere, saying, *All ages can testify enough how profitable that fable of Christe hath bin to us and our companie*".[2] It stands to reason that this remark is a spiteful and monstrous invention of a rabid or unscrupulous Reformer, and the same comment may reasonably be applied to a somewhat similar tale ; namely, that Leo's secretary, the aforesaid Bembo, strictly enjoined his colleague Sadoleto to refrain from studying the Vulgate, lest its indifferent Latin might spoil his elegant and graceful style of writing. On the contrary, there exists much evidence to prove that Leo was personally most conscientious in his public religious duties. No contemporary writer has given the smallest hint as to the Pope's unbelief, open or concealed, nor has modern research in the archives of the various Italian cities revealed the slightest ground for such an insinuation. From his childhood the Pontiff had been expressly educated with a view to his attaining to the

---

[1] John Bale, formerly a Carmelite monk at Norwich and later a staunch upholder of the Reformed religion, was appointed Bishop of Ossory in 1552. On Mary's accession he had to fly to the Continent, but returned to England in 1559, dying at Canterbury in 1563.

[2] " Quantum nobis nostrisque ea de Christo fabula profuerit, satis est omnibus sæculis notum " (Roscoe, vol. ii., p. 490, note 30).

highest rank in the Church—"together with his nurse's milk," writes Politian with genuine enthusiasm, "did he suck in piety and religion, preparing himself even from his cradle for the holy offices". Even if Leo's notorious frivolity and love of amusement may afford some ground for the allegation of vicious habits, Bale's absurd charge of atheism can be accounted scandalous only in its original inventor.

It is certain, that at least outwardly, Leo was always most diligent in his ecclesiastical duties and orthodox in his expressed opinions, exhibiting to the world thereby an edifying contrast with the unseemly behaviour of Julius II., who was habitually careless of all ceremonial, openly showing his impatience thereof both in manner and countenance. Leo, on the other hand, took a dignified part in endless services, and Paris de Grassis describes how during the protracted ceremonies in hot weather he used to observe the exhausted Pope wiping the perspiration with a kerchief from his streaming face. Daily Leo was wont to hear Mass in the beautiful oratory of Nicholas V. with its series of exquisite frescoes from the brush of the holy Fra Angelico. He kept rigorously the days of fasting ordained by the Church; invariably he went to confession before celebrating Mass in public. He took a deep interest in the training of the Sistine choir, lecturing the papal choristers not only on the subject of music but also on their moral behaviour out of service hours. "His religious duties he fulfils conscientiously," comments the Venetian envoy, "but he likes to enjoy life, and takes an inordinate pleasure in the chase."[1] Even Paolo Sarpi, the outspoken friar of Venice, admits that Leo brought many good qualities to

---

[1] He is *buon religioso*, admits Marco Minio.

the papal throne, and proceeds to say he would have made a perfect Pope, if to these good qualities he had but joined some recognition of the claims of Religion and shown some inclination to true piety, but for neither of these things did he care much.[1] These comments of Sarpi, Guicciardini, the Venetian ambassadors and others do not present a very favourable account of Leo's conduct, yet they afford sufficient evidence to contradict these flimsy charges of religious indifference or atheism.

It is no difficult task to detect and point out the real failings in Leo's character, those failings which have earned for him, not altogether with justice, the unenviable reputation of being reckoned amongst the evil Pontiffs of the secular Papacy. It was his extravagance, his constant waste of time and treasure on pursuits which, though not immoral in themselves, had become criminal in his case, because they were carried to excess. Added to this extravagance, which involved the Holy See in endless difficulties, was Leo's besetting sin of frivolity, his persistent refusal to take his position seriously. Extravagance and frivolity ;—to these two moral failings in Leo X. can be traced, directly or indirectly, many of those events which were destined shortly to disturb Western Christendom. If Leo had not been so engrossed in idle and selfish amusements, he could not have failed to discern the religious storm that was brewing in Germany, the storm that the Medici's undeniable tact and ability might have done so much to allay. But Leo preferred to shut his eyes and "to enjoy the Papacy," basking in the sunshine of adulation and luxury beneath a blue serene sky, wherein he deliberately refused to notice the distant shadows of the thunder-clouds of the

[1] *Historia del Concilio Tridentino*, lib. i.

tempest coming from beyond the Alps. That cynical French proverb, *Après moi le déluge*, might even have been taken for the true motto of this papal hedonist.

"In the breast of Leo the Tenth dwelt two souls!" exclaims Professor Pastor, and indeed this sentiment will be echoed by all who have cared to study the life and pontificate of Giovanni de' Medici, Pope Leo X. But it is more kind and pleasant to look upon the brighter side of his character, and to regard Leo as the splendid patron of art and letters, as the learned and genial son of Lorenzo the Magnificent, as the friend of Raphael and the incarnation of the glories of the Leonine Age. Let us try to forget his share in the evil deeds that preceded the movement of Martin Luther, his perfidy towards his old companion Petrucci, his utter failure to fulfil those high hopes that Christendom had formed at his election ; let us think rather of him as the Supreme Pontiff

> Whom Europe views
> With wondering awe, her pastor and her guide,
> From great Lorenzo sprung ; the brightest Star
> Of Medicean fame, with conscious pride
> Whom his own Florence hails ; and from afar
> The sceptr'd rulers of the nations own,
> And as their lord obey ; in towering state
> Imperial Leo named, who bears alone
> The key that opes Olympus' lofty gate.[1]

[1] Roscoe, vol. i., Appendix XXXII. "*Translation of the Greek verses of Marcus Muscarus prefixed to the works of Plato.*"

CHAPTER XII

CLEMENS SEPTIMUS PONTIFEX MAXIMUS

Many a stone has been cast at the memory of Clement VII. by Italian writers of all ages, from his own to the present, for postponing his patriotism to the gratification of less worthy passions. But had the majority of his countrymen been justified in casting the first stone of reproach for such a sin, their unabated longing for such a deliverance of Italy would not have been at the present day (1855) ungratified (T. A. Trollope).

THE interval separating the reigns of the two Medicean Pontiffs was destined to be a brief one. In the middle of December, 1521, the Cardinal de' Medici hurried full of eager hopes back to Rome from the Imperialist camp in Lombardy, and presented himself in ample time for the conclave which opened on the 28th day of the same month. But in spite of the pervading Medicean influence (for more than half the members of the Sacred College had been created by the late Pontiff), a strong faction, headed by Francesco Soderini, the most persistent foe of the House of Medici, was already formed to oppose the expected election of Leo's cousin. So fierce and powerful was this cabal in the College, that ere long Giulio de' Medici thought it useless to prosecute his candidature further, and accordingly declared himself willing to support any fit nominee of the Imperialist party. Notwithstanding the critical and even alarming aspect of the political situation, the utmost desire to obtain the tiara was exhibited by nearly all the cardinals, foremost amongst them being that partially reformed libertine Alessandro Farnese, and the powerful English favourite of Henry VIII., Thomas Wolsey, Cardinal of York. It was finally only by means of something resembling a tacit compromise, that the thirty-nine cardinals assembled almost unanimously decided upon the choice of the most virtuous and also the least known of their number in the person of Adrian of Utrecht, Cardinal of Tortosa. Adrian Dedel, a Fleming of lowly birth, was in his sixty-third year when he was thus called upon to fill the vacant throne of the resplendent Leo X., who had included his humble successor, then tutor to the future Emperor Charles V., in his wholesale creation of cardinals in 1517. This unexpected selection of one who was at once a saintly ascetic, a foreigner, and a plebeian aroused a storm of angry derision in the city and court of Rome; nor on the other hand did the news bring any delight to the recipient of this high dignity. For Adrian, then absent in Spain, heard of his elevation with a deep groan, abandoning himself to genuine despair at the thought of the awful responsibility and the difficulty of the uncongenial task before him. Late in the summer of 1522, the new Pontiff, entitled Adrian VI., the last German and indeed the last non-Italian Pope, entered the gates of Rome, whose regeneration he professed himself so anxious to effect, and at once set to inaugurate a series of pious but fruitless endeavours to inspire some true Christian ideals into the voluptuous and extravagant city, which was the capital of Western Christendom. The melancholy tale of poor Adrian's hopeless attempt to reform the Church and to infuse some jot of Christian conscience and charity into those two selfish potentates, Francis of France and his own inept pupil the Emperor, lies wholly outside the

limits of this work.   After a residence barely exceeding
a twelvemonth in "that sink of all iniquity," the unhappy
Pope (whose reign was marked, amongst other misfortunes which he was powerless to avert, by the capture
of Rhodes and the expulsion of its Christian knights
from their ancient citadel) fell sick of a strange consum-
ing malady, which according to the learned Roman
physicians was due to poison administered by some agent
of the French King ; although a heart chilled by a sense
of complete failure and deeply injured by the callous
apathy or bitter enmity of those around him in Rome
seems to have constituted the true cause of Adrian's
death on 14th September, 1523.   All Rome was delighted at the release from the presence of this spiritual
reformer, whose humble figure, "in immediate contrast
with Leo X. and against the storm-lighted background
of the German Reformation, is one of the most tragic
in the history of the Papacy".[1]   Assuming, probably
not without reason, that the Pope's demise was acceler-
ated by the nostrums of his court physician, the wits of
the city hung grateful garlands to the door-posts of that
functionary, with an inscription naming him the liberator
of the Roman Senate and People from the late foreign
domination : an attention which proved more embarras-
sing than flattering to the personage selected for this
civic honour.

Shortly after Adrian's arrival in Rome, Giulio de'
Medici, fearing the influence of his old rival Francesco
Soderini, who stood high in the new Pope's favour, had
retired to Florence, which he proceeded to govern with
tact and clemency in the name of the family whereof he
had now become the most influential member, since he
was the guardian of the young Lorenzo's heiress,

[1] F. Gregorovius, vol. viii., part ii.

Caterina de' Medici, as well as of the two illegitimate lads, Ippolito and Alessandro. Recalled to Rome towards the close of his brief reign by the reforming Adrian, who was now openly following the Imperialist party, Medici had taken up his abode in the splendid palace of the late Cardinal Riario, who had been forced by Leo X. to cede this building at the time of his downfall in 1517. Here Giulio de' Medici, now consulted and distinguished by the ascetic Pontiff, continued to reside in great state;—indeed, the Cardinal was far more courted and esteemed by the Roman people than the foreign intruder at the Vatican, where the silent halls and empty galleries testified plainly to the unpopular ideas of strict economy and of virtuous simplicity which that despised barbarian was striving to introduce. Driven from the Apostolic palace, the poets and artists, who had recently battened at the court of Leo X., found their way to the Medici's mansion, so that it verily appeared as if the gorgeous mantle of the lamented Leo had fallen on his cousin, the natural son of the murdered Giuliano.

The obsequies of the unhappy Adrian, whose burial-place is marked by the beautiful monument in the national church of the Germans, Santa Maria dell' Anima, were carried out in the latter days of September, and on 1st October thirty-five cardinals entered the Sistine Chapel for the conclave, Medici's cell being by accident or design placed below Perugino's fine fresco of Christ bestowing the keys on St. Peter: a circumstance from which his partisans professed to draw a happy augury. Seven weeks this important conclave lasted, its deliberations throughout being marked by a surpassing amount of intrigue and bribery. Fiercely did the rival supporters of the Imperial and French

CLEMENS. VII. PONT. MAX. IVLIANI MED. F.

GIULIO DE MEDICI (CLEMENT VII)

parties struggle to accomplish the election of a Pope of
their own political views, and even the threat of the
guardians of the conclave to enforce a diet of bread and
water on the obstinate princes of the Church failed to
make their arguments meet in one point.   Farnese, of
whose flagrant immorality even that immoral age had
been ashamed, did his utmost by unabashed promises of
payment to obtain the coveted tiara, and was almost
successful in his frantic efforts; Thomas Wolsey, to
whom the Emperor had once promised his personal aid,
was told plainly his chance was hopeless, since even if
the conclave chose him, the Roman people would positively refuse to admit another foreigner within the city in
the capacity of Pope; Medici, meanwhile, in spite of
bitter enmity, never relinquished hope and kept quietly
but firmly pursuing his own ends.   At last the Imperial
faction, of which Medici was commonly regarded one of
the leading champions, got the upper hand, and with
the withdrawal of the opposition of Soderini and the
shameless winning-over of the turbulent Pompeo
Colonna, who was promised the reversion of Medici's
vice-chancellorship and the possession of the fine palace
of old Riario, the Cardinal de' Medici was enabled to
secure the requisite number of votes, with the result that
on the night of 18th November he was declared duly
elected.   Thus did Giulio de' Medici, within two years
from the date of his cousin's death on 1st December,
1521, ascend the papal throne under the official title of
Clement VII.   Nevertheless, according to the testimony
of Guicciardini,[1] the second Medicean Pontiff at first desired to be known as Julius III., but was dissuaded by
his friends from thus making use of his own baptismal

---

[1] *Storia d' Italia*, lib. xiv.

name; and his subsequent choice of the title of Clement has been variously attributed to his connection with the basilica of San Clemente (of which he was titular cardinal-priest), to the rapid approach of St. Clement's festival, or to the new Pope's intended *clemency* towards Soderini and other late opponents in the conclave.

Giulio de' Medici was in his forty-sixth year when he thus attained to the highest dignity in Christendom : a dignity which his base birth in reality denied him. His early history we have already discussed at length in the preceding chapters, wherein we have tried to show how closely his career was associated with the fluctuating fortunes of Leo X. For as early as the year 1494, at the date of the Florentine revolution which expelled the three sons of Lorenzo the Magnificent, Giulio had attached himself to his cousin, the Cardinal Giovanni, and had rarely been separated from him, either in good or evil plight, until the day of the Pope's death;—in the phrase of an unkind critic, Giulio had consistently played the humble part of jackal to the Medicean lion. The new Pontiff, in short, owed everything to his intimacy with his illustrious kinsman, who was but two years his senior; from Leo he had learned and imbibed all the secret aims and tenets of the ambitious House of Medici; he had carefully copied his master in all matters of policy and patronage; and it was to Leo's favour that he owed the removal (so far as the act was morally possible) of the clinging disgrace of illegitimacy, and had obtained an assured position of wealth and importance at his cousin's brilliant court.

Yet, although Giulio de' Medici had continued the judicious confidant and devoted servant of Leo X. for nigh upon thirty years, the dissimilarity between the cousins had always been most striking; nor was it by

any means confined to personal appearance.   The
frivolity and keen love of enjoyment that were so conspicuous in Leo seemed wholly lacking in Clement VII.,
whose behaviour was ever grave and circumspect, and
whose late share in the extravagant pursuits of Leo's
court had been due to motives of an ingratiating policy
rather than to natural inclination.   Clement's manner in
public was somewhat cold and repellent, which was perhaps one of the many reasons causing him to be so disliked
by his peers in the Sacred College, despite his enormous
influence and his frequent efforts to propitiate those who
might possibly be of service to him in the future.   Yet
his edifying and serious aspect, his reputation for political
sagacity, his supposed desire for public economy and his
strict personal morality made his election acceptable both
to the Emperor and to Henry VIII. of England, whilst
Francis of France had experienced enough of Medicean
diplomacy in the past to rest assured that no Medici was
ever likely to become a mere tool of the Imperial will.
On the whole, therefore, Clement VII.'s elevation, in spite
of the scandalous delays in the late conclave, was well
received by the princes of Europe, whilst it produced
an outburst of popular enthusiasm in the city of Rome,
where all men "trusted to behold again a flourishing
court, a liberal Pontiff, and a revival of the arts and
letters which had been banished under the late barbarian
tyranny of Adrian, since it is the boast of the House
of Medici that it favours the Muses".[1]   The sober
Guicciardini also extols the choice of the conclave, declaring that the new Pontiff was "held in the highest
reputation throughout all Europe;—indeed, the extraordinary delay in the late election seemed excusable,

[1] F. Gregorovius, vol. viii., part ii., p. 457, note 1.

seeing that it had resulted in the elevation to the papal
throne of a person of the greatest power and capacity ".[1]

In appearance, as in manner, the new Pope offered
a strong contrast with the stout and genial Leo X.
Clement's figure was tall, slight, and well formed; his
complexion was sallow; his hair black, his eyes a deep
brown, and he had fine regular features. He was more
of a typical Medici than his cousin Leo, and bore a
strong resemblance to his father, Giuliano, the only
brother of Lorenzo the Magnificent, who was murdered
in the Florentine cathedral a month before his natural
son was born to him.[2]   But although handsome,
Clement's face was rendered unattractive by reason of
its disagreeable expression and the look of suspicion
which was constantly passing over it. At the date of
his election the Pontiff was smooth-shaven, as we can
observe him in Raphael's celebrated portrait of Leo X.,
and in certain of the frescoes in the Vatican, for it was
not until after the sack of Rome in 1527, that Clement,
in sign of mourning for his past indignities, allowed his
beard and moustache to grow naturally, a change which
undoubtedly added dignity to the Pope's general appearance. If Julius was the first Pontiff to wear a beard,
Clement was certainly the originator of the papal
moustache, which continued in vogue amongst the Roman
Pontiffs for nearly two centuries.

Though less liberal and also less learned than Leo,
Giulio de' Medici owned a more discerning as well as a
more catholic taste in contemporary art. It speaks eloquently for Clement's true understanding of art in all its
varied forms, that he showed himself able to appreciate

[1] *Storia d' Italia*, lib. xiv.
[2] Platina, etc., *Vita Clementis VIII.*; also Guicciardini, *Storia
d' Italia*, lib. xii.; Creighton, vol. v., p. 224, etc.

the exquisite inventions of that Florentine prince of
jewellers, Benvenuto Cellini (who as a young man was
then rising rapidly to fame in Rome), and likewise the
gigantic productions of the chisel of Michelangelo, whose
marvellous powers the new Pope, unlike his late cousin,
always held in the highest consideration.   Clement,
" who alone of all the Medici kept a just balance between
the two rivals who were disputing the crown of art," [1]
had also been a constant patron of the late Raffaele
Sanzio, and amongst other commissions he had entrusted
the great artist of Urbino with the erection of a villa on
the slopes of Monte Mario, the prominent cypress-clad
hill above the Flaminian Gate of the city.   This splendid
villa, in the construction of which the natural rise and
fall of the ground had been skilfully utilised to contribute
to the general effect, would probably have afforded one
of the finest examples of the florid art of the Italian
Renaissance, had but circumstances allowed of its completion according to the desire of the Cardinal and the
design of Raphael.   Its style of architecture was com-
posite, a blend of all that was excellent in antique and
contemporary art, whilst the gorgeous decorations of its
halls and loggia were even said to surpass the efforts of
their artists, Giulio Romano and Giovanni da Udine, at
the Vatican itself.   Unfortunately, like so many other
ambitious projects of the Renaissance, this magnificent
palace was never brought to perfection, and in the
squalid dilapidated building, to-day called the Villa
Madama, the stranger will only perceive another of
those dismal unfinished monuments of extravagance and
ambition, with which all Italy is so thickly studded.   A
nobler and more enduring memorial of Clement's good
taste and bounty in those early days is to be found in

[1] Muntz, p. 146.

that matchless creation of the divine Raphael, the picture of the Transfiguration, which adorned the chamber of the dying artist and was borne in that silent procession through the streets of Rome to his honoured tomb in the Pantheon.   For it was the Cardinal Giulio de' Medici, who had expressly commanded this world-famous masterpiece for the high altar of the cathedral-church of Narbonne, as a mark of gratitude for his appointment to that distant bishopric.   We can, however, scarcely blame the Cardinal for his refusal to allow this picture to quit Rome, when we consider the extraordinary beauty of the composition and reflect upon the sad but hallowed memories attending its completion.   The picture (finished in detail, and none too satisfactorily, by Raphael's pupil Giulio Romano) was placed in the Roman church of San Pietro in Montorio, whilst a copy was despatched to remote Narbonne.   After remaining the pride and glory of San Pietro in Montorio for nearly three centuries, Raphael's masterpiece was removed to Paris by the emissaries of the French Republic in 1798, and on its restoration to the papal government in 1815, Pius VII. claimed it for the Vatican picture-gallery, of which it has ever since formed the chief ornament.

With the election of Giulio de' Medici in November, 1523, the Vatican, which had remained silent and half-deserted for the past two years, once more began to resume its normal aspect of intrigue and pleasure.   That corrupt and still unended pageant of the Leonine Age, which the first Medicean Pope inaugurated, had indeed been scarcely suspended anywhere in the city of Rome save in the Apostolic palace itself, where the unhappy and despised Adrian was living frugally on a ducat a day and was being served by a Flemish crone, who did duty for the swarm of valets, lacqueys and grooms whose presence the Magnificent Leo had considered indispensable. But the gloom and torpor that had fallen on the Vatican since Leo's death had in no wise interrupted the follies or vices of Rome at large. Cardinals and prelates of the court hunted, feasted, made music, jested, entertained, led immoral lives, and in short openly set at defiance the commands and threats of their foreign master, whose exhortation to virtue was heard unheeded in this ecclesiastical desert of pride and luxury. With the Vatican once more the acknowledged seat of artistic patronage and with a second Medici on the papal throne, Rome was herself again, and was prepared to forget the brief and ineffectual interlude of a barbarian pontificate.

Foremost of the signs of resumed activity at the Vatican was the renewal of the progress of building and decorating the palace, which had been abruptly abandoned under the pedantic Adrian with his utter ignorance of modern art and his pious horror of all pagan culture. Loud indeed was the outburst of relief from the artists of Rome, who "were all during the reign of Adrian but little better than dying of hunger," so Vasari informs us in exaggerated language. "On that very day," proceeds the Plutarch of Italian painters, "of Pope Clement's election, the arts of design together with all the other arts, were recalled to new life, and Giulio Romano and Gian-Francesco Penni set themselves joyfully to work by command of the Pontiff, to finish the Hall of Constantine,"[1] the fourth and most spacious chamber of the suite of the Stanze di Raffaelo.[2] Here, on the wall facing the windows, Giulio Romano painted the animated battle-piece, the *Triumph of the Emperor Constantine* over the infidel Maxentius, an immense composition crowded with Christian and pagan warriors and with many horses,

---

[1] *Vita di' Giulio Romano.*   [2] See chapter ix.

which in spite of the harshness of its colouring is a splendid performance of the painter, who has throughout followed closely the details of the original cartoon from the hand of his dead master, Raphael. In the adjoining fresco, the *Vision of the Cross to Constantine*, it is only too evident that Giulio Romano has deviated both from the spirit and the design of the original cartoon, whilst the introduction into so solemn a subject of the repulsive Gradasso da Norcia, the hideous dwarf from the household of Ippolito de' Medici, constitutes a flagrant outrage against good taste. Opposite this work, appears the *Baptism of Constantine*, with its valuable representation of the ancient baptistery of the Lateran in the days of the second Medicean Pope and its portrait of Clement himself officiating in the guise of Pope Sylvester. Last of all in artistic merit but of special interest as presenting us with an admirable view of the interior of old St. Peter's with its pillared nave, its tribune and its crude mosaics, is the fourth fresco of this hall, which, being the latest of all in date, exhibits St. Sylvester as Clement VII., grown older and bearded, seated in state to receive the donation of Rome for himself and his successors from the hand of Constantine, who in solemn assertion of his good faith offers the Pontiff the bronze statue of a warrior. Numerous auxiliary figures have been introduced into this picture; courtiers, children, women, beggars, the Grand Master of Rhodes, and even soldiers of the Swiss Guard, who keep the populace at a respectful distance with their halberds. The frescoes of the Stanza di Costantino, though artistically on a far lower level than those of the other three halls, form an interesting historical link with the disastrous pontificate of Clement VII., who tried conscientiously to complete the splendid series of frescoes, emblematic of the secular Papacy, that

Julius II. had commenced and Leo X. had continued; it was the fault of Raphael's pupils and not of the Medici that the decorations of the last hall of the official suite, intended to idealise the origin of the temporal power of the Papacy, should have proved so inferior to Raphael's own creations in the adjoining chambers.

Everywhere in the neighbourhood of the Hall of Constantine are visible the heraldic achievements of the luckless Clement, notably in the pair of splendid carved portals that give on the Loggia of Raphael.   And in the panels of these doors the curious may observe the strange emblem or *impresa* adopted by Clement VII., which represents the rays of the sun in full splendour falling on a crystal globe, that stands on a pedestal marked with the words *Candor Illaesus*, and passing thence so as to set fire to a tree in full leaf.   According to Paolo Giovio, this enigmatic piece of heraldry was the invention of a certain Domenico Buoninsegni of Florence, treasurer to Clement VII., shortly before the date of his master's election in 1523, who strove to show to the world thereby Clement's earnest sincerity and candour of mind, which were so great as to render their owner proof against the manifold slanders and plots of his enemies.   This quaint device seems to have commended itself to the Pope, then Cardinal, although in the whole roll of history it would be hard to discover any sovereign to whom the epithet of "candid" might be applied with less reason than to this Medicean disciple of the tortuous and uncandid principles laid down by Machiavelli.[1]

Of the various artists patronised by Clement VII., "whose election proved to be a great and much-needed restoration and refreshment to the arts of painting and

[1] Geronimo Ruscelli, *Le Imprese illustri*.   In Venetia, 1572, pp. 40, 41.

sculpture,"[1] perhaps the account left by Benvenuto Cellini of his own relations with Clement is the most valuable, as affording us an insight not only into the artistic notions of his papal patron, but also into his disposition and mode of life. For the Pontiff seems to have formed a close friendship with Cellini, then twenty-six years of age, during the awful siege of the castle of Sant' Angelo, and the intimacy begun under these baleful conditions was resumed in happier days, on Clement's return to Rome after his coronation of the Emperor at Bologna. This strange adherent of the House of Medici—exquisite jeweller, vulgar braggart, plebeian roysterer and author of one of the most valuable human documents concerning the social life of the Italian Renaissance—has presented us in his immortal *Autobiography* with a mass of artless details concerning Clement, and has recorded in these pages a number of strange conversations between himself and the Pope, which though highly entertaining in themselves, cannot possibly be accounted veracious, for they are in reality but stray reminiscences of events put down on paper some twenty or thirty years after their actual occurrence.

Rome, at the date of Cellini's arrival thither in 1523, was still the undisputed centre of the intellectual and artistic world, and Clement's election set the seal on its universal reputation. As a master-workman, whose fame had already preceded him in Rome, Cellini had received from Clement a cordial welcome, the warmth of which was doubtless enhanced by the Pope's knowledge of the firm political sympathies of the lowly Cellini family with the lofty House of Medici. With the early securing of the papal patronage, commissions of every kind at once began to pour down upon the conceited but talented

[1] Vasari, *Vita di Pierino del Vaga.*

Florentine youth, who ere long came to be acknowledged as the prince of his profession.

"No labour seemed too minute, no metal was too mean for the exercise of the master-workman's skill, nor did he run the risk of becoming one of those half-amateurs in whom accomplishment falls short on first conception.   Art ennobled for him all that he was called to do.   Whether cardinals required him to fashion silver vases for their banquet-tables; or ladies wished the setting of their jewels altered ; or a Pope wanted the enamelled binding of a book of prayers ; or men-at-arms sent sword-blades to be damaskened with acanthus foliage ; or kings desired fountains and statues for their palace-courts ; or poets begged to have their portraits cast in bronze ; or generals needed medals to commemorate their victories, or dukes new coins for the mint ; or bishops ordered reliquaries for the altars of their patron-saints ; or merchants sought for seals and signet-rings engraved with their device ; or men of fashion asked for medals of Leda and Adonis to fasten in their caps—all these commissions would be undertaken by a workman like Cellini."[1]

These early years in Rome were probably the happiest and most prosperous in all Cellini's career. Assured of the Pope's· sympathy in his work, and later drawing a good salary as master of the papal mint, Benvenuto moved as a figure of no little importance in that brilliant if corrupt pageant of the closing years of the Leonine Age.   For society he enjoyed the intimate friendship of his own revered Michelangelo, of the painter Giulio Romano, and of such of the leading artists of the day as he did not choose to offend.   For his amusements there were the eternal feasting, intriguing

[1] J. A. Symonds, *Renaissance in Italy.*

and brawling of the time, whilst for his health's sake Benvenuto was wont to go daily outside the city walls with his fowling-piece and a well-trained shock-dog in quest of game on the Roman Campagna, or else to sketch the neglected remains of classical Rome, lightening his task of drawing by occasionally shooting at the flocks of pigeons which these ivy-clad ruins sheltered.

But this pleasant existence of mingled work and recreation received a rude shock in the capture and sack of Rome by the lawless troops of the Constable of Bourbon in the spring of 1527. During the fearful siege of the castle of Sant' Angelo, Cellini gladly gave his services to his unfortunate patron, to whom he seems to have borne as genuine an attachment as his conceited and selfish nature would permit. We shall speak in the following chapter of Cellini's vaunted exploits in the beleaguered citadel of Rome, but one curious incident it is more suitable to mention in this place. It seems that at Clement's special request, Cellini undertook to break up the papal crown-jewels, to extract their gems and to melt down their component gold, a delicate operation, for which Benvenuto's unique skill in his profession and undoubted honesty rendered his assistance of extreme value in such an emergency. This signal service to the Medici was, however, destined to bring unmerited evil on the head of the artist in after years under the rule of the terrible Farnese Pope, Paul III., whose mean suspicious nature could not conceive of any artist having undertaken such a task, without the determination to rob his employer of part at least of the stones and gold entrusted to his care and honour.[1]

Ever a faithful adherent of the Medici, Benvenuto openly preferred to return to Rome in the train of

[1] *Vita di B. Cellini.*

Clement rather than to assist in the defence of his native
Florence, which had in the meantime shaken off the
Medicean yoke.   During the years 1530-1534, Clement
was undoubtedly the artist's best patron, and in the racy
narrative of the jeweller-author's own *Autobiography*
we are given many instances of the Pope's varying moods.   For during these four years the artist was
in constant attendance at the Vatican, where he was
sometimes flattered, sometimes soundly rated by His
Holiness, according as a friendly or unfriendly courtier
had previous access to the papal ear, for the perplexed
Pontiff was ever a prey to some temporary influence.
Nevertheless, despite innumerable quarrels between
patron and artist, Cellini executed many commissions for
Clement, besides designing and striking those beautiful
papal medals, which even in the fastidious Pope's opinion
surpassed the finest specimens of the coins of antiquity.
These medals distinguished by Clement's handsome profile
survive as prized possessions in many a cabinet to-day ;
but what has become, we wonder, of those superb if
trivial masterpieces with which Cellini's deft fingers and
keen-sighted eyes contrived to delight the art-loving
Medici?   Where is that golden brooch to fasten the
pontifical cope, "the size of a small trencher, one-third
of a cubit wide," with its design of the Almighty surrounded by cherubim and seated on a glowing orb,
which was to have been formed by the finest diamond
in the papal treasury?   Where is that ornate chalice, the
apple of its artificer's eye, that in its unfinished state had
been contemptuously referred to as *una cipollata*, "a
mess of onions," by the supercilious Cardinal Salviati :
an insult the vindictive genius never forgave?   Or the
model for the setting of "an unicorn's horn"—or rather
the fine narwhal's tusk, a curio that cost the impoverished

treasury 17,000 ducats—with which Clement was anxious to propitiate the King of France at the approaching marriage of the little Caterina de' Medici with the second son of Francis? All have perished; so that the most enduring memorial of Clement's patronage of Cellini is to be found in those chapters of the artist's *Autobiography*,[1] which describe from his own point of view the numerous colloquies and misunderstandings between the two men placed in such widely separated spheres of life. Were both Pope and artist living at this moment, each would express an equal surprise at this circumstance, for little did that gifted but self-satisfied master-workman suspect, as in his declining years he jotted down his pungent reminiscences of the great, that the fame of these carelessly dictated memoirs was destined to outweigh in the eyes of future generations the value of his statues, his coins, and his elaborate designs for plate and jewellery.

We have already made allusion to Clement's unbounded admiration of the talents of Michelangelo, whom as Cardinal de' Medici he had been wont to address with the deepest courtesy as *Spectabilis Vir, amice noster chiarissime*. And immediately upon his election it is not strange that the Pope decided to engage the services of the master for the completion of a Medicean mausoleum adjoining the church of San Lorenzo in Florence, a project that was evidently very dear to the heart of this bastard of the Medici, now risen to be Supreme Pontiff. Together with the proposed mausoleum was included a commission for the erection of a library hard by, suitable to contain the splendid collection of books and manuscripts of Leo X., which was now the property of his heir. "Thou art aware," writes Clement in an autograph note to a formal letter of instruction from his secretary, "that

[1] *Vita di B. Cellini.*

Popes are short-lived, and we are all eagerness to behold the chapel with the monuments of our race, or at least to learn of its completion. So also with the library. Therefore we rely on thy diligence in both our commands. Be assured that commissions and rewards will never be lacking during our lifetime. Farewell, with the benediction of God and ourselves. Julius." [1]

With such a proof of Clement's earnest anxiety, the master set to work with zest upon the domed mausoleum of the Medici, commonly called the New Sacristy of San Lorenzo, in contrast with the existing old Sacristy of Brunelleschi near the southern transept of the basilica. The original intention both of Pope and artist seems to have been the erection of four vast and overladen sepulchral monuments covered with allegorical figures in commemoration of Giuliano the Good, Lorenzo Duke of Urbino, Lorenzo the Magnificent, and Giuliano his brother, the two last being the parents respectively of Leo X. and Clement VII. Other accounts credit Clement with the desire of a splendid tomb to be raised to himself in his lifetime. Eventually, as we know, only the tombs of the two former princes were ever erected.

Within a year the shell of the fabric was finished, and was ready to receive the elaborate masses of statuary and sepulchral architecture, on which the master was now lavishing his genius. Early in 1526 the foundations of the Laurentian Library also were laid, whilst its necessary fittings and decorations were being prepared by a number of skilled craftsmen, prominent amongst them being the celebrated Giovanni da Udine who was likewise instructed to adorn in fresco the cupola of the Sacristy. It was about this time also that Clement, who

[1] J. A. Symonds, *Life of Michelangelo*, vol. i., p. 397. Clement VII. signs with his baptismal name in this letter, dated April, 1525.

from a distance was taking the liveliest interest in the progress of these operations at San Lorenzo, sent to Michelangelo an extraordinary proposal to erect a colossal figure of forty cubits' stature in the piazza before the church, apparently on the very spot now occupied by the mediocre effigy of the father of the first Tuscan Grand-Duke, the famous Giovanni of the Black Bands. This extravagant and tasteless suggestion, although emanating directly from the Pope, was savagely opposed by Michelangelo in a letter filled with most insolent sarcasm, combined with the elephantine humour in which the master occasionally indulged.[1] The contemptuous remarks contained in this communication could not have failed to give offence to the Pope, had its contents been brought to his notice by some mischief-making person (as indeed may actually have happened). Yet Clement seems to have paid no attention to the rude jests of this privileged man of genius, for the scheme was immediately dropped and we hear no more of it. But one cannot help speculating on what the violent Julius II. or the particular Leo X. would have said or done, on hearing such personal ridicule from any architect accepting their pay.

Owing to the Florentine revolution of 1527 and the subsequent downfall of Medicean rule, the work at San Lorenzo was of necessity suspended, whilst Michelangelo was set to labour on another and a nobler task, that of raising the fortifications at San Miniato in order to protect his native city from the assailing army of the Prince of Orange. With the recapture and thraldom of the revolted city, the great artist, whose earnest efforts on behalf of the short-lived Florentine Republic were well known to the now-detested Clement, was forced to lie awhile in hiding. But it was not long ere the Pope,

---

[1] J. A. Symonds, *Life of Michelangelo*, vol. i., pp. 400, 401.

whose intense anxiety to finish worthily his chapel and library at San Lorenzo evidently outweighed any supposed thirst for vengeance on his architect, offered of his own motion free pardon and grace to the patriotic master, who was thus once more recalled to resume his interrupted commission of glorifying the triumphant House of Medici. "Michelangelo," remarks his biographer Condivi, "now came forth from his place of concealment, and took up again his work on the statues in the Sacristy of San Lorenzo, being moved thereto more by fear of the Pope than by love for the Medici."[1]   Yet if the artist himself were sore in spirit, he seems in no wise to have forfeited Clement's favour, for in one of the letters of his chief friend and gossip in Rome, Sebastiano del Piombo (who also accepted the bounty of Clement VII.), that distinguished painter implores Michelangelo to lay aside all resentment against the Pope, "who speaks of you in such honourable and affectionate terms, that no parent could praise a son more highly.   It is true he has been annoyed by whisperings as to your conduct during the late siege of Florence, but he shrugs his shoulders and only remarks, *Michelangelo is mistaken, for I never did him any wrong.*"[2]

Thus for nearly four years did Michelangelo toil with a heavy heart at his uncongenial task at San Lorenzo, but on the Pope's death in 1534 the work ceased abruptly, nor was it ever resumed, though the Grand-Duke Cosimo I. tried later to persuade the master to achieve the original design.   The result of Clement's premature decease and of his artist's consequent escape from an irksome duty is therefore that to-day we possess only the chilly vaulted apartment of perfect proportions covered

[1] J. A. Symonds, *Life of Michelangelo*, vol. i., p. 438.
[2] *Ibid.*, vol. i., p. 348.

with meaningless niches, cornices and brackets, which cry aloud for their intended pieces of statuary; and disfigured by the blank wall-spaces which were meant to glow with frescoes from the master's own hand or with graceful arabesques from the brush of Giovanni da Udine. A first inspection of this famous building with its white-washed walls and its abundance of the sadcoloured *pietra serena*, the grey stone which renders gloomy so many of the finest edifices of Florence, strikes a chill, moral as well as physical, in the traveller, who probably experiences a sense of disappointment that he dares not openly express on his first acquaintance with the New Sacristy of San Lorenzo. Of its two completed sepulchral monuments to Giuliano and Lorenzo de' Medici we have already spoken, and therefore shall refrain from adding another word of praise or criticism concerning that which has given rise to endless speculation and poetical rhapsody from generations of artists and authors. To the passing stranger we offer but this humble suggestion: that in fairness to the execrated memory of Clement VII. he should bear in mind that to this hated Pontiff is due the erection of this drear but splendid sanctuary of art, which has drawn hither for nearly four centuries so many pilgrims of every race and from every clime.

CHAPTER XIII

THE SACK OF ROME

Alas, how many a courtier, how many a high-born and delicately nurtured noble, how many a gracious prelate, how many a pious nun, how many a virgin, how many a stately matron with all her infants fell a prey to those cruel Barbarians! Think of the chalices, the crosses and the images; think of the goodly vases of gold or silver that were snatched by bloody and sacrilegious hands from the altars and holy places where they were wont to repose! Alas, for the fate of those marvellous and venerable Relics, which were first robbed of their coverings of precious metal, and then flung to earth by murder-stained hands in insult to our Faith! The sacred heads of the holy Apostles Peter, Paul and Andrew, the Wood of the True Cross, the Crown of Thorns, the Holy Oils, and even the consecrated Hosts, all trodden underfoot by those remorseless Barbarians! (L. Guicciardini, *Il Sacco di Roma*).

ALTHOUGH reckoned at the time of the conclave one of the Emperor's most ardent supporters, it was not long before Clement took up the threads of the old Medicean policy of vacillating between King and Cæsar, and of trying to turn every chance to the private advantage of the House of Medici. By constant shuffling, intriguing and deceiving, the Pontiff proceeded to an open rupture with Charles V. and to a close alliance with Francis of France, until in 1525 the startling news of the decisive victory of Pavia burst like a thunder-clap over Rome and the Papal court. "On the 26th day of February about four o'clock in the evening were brought tidings to the Pope that the army of the King of France had been worsted by the army of the Emperor and the Duke of Milan, and that King Francis was actually taken prisoner. The whole of that night the Spanish residents of Rome paraded the streets, applauding the victory and celebrating it with bonfires and explosions of mortars. . . . And on the final day of February a messenger arrived in the city, who confirmed the report of the capture of the king, of the destruction of his army, and of the slaughter of numbers of the nobles of France."[1]

Yet even this absolute upheaval of the European balance of power, on which the Pope had been so artfully calculating, proved insufficient to teach wisdom to the secretive Clement, who unlike Leo, never recognised the right moment to yield, or at least to pretend to yield, with a good grace. However disagreeable and humiliating his position may have appeared after the battle of Pavia, it was obviously Clement's only chance to implore the pardon of the irate Charles and to seek his protection for Florence and the Holy See. Yet although the Emperor had been made all-powerful beyond the shadow of a doubt since the fatal day of Pavia, we find the infatuated Clement in the following year actually at the head of a League, composed of the independent Italian states in conjunction with the broken realm of France and the distant kingdom of England, for the avowed purpose of driving the victorious Spanish arms out of Italy. Thus by this irrevocable act of folly unspeakable was the true aim of Medicean statecraft revealed. The army of the League under the command of the treacherous Francesco-Maria, Della Rovere, Duke of Urbino, who must have hated the House of Medici after his treatment by Leo X., now advanced into Lombardy, where that renegade prince, the cele-

[1] Creighton, vol. vi. *Diary of Blasius de Martinellis*, p. 380.

CLEMENT VII AND THE EMPEROR CHARLES V

brated Constable of Bourbon, was holding the unhappy
city of Milan in the name of his present master, Charles
V. In the autumn of this very year moreover the Pope
received yet another warning against the terrible doom
his rashness and duplicity were preparing for his House,
for the Papacy, and indeed for all Italy. For in September, 1526, the irrepressible Cardinal Pompeo Colonna,
with the followers of that great feudal House, suddenly
swooped down upon Rome with the connivance of the
Imperial envoy, the unscrupulous Moncada, and invaded
the defenceless suburb lying round St. Peter's. The
open indifference of the Roman people, whose sympathy
Clement had contrived to alienate, and the cowardly
indecision of the Pontiff himself, allowed the angry
Colonna, the self-styled deliverer of Rome from papal
tyranny, to pillage the Apostolic palace, which the Pope
had ignominiously abandoned for the security of the
castle of Sant' Angelo. In an agony of distress,
Clement at once applied to Moncada, who assisted the
Pope to escape from his undignified position, by patching
up a treaty wherein Clement swore faithfully to secede
from the League and also to pardon the Colonna for
this late exploit.

But Clement, "the very sport of misfortune," never
made a promise but to break it at the earliest opportunity.
In November of the same year the papal troops were
unexpectedly despatched into the plains and mountains
of the Roman State, to storm and raze the strongholds
of the unsuspecting Colonna, when defenceless tenants
and *contadini* of this House were treated with a measure
of cruelty which would have put the Turk to shame;
whilst the Cardinal Pompeo and every member of his
family were formally deprived of all their titles and
declared outlaws. That such an act of treachery and

insolence was caused by abject fear rather than by wanton aggression cannot excuse Clement's conduct, and it is not hard to understand the position subsequently assumed by the Emperor, thus openly cheated and flouted, towards a Pope whose election had been mainly secured by Imperial influence.

But retribution was very near at hand. On 1st December, the Imperial viceroy of Naples, Lannoy, reached Gaeta with a large force by sea, and he was immediately joined on his landing by the infuriated Cardinal Colonna, burning with vengeance against the perfidious Medici. Bad, however, as was this piece of news, the reports from the north of Italy were even more calculated to alarm the guilty Pope. For during the autumn months the famous veteran George von Frundsberg had been collecting an army of *Landsknechts* to march under his banner into Italy, to subdue and even to punish with death the perjured enemy of the Emperor. These *Landsknechts* were volunteer foot-soldiers, drawn from the sturdy peasantry of the Franconian plains or from the mountains of Bavaria. A large proportion of them were confessedly Lutherans, filled with the anti-papal sentiments of their religious leader, so that the prospect of hanging Anti-Christ in the person of Clement and the expected plunder of the richest city in Europe appealed to their minds with almost equal force. Crossing the Alps amid fearful storms of rain and snow, and surmounting precipitous passes where the aged and corpulent Frundsberg had to be pushed or carried by his men, this picked body of German adventurers finally reached the neighbourhood of Brescia, almost at the precise moment of Clement's treacherous raid upon the castles of the Colonna. It is easy to comprehend the consternation of the Pope and the Roman court, when it was realised in

Rome that Frundsberg and his Protestant myrmidons
had actually gained the plain of Lombardy and that the
viceroy Lannoy's Spanish fleet was riding safe in the
roads of Gaeta. "We are on the brink of ruin!" was
the only too prophetic utterance of Clement's patriotic
but headstrong secretary, Gian-Matteo Giberti, whose
advice was ever in strong·conflict with the Pope's other
favourite counsellor, the German Imperialist, Nicholas
Schomberg. For the feeble Clement was ever wavering
between Giberti's exhortations to prosecute the war of
Italian independence at all costs, and Schomberg's more
prudent recommendation to make peace, even at the
eleventh hour, with the enraged Emperor, no matter how
severe the terms demanded.

At the battle of Frosinone, the advance of Lannoy
and Pompeo Colonna upon Rome was temporarily
checked at the close of January, 1527, but all efforts of
the army of the League in Lombardy proved unavailing
to arrest the progress of Frundsberg's force, which was
slowly but surely fighting its way from the Alps towards
the Tiber. The kind offices of Alfonso of Ferrara,
whom Clement had been foolish enough to exasperate,
enabled the hard-pressed Germans to surmount all
obstacles natural and military in their path, whilst Fortune
at the same time deprived the Pope and indeed Italy of
an able and most trustworthy leader in the person of the
brave but brutal Giovanni delle Bande Nere, head of the
junior branch of the House of Medici and father of the
future first Grand-Duke of Tuscany. For Giovanni of
the Black Bands was struck down by a bullet in a small
skirmish on the banks of·the Mincio, and though his indomitable pluck permitted him to hold with his own hand
the torch so as to assist the attending surgeon to amputate
the injured leg, he died of his wound at Mantua five days

later. On 1st December, the day succeeding Medici's death, Frundsberg was joined by a princely adventurer, the young Philibert of Orange, now in the service of the Emperor ; but it was not until two months later that the Constable of Bourbon was able to quit Milan with the Spanish forces and to form a junction with the army of advancing *Landsknechts* at Pontenuro. The combined forces of German volunteers and of Spanish soldiers now reckoned in all some 30,000 men, well supplied with cavalry but greatly deficient in artillery. " It was a formidable host of veteran soldiers, whom a hundred battles had made as hard as steel, and whom no hardships could bend : Catholics and Lutherans all fired with the same fierce hatred of the Papacy and impelled by the same thirst for spoil." [1]

Meanwhile, as the united army of Frundsberg and Bourbon was marching towards Bologna, an eight months' truce was arranged between the Pope and the viceroy Lannoy, which under the circumstances was probably the best diplomatic move Clement could have made, had he not followed the signing of the terms by a general disarmament of his forces, thus leaving the city defenceless in the event of a hostile army assailing Rome from the north. But the armistice, though certainly excellent from the selfish view of the wavering Pope, was loudly execrated both by the Colonna, who thought Lannoy's terms far too lenient to Clement, and by the patriotic party in Italy, which was furious at this papal surrender to the Emperor after the late victory of Frosinone. Clement became therefore distrusted, hated, and anathematised all round for his cold, crafty and truly Medicean policy. But, truce or no truce, the Imperialist

[1] Gregorovius, vol. viii., part ii.

army of the north was determined to proceed.   On
news of the negotiations recently opened between
Clement and Lannoy, a mutiny at once broke out in
the camp, where even the *Landsknechts*, furious at the
prospect of being baulked of their expected prey, set
their old leader Frundsberg at defiance, and loudly
clamoured for pay or pillage.   Seized with an apoplectic
fit in the midst of this tumult, the aged general was now
removed helpless to Ferrara, so that the advance southward of the vast but undisciplined Imperialist army was
undertaken solely by Bourbon, who was practically as
much the servant as the leader of this Spanish-German
host.   In vain did Lannoy himself proceed in person to
expostulate with Bourbon and in the Pope's name to
offer higher and higher ransom, if only the army would
retire to Milan; the penniless Bourbon durst not turn
back, even if he would.   In despair the viceroy returned
to Rome, whilst towards the close of April, Bourbon
found himself in the neighbourhood of Arezzo, and
within a few leagues of Florence.

The governorship of Florence had been entrusted
by Clement to Cardinal Silvio Passerini of Cortona,
whilst the House of Medici was represented in that city
by the presence of the little Catherine, heiress of her
House, and the two lads, Ippolito and Alessandro.   Of
these two youths, Ippolito was now grown into a handsome, attractive stripling, filled with martial instincts and
by no means amenable to the Pope's intention of forcing
him to embrace an ecclesiastical career.   Alessandro, on
the other hand, swarthy, ill-featured and ungracious, was
undoubtedly the papal favourite; a strange circumstance
which was popularly attributed to the Pope's paternity
of this unprepossessing bastard, who was later created

Duke of Florence.[1]   Besides these three Medici, there was the proud and arrogant Clarice de' Medici, wife of Filippo Strozzi, who was at this moment a hostage at Naples for the Pope's good faith, a position which caused much anxiety to Clarice, since she was only too well acquainted with Clement's innate selfishness and constant double-dealing.   The city of Florence, however, was well prepared for any emergency, the Duke of Urbino having been engaged to take up a position with his army in the Val d' Arno at Incisa, in case Bourbon, or rather his unruly followers, might be tempted to approach and plunder the city.   But for this act of forethought, it is not improbable that Florence might have anticipated the horrors of the evil fate which was to overtake Rome within a few days.   But seeing his avenue to Florence barred by a resolute general with an adequate army, the Constable of Bourbon decided to quit Tuscany and to continue his course direct towards Rome, the admitted goal of this savage armament.

Nearer and nearer towards Rome drew the force, yet Clement remained immovable, half-paralysed, like some small bird fascinated by a snake.   Amid torrents of rain the mingled host of German Protestants and of Spanish fanatics slowly continued to advance, the ragged and starving men fording the swollen mountain-torrents with clasped hands in gangs of thirty, and forgetting their hunger and nakedness in the dazzling prospect of the luxury and wealth that awaited them in Rome.   At Viterbo, the Knights of Rhodes[2] contrived

---

[1] Modesto Rastrelli, Duke Alexander's sole biographer, stoutly denies this common belief, and declares him to have been the son of Duke Lorenzo of Urbino by an unknown mother (*Storia d' Alessandro de Medici, Primo Duc a di Firenze*, Firenze, 1781).

[2] The Knights of Rhodes, recently expelled from their ancient citadel, had been placed by Adrian VI. at Viterbo.   The island of Malta was granted to them by Charles V. in 1513.

to save their town from pillage by contracting to supply the famished soldiers with provisions, a circumstance which enabled Bourbon's army to hasten southward, so that on 4th May the vast assembly found itself encamped at Isola Farnese, the site of ancient Veii, within a few miles of Rome itself. As a general anxious to avoid the possible disgrace of a military repulse and also as a Catholic prince, Bourbon was certainly willing to avoid the inevitable horrors of a sack of the Eternal City in the present temper of the men nominally under his command. Accordingly, from this point he began to send heralds into the city to open negotiations with Clement for the exaction of a ransom heavy enough to satisfy even his clamouring and mutinous troopers. But the Pope, whom it is kind to regard as temporarily insane through sheer terror,[1] would make no reply to any overtures coming from the discredited Constable of France. On the contrary, now that it was really too late, a feverish activity of defence was reigning in the doomed city, where Renzo da Ceri had been appointed commander of the force it was intended to raise. More prudent than their vacillating sovereign, the nobles and prelates of Rome had for some time been making ready for the disaster that Clement's continued folly was certain to bring on the city. Not a few had fled, in spite of the Pope's severe edict against any desertion or removal of treasure, and of those who remained, several had fortified their houses and engaged young men, *ben pagati e ben trattati*, to protect their property. Amongst these private residences carefully garrisoned against coming trouble, was the palace of the Santi Apostoli, at that moment inhabited by the Marchioness of Mantua, the intrepid Isabella d' Este, who had been staying some time in Rome, im-

---

[1] Quem Deus vult perdere, prius dementat.

portuning the unwilling and perplexed Clement to bestow a scarlet hat on her son Ercole.   This boon the fascinating Marchesa had at last secured, but only on the eve of the catastrophe which we are about to relate.   For on 4th May, Clement had held a consistory, whereat, in order to raise funds in this emergency, he had bestowed the rank of cardinal on four persons, Ercole Gonzaga being amongst them, and had thereby obtained the sum of 200,000 ducats for the papal treasury.   But even this step, which in all fairness it must be stated Clement only took with the greatest reluctance and after much entreaty from his counsellors, proved eventually useless.   On Sunday, 5th May, the Constable had marched from Isola Farnese to the Janiculan Hill on the western side of Rome, where he himself established his headquarters in the convent of Sant' Onofrio, whilst his army, composed of Spaniards, Germans and the Italian followers of the Colonna to the total number of 40,000, bivouacked in the form of a vast semicircle stretching from the Porta San Pancrazio to the Torrione, at the rear of the Vatican gardens.

At the first flush of dawn on Monday, 6th May, a general attack was made with improvised scaling-ladders, but these efforts were at first checked by the papal bombardiers, among them being Benvenuto Cellini, who were serving the guns at Sant' Angelo.   To aid the assailants at this critical moment, there arose however a thick white mist from the Tiber, enveloping the attacking force and obstructing the aim of the Roman gunners. In the confusion wrought by this sudden fog, the Constable of Bourbon, conspicuous in his shirt of silver mail, rode hither and thither, encouraging and directing the operations of attack, until a stray bullet struck the prince in the thigh, so that he fell mortally wounded to earth, crying aloud in his agony, "Ha, Notre Dame, Je suis mort!" The young Prince of Orange, who stood next in command, at once covered his dying leader's body with his military cloak and bore him to a chapel hard by, where a few hours later Bourbon expired. Although Jovius ascribes Bourbon's violent end to the direct vengeance of Heaven and although numbers of persons in Rome, including that irrepressible braggart Benvenuto Cellini, dared to claim the honour of having fired the fatal shot which slew the Constable of France, the death of Bourbon proved in reality the worst misfortune that could have afflicted the Romans at this juncture, for it meant the loss of the solitary general who owned any restraining influence (and that was little enough) over the hungry and infuriated hordes, who were thirsting for the blood and treasure of the Eternal City. As it so fell, this untimely slaughter of a popular leader roused the passions of his men to fever heat, without giving any perceptible advantage to the besieged. For it was not long before the assailing party under cover of the mist had scaled the walls at several points, and was forcing its way into the Città Leonina, the walled suburb that lies round St. Peter's.

Although Germans, Spaniards and wild mountaineers from the estates of the Colonna were now beginning to pour into the devoted city, shouting triumphantly in three languages, plundering and slaying, yet so far the assailants had only carried the quarter round St. Peter's, so that there was still time for the Pope and his troops to withdraw across the Tiber, for the bridges to be demolished and for the passage of the stream to be vigorously defended against the huge mass of undisciplined foreigners, until the expected arrival of the Italian army under the Duke of Urbino, who was supposed to be pursuing

Bourbon. The papal general, Renzo da Ceri, however, seems to have lost either his courage or his wits in this terrible crisis, for he is reported to have given the signal for a general stampede into the neighbouring castle of Sant' Angelo. Yet the folly of such a step must have been obvious on reflection, for by filling the castle to its utmost capacity the defending party was cut into two divisions, each separated from the other by the intervening Tiber. A fearful scene of slaughter, confusion and struggling was thus brought about, the like of which had never yet been witnessed in all the previous sieges of Rome, and perhaps in the world's history. All persons, in every rank of life, from cardinals and prelates to servants and apprentices, pressed in one jostling mass towards the open drawbridge of the castle, whilst the crush of terrified humanity on the adjacent bridge of Sant' Angelo was so fierce that the plucky old Cardinal Pucci of Florence was with difficulty rescued from being trodden underfoot, and had finally to be hauled by means of ropes from the ground to a convenient window. Others, less fortunate than this prince of the Church, failed to effect an entrance and were quickly despatched by the on-rushing bloodthirsty invaders. In all, some 3000 persons, of either sex, found shelter within the walls of this almost impregnable fortress, once the tomb of the Emperor Hadrian.

Meanwhile the Pope himself, whose past deceit and vacillation had brought the unhappy city to this awful extremity, had been praying since dawn for the success of the papal arms, "vainly importuning an angry Providence at the altar". The tidings of Bourbon's death had given him a passing gleam of hope, and with an assumed air of majesty the Supreme Pontiff now declared himself ready to await the onset of the Barbarians in the event of their victory, clad in the pontifical robes and seated on the throne of state. But on hearing the uproar succeeding the entry of the foreigner and on learning the truth of the situation, Clement fell at once into an abject state of utter fear and indecision, and like most weak characters began to prate wildly of betrayal and ingratitude. Whilst weeping and complaining thus, the historian Paolo Giovio earnestly implored the distraught Pontiff to join the crowd of officials who were already hastening from the Vatican to the castle of Sant' Angelo by means of the stone corridor, whereby the prudent Alexander VI. had connected the Apostolic palace with its adjacent fortress. Leaving his oratory and proceeding along this passage, the eyes of the terrified Pope could perceive through its many apertures sickening sights of priests and citizens pursued and butchered by the halberds of the furious *Landsknechts*. "As Clement was hurrying with immense strides," so Giovio relates in his graphic narrative of this awful moment, " I, Paolo Giovio, who have written this account, held up the skirt of his long robe, so as to enable him to run faster, and I flung my own purple cloak about his head and shoulders, lest some Barbarian rascal in the crowd below might recognise the Pope by his white rochet, as he was passing a window, and take a chance shot at his fleeing form."[1] Thus with the timely aid of the Bishop of Nocera, did the miserable Clement VII. save his own life amid the general carnage and confusion by abandoning his palace and running with undignified speed into the shelter of the castle.

With the Pope and thirteen of the cardinals and numberless prelates thus self-immured inside the strong walls of Sant' Angelo, the citizens of Rome were forcibly driven out of the Trastevere, whilst before sunset the

[1] *Vita Pompeii Colonnae.*

Imperialists had carried by storm the Ponte Sisto, which was being held with a desperation worthy of the old Roman valour. With the capture of this bridge the whole city lay entirely at the mercy of the Imperialists, who at once proceeded to massacre every man, woman or child that had not as yet found a temporary refuge in the fortified palace of some prince or cardinal. Yet even these horrors constituted but a mild prelude to the rapine and villainy of the morrow. For at daybreak of the seventh day of May the terrible Sack of Rome, which marks an era in the annals of Italy and indeed of Europe, began in deadly earnest. The outrages of the savage troopers, maddened with wine and fanaticism, are too terrible to relate, and the existing descriptions of eye-witnesses, even at this distance of time, still arouse the liveliest feelings of horror, pity and indignation, for the event was a repetition of the sack of Prato, but on an extended scale and with many additional barbarities. The men of the three nations engaged in this fiendish task exhibited their national vices in the horrible work, for the German *Landsknechts* distinguished themselves by their drunkenness and their profanation of the churches and convents; the Spaniards by their heartless and re-volting tortures upon every unhappy creature that fell into their clutches; and the Italians by the thorough manner in which they pillaged every house, even the hovels of the poor watermen, carrying away the very nails and hinges of the doors. An exorbitant ransom was first demanded of all holders of the fortified resid-ences in the city, but this was only a preliminary step to the raiding and ransacking of all the buildings of Rome with the exception of the strongly fortified mansions of the Colonna—the palaces of the Cancelleria and of the Apostoli. In vain did the Imperialist cardinals and prelates, the foreign nobles and even the ambassadors, cry out for exemption; all were forced to surrender their goods and were brutally slaughtered at the first sign of argument or resistance.   Many of the pampered princes of the Church were carried as hostages from one place to another in quest of an increased ransom, and amongst others thus maltreated was the Cardinal of Gaeta, the late opponent of Martin Luther, who with a fool's cap on his head was hustled with kicks and buffets from the jeering Lutherans towards the castle of Sant' Angelo, so that the imprisoned Pope might perceive the fate awaiting himself on the capture of the fortress.   Noble ladies had their ears and arms cut off by the sword for the sake of pendants or bracelets, and even the fingers of prelates were thus mutilated to secure the episcopal seal rings.   The sewers and the very tombs were rifled in the mad search for hidden treasure, the corpse of Julius II. being dragged from its coffin and the papal ornaments fought for and sold to the active Jews, who as usual were reaping a rich harvest out of the public misfortunes.   The relics of St. Peter's and the Lateran, even the most revered and venerable, were bandied about the streets and made the objects of insult and blasphemy by the Lutheran soldiers.   The rich vestments of the sacristies were seized to clothe the many courtesans of Rome, who drank and gambled on the altars of the polluted churches with their swinish protectors.   Priests were forced to take part in blasphemous orgies, or were murdered for refusing to obey.   In the halls of the palaces of cardinals, nobles and ambassadors, the plebeian masters of the Eternal City ate and drank to excess with Roman matrons or high-born prelates to wait humbly on every behest.   Everywhere was strewn the wealth of the richest city in Christendom; valuable

manuscripts from famous libraries were used to form the
litter of the troopers' horses ; and it was only with difficulty that Philibert of Orange saved the priceless Vatican
collection from a similar fate, although this nominal
general was himself dwelling in the Apostolic palace.
Such was the condition of the city of the Cæsars and
the Popes, when Cardinal Pompeo Colonna returned
thither in haste on hearing of the siege and sack. Even
this fierce enemy of the Medici and the secular Papacy
was overwhelmed with dismay and fell to shedding bitter
tears of remorse at the appalling spectacle of desolation,
mourning and massacre that met his eyes. If Giovio
is to be credited, the Colonna did what he could to
ameliorate the state of Rome, and his presence was
probably of some use later in arranging negotiations with
the culpable fugitive in the castle of Sant' Angelo.[1]

Meanwhile, the unhappy Clement remained secure in
the stronghold of Sant' Angelo amid sounds, sights and
stenches that must have sickened him both morally and
physically, and with the prospect of an ignominious and
painful death before him in the possible event of the
capture of the castle through treachery or a successful
assault. Once more, as in the days of Pope Boniface
VIII., was Christ openly insulted and threatened in the
person of His Vicar on earth ; once more was the ill-
omened banner of France with the golden lilies (that
Bourbon bore) publicly displayed in the purlieus of the
Holy City.[2] Vainly, by the clear light of morning and
evening, did the harassed Pope cast his eyes anxiously

[1] Jovius, *Vita Pompeii Colonnae ;* C. Milanesi, *Il Sacco di Roma
del MDXXVII.,* etc., etc.
[2] Veggio in Alagna entrar lo Fiordaliso
E nel Vicario suo Cristo esser catto, *etc.*
—*Purgatorio,* canto xx.

across the distant Campagna for any sign of the army
of the supine and perfidious Duke of Urbino, on which
with folly unutterable Clement always professed to rely.
Against the great circular mass of the castle, as around a
solitary rock buffeted by an angry sea, surged one after
another the fierce assaults of the besiegers, who openly
shouted their intention to hang the immured Pontiff;—
the Spaniards, because he was the enemy of their Emperor, and the Germans for his late persecution of their
beloved Martin Luther.   The fortress was, however,
defended meanwhile with great skill and devotion by its
lieutenant, Antonio Santacroce, his efforts being ably
seconded by Benvenuto Cellini, whose vivid if egotistic
account of the siege of Sant' Angelo reads like a lurid
incident from some historical romance.[1]   Living on the
coarsest of food and enduring the sweltering heats of
a Roman May, Clement and his companions spent in
the ancient tomb of Hadrian some five weeks of hunger,
misery, privation and uncertainty, whilst the overwhelming indignity of his position almost slew the Pope with
mingled grief and shame.   For within a fortnight of the
capture of Rome, the news was brought to the helpless
Pontiff that his agent Cardinal Passerini had been expelled from Florence; that a new republic had been
proclaimed amidst general rejoicings ; that his own effigy
had been dragged from the church of the Anunziata and
hacked to pieces with contumely in the streets.   And
this evil intelligence was still further aggravated by the
report of the conduct of Filippo and Clarice Strozzi on
this occasion, for that intrepid niece of Leo X.,[2] who
hated and despised the bastard Clement, had railed in
public at the two youths Ippolito and the beloved Ales-

[1] *Vita di B. Cellini.*
[2] Her father was Piero II., eldest son of Lorenzo the Magnificent.

sandro, and in the plainest of terms had denounced their
base birth, even adding her opinion that Clement himself
had no right to fill the office of Pope.   With the continual thunder of cannon in his ears ; with the horrible
scenes daily enacted below the walls of the prison-fortress ;
with fever and famine hourly gaining ground amongst
the refugees of the castle, did Clement drag out a miserable life-in-death for more than a month.   With Rome
in ruins at his feet and with Florence revolted from his
yoke, and with himself an universal object of contempt
and execration throughout all Italy, Clement at last
decided to capitulate unconditionally to the Emperor's
representative on 7th June after thirty days of misery
untold.

   .   .   .   .

    Although the Emperor affected to feel extreme com-
passion for his helpless captive and had even commanded
the Imperial court to don mourning in atonement for the
barbarities of the sack of Rome, he nevertheless per-
sisted in keeping Clement a close prisoner within the
castle walls, where the long hot summer and autumn were
passed in sickness, lamentation and dire suspense.   At
length the Pope, who for some time past had noticed a
decreasing vigilance amongst his personal guards, plucked
up sufficient courage to meditate escape, with the result
that on 5th December in the disguise of a gardener he
eluded the night-watch and got clear of the citadel which
had been his prison for so many weary months.   Hastening northward towards the Umbrian mountains, Clement
hurried with a few followers to the almost impregnable
city of Orvieto, set upon lofty precipices of tawny rock
and approached from the deep valley of the Paglia by a
solitary mule track.   Taking up his residence in the
drear deserted episcopal palace, the cowering and humi-

liated Medici found some degree of liberty, but even less actual comfort than he had experienced in his Roman fortress. In any case, Clement by his flight obtained no respite from political cares and dangers, for scarcely had he arrived weary and alarmed at Orvieto, than there was announced the advent of an important embassy from the English court, including Dr. Stephen Gardiner and Dr. Edward Foxe, who were come to demand a most difficult and dangerous favour of the fugitive Pontiff. For the object of the embassy was to obtain the Pope's authority to annul Henry VIII.'s marriage with his Queen, Catherine of Aragon, the aunt of the omnipotent Emperor, on whose caprice or policy depended at this moment the very salvation of the secular Papacy itself. Rousing himself to face this new dilemma with Medicean cunning if not with manly courage, Clement proceeded to temporise with the English envoys by holding out vague hopes of his ultimate consent to King Henry's petition, if only his former position of independence could be recovered. Foxe and Gardiner, who were thus dismissed half-satisfied with the nebulous promises of the wily Medici, gave on their return home a most melancholy account of the miserable plight of Clement and his court, as well as of the squalor of Orvieto, "where all things are in such a scarcity and dearth as we think have not been seen in any place; and that not only in victuals, which can not be brought into the town in any great quantity, by reason that everything is conveyed by asses and mules, but also in other necessaries. . . . Orvieto may well be called *Urbs Vetus*, for every man in all languages at his entry would give it none other name. We can not well tell the Pope should be noted in liberty, being here, where hunger, scarcity, ill-favoured lodging, ill air, and many other incommodities keep him and all his as straitly as he was ever kept in Castle Angelo. It is *aliqua mutatio soli, sed nulla libertatis;* and in manner the Pope could not deny to Mr. Gregory,[1] 'it were better to be in captivity in Rome than here at liberty'. The Pope lieth in an old palace of the bishops of the city, ruinous and decayed, where or we came to his privy chamber, we pass three chambers, all naked and un-hanged, the roofs fallen down, and as one can guess, thirty persons, rifraf and others, standing in the chambers for a garnishment. And as for the Pope's bed-chamber, all the apparel in it was not worth twenty nobles, bed and all."[2]

In four months' time, however, the harassed Pope, who must have detested the Emperor, and the Emperor, who must have despised beyond measure the ever-scheming Pontiff, were again re-united in supposed amity by the terms of the treaty of Barcelona, to which selfish compact of mutual convenience Francis of France gave his adhesion during the summer of 1529. This cynical triumvirate of Pope, King and Emperor was destined to prove fatal to the newly proclaimed liberties of the Re-public of Florence, now the sole Italian city of importance, save Venice, which remained free from foreign domina-tion. Abandoned by her historic ally of France and now marked out for his certain prey by the vindictive Clement, the Florentine Republic possessed scarcely a chance of retaining her independence in face of this recent political combination, which had been called into existence by Clement chiefly with the object of recovering the city for himself and the papal favourites. And to carry out this unholy scheme of aggression, Clement, with a callous villainy that to this day has been neither forgotten nor for-

---

[1] Gregorio da Casale.
[2] *State Papers*, vol. vii., p. 63.

CLEMENT VII AND FRANCIS I OF FRANCE

given in Italy, must needs contract with the Prince of
Orange, who had been his own gaoler in Rome and whose
troops had so lately desecrated his capital, to take command of this armament necessary for the reduction of
Florence.   Not a small portion of the Pope's hastily levied
force consisted of German and Spanish adventurers
openly urged to enlist by promise of an expected sack of
the rebellious city of the Medici.   "Aha, Signora Fiorenza,
get ready your rich brocades, for we are coming to
measure them by the pike and not by the ell!" became a
constant and mirth-provoking witticism amongst these
savage and spoiled mercenaries, as they were busily
furbishing their weapons in readiness for the expected
march northward, towards the valley of the Arno.

On the 24th day of October, 1529, appeared the
army of the Prince of Orange before the walls of the
devoted city, and for the third and last time in history
did the venerable Republic of Florence prepare to do battle
for existence against the wealth, power and influence of
the House of Medici.   But whilst the siege was being
prosecuted with varying fortune, the formal act of reconciliation between Charles and Clement took place in
the opening month of the following year, 1530, at Bologna
which had been fixed upon as the most convenient place
for the Imperial coronation.   This splendid public investiture of Charles V. with the Iron Crown of the Holy
Roman Empire may be said to have sealed the fate of
the struggling Florentines, who had now to chose between
the inevitable issues of a successful assault on the city
followed by the horrors of a sack, or of a peaceful surrender to the Medici on the most humiliating terms.
Fortunately perhaps for the people of Florence, the latter
course was thrust upon them through the death of their
brave citizen Federigo Ferruccio in the battle of Gavinana

and the appalling treachery of the Republic's own paid commander, Malatesta Baglioni; these two disasters combined to enforce a bloodless capitulation upon the unhappy city, which formally opened its gates to the Imperial and papal army on 12th August after a siege of nearly ten months.

And although a clause actually providing for the preservation of the time-honoured liberties and privileges of the city had been inserted amidst the terms of surrender, the Florentines themselves must have been only too well aware, from Clement's notorious political reputation, that such a safeguard would never be respected by the unscrupulous Pope. Indeed, it was evident to all men that Florence lay absolutely at the mercy of the triumphant Clement, the relative and patron of the two youths, Ippolito and Alessandro de' Medici, who had three years before been ignominiously chased hence. Even assuming Clement's determination to win back Florence was natural if not laudable, it becomes impossible to censure too strongly his brutal and unpatriotic methods of regaining the city; whilst the common belief that his extreme eagerness to accomplish this end was prompted by paternal anxiety to push the fortunes of his supposed natural son, the ill-favoured Alessandro, now Duke of Città Penna by the Emperor's favour, only makes the Pope's conduct appear less edifying and excusable. Although later historians have perhaps painted Clement's tyranny over recaptured Florence even blacker than its reality, yet it speaks eloquently for the Pontiff's own sense of his shame in the late transaction that he no more ventured to show his face in the streets of his native city during his lifetime, but ever contented himself with arranging and controlling the new Florentine government from a distance.

CHAPTER XIV

LAST YEARS OF CLEMENT VII

Pope Clement VII. died unregretted even by those nearest to his person ; deceitful, avaricious, cruel and heartless, he had all the bad without any of the redeeming qualities of his race ; he was acute, able and clear-sighted as a statesman, but weak and unsteady in his resolutions, and never by any chance sincere. He was detested by the Romans as the author of all their calamities and by everybody else as one of the basest men and worst Pontiffs that ever wore the sacred seal of the Fisherman (H. E. Napier, *Florentine History*).

DURING the summer months of 1528, shortly after his return from dismal Orvieto to his devastated capital, Clement, once again reconciled to the Emperor, began to take active measures to further the career of the younger and more favoured of his relatives, Ippolito and Alessandro de' Medici. As Leo X.'s Italian policy had largely been based upon his ambitious projects on behalf of the papal nephew Lorenzo de' Medici, so Clement VII., a true imitator of his cousin Leo, now concentrated all his efforts on obtaining a principality for the boy Alessandro, whom shrewd but ill-natured persons were inclined to designate as the Pope's offspring rather than as the unacknowledged natural son of the late Duke Lorenzo of Urbino. As neither Ippolito nor Alessandro were in reality closely related to the Pontiff, the latter in particular being (if his presumed parentage were admitted) only the grandson of Piero il Pazzo, Clement's first cousin, it seems scarcely possible to deny the probable correctness of this supposition of

the Pope's true paternity of this hideous and horrible
youth, who through papal and Imperial influence was ere
long to be acclaimed as Duke of Florence.   Towards
Ippolito, however, the attractive if headstrong son of the
gracious Giuliano and the favourite of his late uncle
Leo X., the Pope bore far less affection ; and although
Ippolito was a year or more older than Alessandro, was
comely and courteous, and was far from being unpopular
with the Florentines, yet Clement was evidently bent on
removing this young prince out of the path of Alessandro's
advancement by forcibly raising him to the purple.   In
vain did the high-mettled and pleasure-loving Ippolito
plead against this imposition of an ecclesiastical career for
which he was so obviously unsuited by natural inclination ;
the Pope, who had his own private and selfish reasons
for this resolve, was inexorable, and eventually this
prince, in spite of his base birth, his own protests and his
manifest unfitness, was compelled to enter the ranks of
the Sacred College.   By this step, so shamelessly repugnant on all moral grounds, did Clement accomplish a
cherished piece of statecraft, whereby he might not only
secure the hoped-for dominion of Florence for his beloved
Alessandro, but might also at the same time set a definite
barrier to any marriage in the future between Giuliano's
son and his cousin, the " Duchessina," Caterina de' Medici.
For a youthful attachment had, it seems, already been
formed between the handsome stripling and the little
pale-faced big-eyed girl, the sole heiress of her House,
who of these two papal nephews detested the ugly
Alessandro (her so-called half-brother) and adored the
good-looking, generous and high-spirited Ippolito.   Upon
the mere possibility of such an union Clement looked with
a most jealous eye for two reasons : first, because such an
alliance would operate to spoil the chance of Alessandro's

sovereignty over Florence ; and second, because he hoped to bestow Catherine's hand upon some prince of a reigning European House, whereby certain political advantages might accrue to himself and the Holy See.

Having thus compelled the reluctant Ippolito to accept a Cardinal's hat, Clement, who had for some time past been ailing with a sickness accounted mortal, made a forcible appeal to the Emperor to employ his good offices for the furtherance of the career of Alessandro, now an exile in Rome ever since his ignominious expulsion from Florence in the previous year. "If it be the will of His Divine Majesty," wrote Clement from his sick-bed, "to take me, His unworthy servant, to Himself, I recommend to your Sovereign Power mine exiled nephew,[1] since no longer can I urge forward his interests by mine own exertions. It is my sincere petition that you will replace him in that position which of justice he lately filled, and of which he has recently been deprived by the evil behaviour of others. O let your performance of this meritorious service be made as an atonement and compensation for all that has been done in the past against my proper dignity ! Further than this I crave nothing of you, and I give you my paternal blessing."[2]

To this urgent appeal of a doting parent or patron, the Emperor replied by creating Alessandro Duke of Città Penna, and later by abetting and assisting in Clement's schemes for the reduction of Florence. Moreover, a suitable match for this lucky young prince was suggested by the magnanimous Charles himself, who offered to bestow his own natural daughter, Margaret of Austria, in matrimony with this Medicean upstart. Pope

---

[1] *Nipote.* The word is very loosely used in Italian to express nephew, grandson or (as in this case) any near relative.

[2] Rastrelli, *Vita di Alessandro de' Medici*, p. 41.

and Emperor being completely in accord as to the necessity of erecting some principality for this base-born pair
in the ultimate event of their marriage, it became an easy
matter for Clement, with the Emperor's connivance, to
form the reconquered city of Florence into a duchy for
this purpose.   On 26th July, 1531, Alessandro de' Medici,
aged scarcely twenty years,[1] was proclaimed Duke of
Florence, and thus in the person of this ignoble youth
was every lingering vestige of the old Florentine
Republic definitely and forever swept away.   Clement,
it is true, did not survive to witness this cherished union
between his favourite and the young Margaret of Austria,
but he lived long enough to be tormented in mind by
the sinister reports from Florence of the conduct and
reputation of the duke, whose reign of five years was
marked throughout by acts of violence, despotism and
illegality, and ended worthily in the brutal murder of the
tyrant himself within the ancient palace of the Medici.[2]

Seeing that the final extinction of the old civic
liberties and the subsequent rule of this repulsive young
prince were due solely to the selfish ambition of Clement,
it is not surprising to find that the memory of the second
Medicean Pontiff is still held in deep abhorrence by the
descendants of his countrymen.   Yet the " Sala di
Clemente Settimo," with its frescoes and portraits by
Vasari, still exists for a memorial in that Florentine
palace, whose great hall likewise contains a fine piece of
statuary representing the Pope conferring the imperial
diadem on Charles V., who kneels at his feet.   Never-

[1] The date of Alessandro's birth is unknown, but it probably belongs to the year 1512.   Ippolito de' Medici was born in 1511.

[2] Amongst the few existing memorials of this evil Duke of
Florence may be mentioned the coronet and coat-of-arms, in
coloured terra-cotta, affixed to the façade of the Florentine church
of Ogni Santi.

theless, it is remarkable that, either by design or accident, the vast picture galleries of Florence contain no
prominent portrait of this papal betrayer of his native
city; although in the roof of one of the gorgeous saloons
in the Pitti Palace the observant stranger may detect the
form of Clement VII. seated beside that of his popular
cousin, Leo X.

Having thus set Alessandro firmly in the seat of
power over the helpless Florentines and having curbed
the highly inconvenient energy of the young Ippolito by
creating him a cardinal, Clement now found himself free
to turn his attention to the third member of the family
who had fallen under his personal guardianship. This
was of course Caterina de' Medici, who is described by
the Venetian ambassador Soriano at this time as being
"small in stature, thin and with indifferent features, but
with the large eyes that are characteristic of all the
Medici".

The unfortunate orphan girl, the last legitimate survivor of the senior branch of her House, had already
entered her fourteenth year when the Pope began to
entertain proposals for her speedy marriage from all
quarters of Europe, for with an ample dowry and various
political pretensions the youthful heiress found no lack of
aspirants to her hand. Amongst her many suitors by
proxy at this time was numbered the young Duke of
Richmond, the favourite natural son of Henry VIII. of
England; but it is needless to state that the crafty and
cold-blooded Clement looked to secure a far more brilliant
husband for his ward than a mere English duke. In the
delicate art of matchmaking indeed the innate cunning of
Clement's unpleasant character was fully revealed, for
the Pope was now scheming steadily to ensure the
promised union of Margaret of Austria with the Duke of

Florence and at the same time to arrange a marriage for the little Catherine with a royal prince of the House of France.   For by this dual alliance of a daughter of the Emperor and a son of King Francis with his own re- lations, the restless Pope fancied he was going to strengthen enormously his own political position.   Yet even on this meditated match with the French court the shifty Clement outwardly seemed scarcely to know his own mind, for "he speaks about it," comments the Venetian envoy, "at one moment cordially, and at another coldly, according to his irresolute nature".   But in all probability Clement was merely anxious to conceal both from Francis and the Emperor his extreme eager- ness to grasp at so brilliant and valuable a family con- nection as this French alliance which he had good reason to fear the Emperor might flatly forbid.   The final settlement of Catherine's betrothal to one out of her host of suitors was therefore deferred, until the projected meeting which Clement and Charles had arranged should take place at Bologna towards the close of the year 1532.

Ill and depressed, yet preferring at any cost to under- take this second arduous journey to Bologna rather than to give Charles the opportunity of traversing the Papal States so as to confer with him in Rome itself, Clement set out for the appointed place about the middle of November, 1532, choosing the more difficult and danger- ous route by way of Perugia in order to avoid a halt within sight of Florence, although his favourite Alessandro was now reigning there as duke.   In the papal retinue during this journey northwards rode King Henry VIII.'s envoy, Dr. Edmund Bonner, afterwards Bishop of Lon- don, and it is through the pen of this English prelate that we possess a curious account of the trials and difficulties the ailing Pontiff was forced to endure on his way to meet a master whom he cordially detested, yet had perforce ever to humour and reverence.[1]

"To advertise your Mastership of our news," so writes Bonner to Thomas Cromwell on Christmas Eve, 1532, "you shall understand that the 18th of November the Pope, taking with him only in his journey and company six cardinals with no great number, entered his journey towards Bologna, not keeping the common way, which, as you know, is by Florence and foul enough, but by Perugia and the lands of the Church; six other cardinals to make up a brown dozen, and yet not all good saints, taking their journey by Florence with the rest of the company. The said journey to the Pope, by reason of the continual rain and foul way, with other unfortunable accidents, as the loss of certain of his mules and the breaking of the leg of one Turkish horse that he had, special good, and above all for the evil lodging that he had with his company, was wondrous painful; the Pope divers time compelled, by reason of the foulness and danger of the way, to go on foot the space of a mile or two, and his company; besides that pleasure and pastime, for lack of a feather-bed, compelled to lie in the straw."

Yet Clement, though sick in mind and body, struggled onward through wet weather and over miry roads, finally reaching his goal on 7th December. "The Pope's entry into Bononie," continues Bonner in his letter to Cromwell, "was two times, the first upon Our Lady's Even[2] secretly, without ceremonies or pride, only within the walls of the city; the other was *in Die Conceptionis* with ceremonies accustomed, and yet no great company; the Pope riding in his long white kirtle, hav-

[1] *State Papers of Henry VIII.*, vol. vii., p. 394.
[2] Eve of the Feast of the Immaculate Conception, 8th December.

ing his rochet upon the same and a stole about his neck, and so coming to his palace. Of any miracles done upon any halt or lame or otherwise, I heard not of." [1]

This second meeting arranged between Pope and Emperor proved neither so gorgeous nor so animated an affair as the late spectacle of the Imperial coronation in this very city of Bologna, held only two years before. A splendid pageant, gratifying alike to the ambition of Charles and to the pride of the Medici, had then contrived to shed a lustre of cheerfulness and content upon the participants in the ceremony of 1530; whereas at this moment it was but a question of urgent business. The harassed and anxious Clement had two special objects to obtain out of the conference ;—the postponement of the calling of a General Council of the Church, which the Emperor was being strongly urged to convoke ; and the settlement of the little Catherine's matrimonial prospects. As to the first, it was openly said that the very sound of the word "Council" always struck a pallor into the nervous face of the Medici, who had risen by a course of unprecedented intrigues to the highest dignity in Christendom, and consequently was ever haunted by the fear that such a representative assembly would immediately clamour for the deposition of the impostor Clement VII., on account of his illegitimacy. With regard to the second matter of importance, the Pope was most anxious to obtain Charles's approval of the suggested French marriage, and yet at the same time to make certain of the projected match between his favourite Alessandro and the Emperor's daughter, Margaret.

Clement's methods of gaining a political point were

[1] *State Papers of Henry VIII.*, *op. cit.*

always deceitful, mean and tortuous, yet they were not unfrequently successful, as in this instance, when he was able to return to Rome early in the year 1533, well satisfied with the reflection that he had staved off, if only for a time, the dreaded convocation of a General Council of the Church, and had also secured the Emperor's grudging assent to the French marriage; an assent, however, which Charles had given carelessly, since in his own mind he could not conceive of the splendid Francis of France seriously intending to allow any son of his House to mate with the daughter of a Florentine burgher line, with "one who was little more than a private gentlewoman". In the late duel of diplomatic skill, therefore, at Bologna the wily Pope certainly outwitted the Emperor, for Clement had made sure beforehand of the sincerity of the French King's professions with regard to the disposal of the poor little heiress, who chanced to be the Pope's most valuable political asset. Instructions were hurriedly conveyed to the French envoys at Bologna, the Cardinals Tournon and Grammont, to hasten with the documents bearing on the forthcoming nuptials of Caterina de' Medici, titular Duchess of Urbino, with Henri de Valois, Duke of Orléans, second son of King Francis I. Much to his surprise and annoyance, Charles perceived too late that his rival of France was desperately in earnest, whilst his contemptuous hatred of Clement must have been immeasurably increased, when he learned of the Pope's intention to preside in person at the approaching wedding festivities at Marseilles, which had by mutual consent of King and Pontiff been fixed upon as a convenient spot for the important event.

Early in September, 1533, Catherine prepared to leave Florence, where she was then residing, in order to proceed on her journey to France. Attended by her uncle-in-law, the brilliant but dissolute Filippo Strozzi[1] and by her cousins Palla Rucellai and Maria Salviati, she made her way to Porto Venere on the Tuscan coast, and thence taking ship after a week's voyage she disembarked at Nice, there to await news of the coming of the Pope.   Clement meanwhile had set out from Rome, and sailing from the mouth of the Arno in the first week of October, reached Marseilles on the eleventh day of that month.   At this port Francis and his court had already arrived some days previously in order to do honour to the expected bride and to the presence of His Holiness, the approach of whose flotilla was duly reported to those on shore by watchers posted on the towers of the Chateau d'If.   Stepping on to the quay at Marseilles, Clement was received in solemn form by a deputation of French bishops, cardinals and abbots ; and on the following morning, which was a Sunday, the Pope entered the city in full panoply of state, the two young Dukes of Orléans and of Angoulême each holding one of the Pontiff's hands.   On Monday, 13th October, the King and Queen of France with a magnificent equipage approached to welcome their illustrious guest, and after this meeting of Clement and Francis nine days were consumed in an endless round of gorgeous banquets and ceremonies, varied by occasional conferences of a political nature. Thus was passed the interval of waiting for the bride's arrival, which was delayed until the twenty-third day of the month, when Caterina de' Medici, attended by twelve maids-of-honour, at last made her appearance.   As at the nuptials of Catherine's own father, the young Lorenzo, Duke of Urbino, the French court was deeply impressed

----

[1] Husband of Clarice de' Medici (d. 1528), the only sister of Lorenzo, Duke of Urbino, Catherine's father.

CATERINA DE' MEDICI, QUEEN OF FRANCE

by the marvellous ostentation of the Medici,[1] nor did any of those present care to reflect upon the recent severe measures of taxation applied in Rome and Florence, in order to obtain the wherewithal to make so brave a display. On Tuesday, 28th October, Clement himself, to give greater solemnity and weight to the event, performed the ceremony of the marriage which constituted his ward the lawful wife of the young Henri de Valois, Duke of Orléans. As the bride of fourteen years old was thus united to the youthful bridegroom of fifteen amidst all the pomp incidental to the wedding of a scion of the royal House of France, Clement must have felt an exquisite thrill of complete and satisfying triumph in the successful issue of his restless intriguing ; a sense of triumph which neither past failure nor present ill-health nor encroaching age could at such a moment blight. In truth, the chief diplomatic fruit of all his past intrigue and deceit was represented by this political union of the great niece of Leo X. with a prince of France, the first truly royal marriage to which a Medici had as yet aspired ; and it is again to Clement's ambition that the forthcoming crimes and troubles of the Medicean Queen's subsequent regency in France must indirectly be ascribed.

The unavoidable fatigues and constant excitement of this late visit to the French court at Marseilles seem to have undermined the waning powers of the Pontiff, who survived the consummation of his diplomatic success less then a twelvemonth. Returning from the shores of

[1] A splendid relic of Clement's liberality towards Francis I. on this occasion is to be found in the magnificent casket by Valerio of Vicenza, preserved in the Gem Room of the Uffizi Gallery in Florence. This beautiful work of art contains twenty-four panels of rock-crystal set in silver gilt, and elaborately engraved with subjects from the New Testament. It bears also the arms and papal insignia of its donor, Clement VII.

France to his capital, Clement found discontent openly
exhibited in Rome, whilst his private life was made miserable by the ceaseless strife waged between the two papal
nephews. For the martial Ippolito was appearing
anxious to divest himself of the purple, so as to dispute
for the mastery of the enthralled Florentines with the
unpopular tyrant already in possession ; nor could any
threats or entreaties on Clement's part terminate the
endless and unseemly quarrels between the Cardinal and
the Duke of Florence ; a city that, for reasons previously
mentioned, the Pope was determined nevermore to visit.
A constant dread of the Imperial vengeance for his late
alliance with the French King likewise haunted the
scheming Pope, who perceived the Emperor deeply
incensed by the recent papal policy and more than ever
filled with the idea of convoking a General Council of
the Church to discuss and settle the many burning questions that were vexing Western Christendom.   The
personal quarrel with Henry VIII.—once his warmest
royal supporter—over Queen Catherine's divorce proceedings, and the consequent formal revolt of England
from the supremacy of the Holy See, must also have
weighed heavily on the mind of Clement, who but for
an ever-present dread of the Emperor would in all probability have granted Henry's petition a dozen times over
rather than risk the catastrophe, which the helpless Pope
was himself, by the irony of an inexorable fate, called
upon to hasten. Yet Clement continued to the last
contriving, trifling, proposing, prevaricating through all
his troubles, finding apparently no relaxation from the
cares wherewith he was beset save by creating fresh
embarrassments on all sides.

Harassed on all sides by domestic quarrelling and political difficulties, it is not surprising to find that by the

summer of 1534 the exhausted Pope was sinking fast to the
grave, a prey to one of those slow intermittent fevers for
which the climate of Rome was once so notorious.   All
Italy, and indeed all Europe, awaited his expected end with
ill-concealed satisfaction, so that almost the only known instance of regret or sympathy with the dying man on this
occasion came from a humble source, namely, from the
jeweller Benvenuto Cellini, whom Clement had patronised
in the past and with whom he not unfrequently deigned
to hold conversation on artistic matters.   During the last
few months of Clement's existence, Cellini had been engaged in preparing and stamping certain medals for the
Pope, amongst them one showing a design of Moses
striking the rock to obtain water, with the explanatory
legend *Ut bibat populus*.   "Having finished my work,"
narrates the prince of jewellers in his famous *Autobiography*, "on 22nd September, I waited on the Pope,
whom I found very ill in bed.   Yet he gave me the
most kindly reception, telling me of his wish to inspect
both the medals themselves and the instruments wherewith I had stamped them.   He ordered his spectacles and
a candle to be brought, but nevertheless he could discern
nothing of my workmanship.   So he set to examine the
medals by the touch of his fingers, but after feeling thus
for some length of time he fetched a deep sigh, and told
one of the courtiers he was sorry for me, but if it pleased
God to restore his health, he would make me a satisfactory payment.   Three days later he died, and I had
only my labour for my pains.   I took courage notwithstanding, comforting myself with the thought that I had
acquired so much renown by means of these medals, that
I might depend on future employment from the next
Pope, and perhaps with better results.   By such reflections did I prevent myself from feeling dejected."

Proceeding with this account of his private affairs, Cellini adds that some days later, on the occasion of Clement's lying-in-state, he "put on his sword and repaired to St. Peter's, where he kissed the feet of the deceased Pontiff, nor could he refrain from tears".[1]

This curious expression of modified sorrow exhibited by Cellini for his late patron stands, however, almost alone amidst the universal outburst of relief and jubilation at the news of the long-desired death of the despised and discredited Medici, which occurred on 25th September, 1534, in the fifty-seventh year of his age and after a reign of ten years and ten months. "The joy at Rome is two-fold," writes Gregory of Casale three weeks later to the Duke of Norfolk, "the election of the new Pope (Alessandro Farnese, Paul III.) and the death of the old one being alike cause of rejoicing."[2]   Nor was this bitterness of feeling limited to mere verbal execration, for the Roman populace made efforts each night to pollute or deface Clement's temporary tomb in St. Peter's.   Several times in the morning was the pontifical monument found smeared with filth; whilst on one occasion some vindictive wag during the night hours contrived to alter the lettering of the inscription, by substituting the words "Inclemens Pontifex Minimus" for the proud title "Clemens Pontifex Maximus," besides making other changes of a derogatory nature in the late Pope's epitaph. It was even planned by some indignant Romans to drag the corpse itself from its coffin and draw it ignominiously with a hook through the streets of the city; an intended insult that was only averted by the prompt action of the Cardinal Ippolito de' Medici who set a strong guard over the tomb, so long as the lawless interval during the sitting

[1] *Vita di B. Cellini.*
[2] *State Papers of Henry VIII.*, vol. vii., p. 373.

of the conclave lasted.   The election of the Farnese
Pontiff naturally restored order in Rome, so that the remains of Paul III.'s unpopular predecessor were hence-
forward at least allowed to rest undisturbed, until their
removal to the choir of the Church of Santa Mariasopra
Minerva, which already contained the ashes of Leo X.
Not many years later was raised on this spot the ponderous but unlovely monument, the work of Antonio da
San Gallo and Baccio Bandinelli of Florence, which
commemorates in imperishable marble "this weak and
clumsy disciple of the principles inculcated by Machiavelli's *Prince*,"[1] Giulio, bastard son of Giuliano de'
Medici, Pope Clement VII.

It is a general maxim of history that those sovereigns or exalted personages who have signally failed in
their public careers should be invariably regarded by
posterity with a greater measure of interest and sympathy,
from the very circumstance of their misfortunes.   And
with regard to this statement, it will be sufficient to cite
from our own annals the striking examples of the
scholar-saint Henry VI., of Queen Mary of Scotland and
of the still-idolised Charles Stuart.   But to this general
rule Giulio de' Medici, Clement VII., offers a notable
exception.   For although the second Medicean Pope was
perhaps the most unfortunate of all the Roman Pontiffs,
and although his disastrous reign belonged to a picturesque
and turbulent age, the historian cannot obtain the smallest
amount of satisfaction or interest from a close contemplation of his private character.   Indeed, few persons
have perhaps been detested or reviled by mankind with
better reason than this papal bastard of the House of
Medici ; this cold, cunning, calculating Pontiff, who was
the indirect cause of the Sack of Rome, the patron of the

[1] Gregorovius, *Tombs of the Popes.*

odious Duke Alessandro, the pitiless destroyer of the liberties of Florence. Yet in reality the man, as we have already shown, was not without his virtues, since he was frugal, industrious, serious ; singularly free, in short, from those failings which have been so properly censured in the case of his cousin, Leo X. Nevertheless, the very absence in Clement of the frivolity, the extravagance and the idleness of the splendid Leo seems scarcely to be accounted commendable, when we reflect upon the chill indifference of his natural disposition, his parsimony and avarice, and that perpetual selfish scheming, which was ever adding new troubles and turmoils to the existing evils of the age. A comparison between Leo X. and Clement VII., drawn from a perusal of these pages, ought to exhibit clearly the reasons why the former, in spite of his faults and even his misdeeds, was sincerely mourned at his death ; whereas the latter sank, loathed, despised and dishonoured into a tomb whereon the indignant and outraged populace of Rome endeavoured to wreak a posthumous vengeance.

It is difficult to palliate or to suggest any reasonable excuse for the conduct and character of Clement, beyond quoting Ranke's expressive phrase, that he was "the very sport of misfortune, without doubt the most ill-fated Pontiff that ever sat on the papal throne". No one can extend a jot of sympathy to this callous adventurer, who by ceaseless intriguing rose to be created a cardinal and later to be elected Supreme Pontiff, and whom a General Council of the Church, sincerely bent on religious reform, would have promptly deposed. Cautious, scheming, shuffling, selfish, suspicious, mean, heartless, insincere, untruthful—such was Clement VII. ; and it only remains to add that on occasions this repellent personage could show himself guilty of the most vindictive and ferocious cruelty ;—as in the case of the helpless monk, Benedetto da Fojano, who for taking an active part in the defence of Florence was thrust into a filthy dungeon of the castle of Sant' Angelo and there slowly and deliberately starved to death by Clement's expressed desire. History can afford many examples of princes or private persons who were monsters of crime or vice, but it can scarcely exhibit another character more worthy of oblivion than the cowardly tyrant, whom the haughty Clarice Strozzi, the niece of Leo X., had once openly denounced as an intruder into the august House of Medici. For it was during the brief moment of the Florentine Republic's triumph in the spring of 1527, when Clement was being held a prisoner in Sant' Angelo, that the impetuous Clarice, urged to use her influence to save from the angry mob the trembling Ippolito and Alessandro with their guardian Cardinal Passerini, had hastened to the ancient palace in Via Larga and there had openly expressed her contemptuous denial of any relationship between herself and the three bastards bearing her family name, the two cowering youths before her and the absent Pontiff.

"Standing in the vast corridor of the palace," narrates the Florentine historian Bernardo Segni, "did she pour forth her scorn of these spurious scions of her House, saying, 'You show plainly what is already known, that you are not of the blood of the Medici ; and not only you, but also Pope Clement, wrongfully a Pope and now most righteously a prisoner in Sant' Angelo!'" Reflecting on Clarice's fiery speech and on Clement's despicable character and inglorious reign, we are led to feel both surprise and regret that in his hour of complete victory the Emperor Charles V. did not depose and remove this papal impostor from the scene of his late misdeeds to some secure and remote fortress, where, deprived of his

ill-gotten honours and powerless to vex henceforth the
peace of Italy and of Europe, this Medicean bastard
might have found time to meditate upon and to repent
of the appalling mischief he had already wrought in the
brief interval of three years between his election and the
Sack of Rome.

CHAPTER XV

THE LATER MEDICI POPES

AFTER the death of Clement VII. the illustrious name of Medici occurs twice in the annals of the Papacy, but in both cases it was borne by Pontiffs who were very distantly connected with the senior branch of the Florentine House that produced Leo X.

The former of these is Gian-Angelo, younger son of Bernardino Medici of Milan, who was elected Pope on Christmas Eve, 1559, under the title of Pius IV., and reigned for nearly six years, his pontificate being distinguished, amongst other events of importance, by the closing of the protracted sittings of the Council of Trent. Pius IV., "who was a man of worldly instincts, a lover of the good things of this life,"[1] but who ever showed himself moderate and conciliatory in his political dealings, is said to have been of humble birth. Nevertheless, the Pope's forefathers claimed, on very doubtful grounds, to be descendants of one Giambuono de' Medici of Florence,[2] in the thirteenth century, who is supposed to have migrated to Milan. Both the sons of Bernardino were successful in life, for the elder, Gian-Giacomo, was created Marquis of Melegnano by the Emperor Charles V., whilst the younger, Gian-Angelo, as we have said, attained to the pontifical throne. Pius IV. is celebrated, moreover,

---

[1] Gregorovius, *Tombs of the Popes.*
[2] Belviglieri, *Tavole Sincrone e Genealogiche,* etc.

as the uncle of St. Charles Borromeo, the son of his only sister, whom this Pope raised to the purple at the early age of twenty-two. After his decease on 10th December, 1565, Pius IV. was interred in the great Roman church of Santa Maria degli Angeli, wherein he possesses no monument other than a simple tablet: a circumstance that may be fairly attributed to the manifest humility and hatred of pomp ever shown by his favoured nephew, St. Charles Borromeo, Cardinal Archbishop of Milan.

But if Pius IV. possessed nothing save his family name to link his personality with the city of Florence, the fourth and last Medici Pope, Leo XI., was at least a Florentine by birth and a true descendant of a collateral branch of that great House. For he was one of the sons of Ottaviano de' Medici, dwelling in a palace near the famous convent of San Marco and for many years a favourite both with Clement VII. and the worthless Duke Alessandro, who had entrusted their distant kinsman with the administration of the vast estates of the Medici throughout Tuscany. Of Ottaviano's children, the eldest son, Bernardetto, espoused Giulia de' Medici, the natural daughter of his father's patron, Duke Alessandro, and eventually was invested with the lordship of Ottajano in the kingdom of Naples, where his descendants are still flourishing. The younger brother, Alessandro, being "pious, learned and most energetic,"[1] was devoted to the service of the Church, wherein he quickly rose to positions of wealth and eminence. Highly favoured by the Grand-Ducal family of Tuscany, Alessandro was appointed Archbishop of Florence and was created a cardinal, whilst it was through his bounty that the official residence of the Florentine Archbishops, facing the ancient Baptistery, was greatly altered and enlarged; a fact which is

[1] Ranke, *History of the Popes*, vol. i.

commemorated by the fine escutcheon in polychrome now affixed to the north-eastern angle of the present palace.

At the death of Clement VIII. in the spring of 1605, on 1st April the Cardinal Alessandro de' Medici was elected Pope to the exorbitant joy of the French court, Henry IV. ordering salvoes of artillery to be fired on the receipt of the tidings from Rome. But this outburst of satisfaction in France was fated to be of brief duration. The new Pontiff, who probably out of compliment to the first fortunate and resplendent Pope of his House, assumed the title of Leo XI., had already entered his seventieth year and was suffering from an incurable malady. The excitement of the conclave and the fatigue of the lengthy ceremonies served to diminish his remaining strength, so that at his own coronation he contracted a feverish chill which produced a fatal result on 27th April. Leo XI.'s reign, one of the shortest in papal annals, lasted therefore but twenty-six days, whilst his sudden decease caused no small degree of disappointment at the courts of Paris and Florence, where high hopes had been entertained of the newly-elected Medici's foreign policy. But although Leo's death was sincerely deplored both in France and in Tuscany, " no one," quaintly observes an old English translator of the *Vite dei Pontefici*,[1] " had so much reason to lament his loss as his own family, who had not the time to receive the honours designed for them, and particularly his great-nephew Ottaviano de' Medici, on whom Leo intended to bestow his own Cardinal's hat". Indeed, it is not difficult to believe in the genuine regret of the short-lived Pontiff's expectant but now dejected relations.

[1] *The Lives of the Popes.* From the Latin of Baptista Platina and others. Translated by Paul Rycaut, London, 1685.

Leo XI.'s fine monument by Algardi with its stately allegorical figures of Minerva and of Abundance adorns the northern aisle of St. Peter's. If it appear peculiar to the inquiring stranger that so vast a memorial should have been erected to a Pontiff who reigned for less than a month's space, let such an one draw a lesson from the sculptured garlands that decorate this papal tomb, for they speak eloquently of the brevity and variableness of all earthly honours, even the hardest won and the best deserved. *Sic florui,* such is the terse motto borne by the blossoming wreaths on Leo's sepulchre, which delicately conveys thus the ancient warning of the Psalmist that "the days of Man are but as grass ; for he flourisheth as a flower of the field".

APPENDIX

LEON. X. PONT. MAX. IAMBICI[1]

In Lucretiae Statuam

Libenter occumbo ; mea in praecordia
Adactum habens ferrum ; juvat mea manu
It praestitisse, quod Viraginum prius
Nulla ob pudicitiam peregit promptius.
Juvat cruorem contueri proprium,
Illumque verbis execrari asperrimis.

Sanguen mi acerbius veneno colchico
Ex quo canis Stygius, vel Hydra praeferox
Artus meos compegit in poenam asperam ;
Lues flue, ac vetus reverte in toxicum.
Tabes amara exi, mihi invisa et gravis,
Quod feceris corpus nitidum et amabile.

Nec interim suas monet Lucretia
Civeis, pudore et castitate semper ut
Sint praeditae, fidemque servant integram
Suis maritis, cum sit haec Mavortii
Laus magna populi, ut castitate foeminae
Laetentur, et viris mage iste gloria
Placere studeant, quam nitere et gratia.
Quin id probasse caede vel mea gravi
Lubet, statim animum purum opertere extrahi
Ab inquinati corporis custodia.

[1] Lines addressed to an antique statue of Lucretia, unearthed in the Trastevere of Rome, by Cardinal Giovanni de' Medici, afterwards Pope Leo X. (Roscoe, vol. ii., Appendix XCVIII.)

(Lucretia speaks, after driving the dagger into her breast :)

Gladly I fall to earth, the cruel steel
Driv'n to my heart ; and yet I find delight
In this self-slaughter, since it needs must prove
That none was ever shown more prompt than I.
With joyful eyes I mark my life-blood flow,
And curse the crimson stream with scathing words.

O Blood of mine, more hateful than the drugs
Which Cerberus or Hydra can produce,
Depart all-tainted to thine ancient source !
Hence bitter-sweet and vile disease of Life,
That once did fill my frame with comeliness !

Thus doth your Lucrece warn her happier peers
Ever to bide in purity and grace,
And ever hold intact the marriage vow.
For is it not the chiefest boast of Rome
That all her matrons walk in Virtue's path,
Seeking to rule their lords by chastity,
And not by beauty or the art to please ?
Thus am I willing by mine own sad end
To preach this lesson ;—that the faithful soul
Must not survive in the polluted clay.

INDEX

353

DATE DUE
